# ACCOUNTING DESK BOOK

## The Accountant's Everyday Instant Answer Book

## 2000 SUPPLEMENT

# TOM M. PLANK
### with Lois R. Plank

PRENTICE HALL

© 2000 by Prentice Hall, Inc.

This publication is designed to provide accurate and authoritative information in
regard to the subject matter covered. It is sold with the understanding that the
publisher is not engaged in rendering legal, accounting, or other professional service. If legal advice or other expert assistance is required, the services of a competent professional person should be sought.

*. . . From the Declaration of Principles jointly adopted by a Committee of the
American Bar Association and a Committee of Publishers and Associations.*

*Printed in the United States of America*

*10  9  8  7  6  5  4  3  2  1*

ISBN   0-13-012414-1

ISSN   1090-039X

---

**ATTENTION: CORPORATIONS AND SCHOOLS**

Prentice Hall books are available at quantity discounts with bulk purchase
for educational, business, or sales promotional use. For information, please
write to: Prentice Hall Special Sales, 240 Frisch Court, Paramus, NJ  07652.
Please supply: title of book, ISBN, quantity, how the book will be used, date
needed.

---

**PRENTICE HALL**
Paramus, NJ 07652

---

**On the World Wide Web at http://www.phdirect.com**

---

# Contents

CHAPTER 2
## INTERNATIONAL ACCOUNTING STANDARDS COMMITTEE                                    49

CHAPTER 3
## RECENTLY ADOPTED OR REVISED INTERNATIONAL ACCOUNTING STANDARDS                                    65

CHAPTER 4
## PLAIN ENGLISH DISCLOSURE RULE

CHAPTER 5
## MUTUAL FUND "PROFILE" DISCLOSURE OPTION

## CHAPTER 6
### MUTUAL FUNDS                                                119

## CHAPTER 7
### BUSINESS USE OF A HOME                                       126

## CHAPTER 10
### MORE "TAXPAYER RIGHTS" AND SOME IRS CHANGES    169

# About the Authors

**Tom M. Plank** is a specialist in SEC Accounting Rules and Regulations, new security issues registration, and annual report filings with the SEC. He holds his degrees from the Graduate School of Management, University of California at Los Angeles.

Mr. Plank has served on the accounting and finance faculties of various major universities in Chicago and Los Angeles. His business experience includes that of an officer and economist for a large commercial bank, a securities analyst for an investment banking firm, an account executive for a large securities firm, and a consultant for various corporations.

Mr. Plank has published several articles in various journals and is the author of many business books: *SEC Accounting Rules and Regulations, The Age of Automation, The Science of Leadership,* and four editions and seven supplements to the *Accounting Desk Book.*

**Lois R. Plank** received her B.A. in Public Administration and International Relations from Miami University in Oxford, Ohio, with additional work in investments at the University of Illinois and the University of California at Los Angeles.

Mrs. Plank co-edited *The Encyclopedia of Accounting Systems.* She has been involved in budgeting and financial management with a government agency in Washington, D.C., and instituted a public relations and marketing program for a suburban Chicago school district.

She is an editor of professional publications and books, and is a public relations consultant. Additional experience includes chief copy consultant for a national magazine, and newspaper reporting.

# How to Use This Supplement

The objective of this *Supplement* is to furnish users of the *Accounting Desk Book, Tenth Edition,* with recent developments in the financial accounting rules and regulations both in the United States and internationally. Since the *Desk Book* was published, significant Financial Accounting Standards Board Statements governing the presentation of financial reports have been issued, and are reviewed in this book.

A gigantic step forward in global accounting was taken when the International Accounting Standards Commission adopted its statement on the recognition and measurement of financial instruments, including derivatives, to complete the core set of Standards to be presented to the International Organization of Securities Commission for consideration for cross-border offering and listing.

Of particular interest to both issuers and users of financial reports are two Final Rules of the Securities and Exchange Commission: the "Profile" disclosure document for mutual funds and the Plain English Disclosure rule.

Among the topics featured in the *Supplement* are:

- Financial Accounting Standards Board Statements Nos. 120 through 137 and Proposals
- International Accounting Standards Committee and Recently Adopted International Accounting Standards
- Plain English Disclosure Rule
- Mutual Fund "Profile" Disclosure Option

- Business Use of a Home
- Miscellaneous Deductions
- Change in Accounting Methods and Consideration of Accounting Periods
- More "Taxpayer Rights" and Some IRS Changes
- Higher Educational Incentives
- Derivatives and Hedging

The discussions throughout the *Supplement* are self-contained. References to text found in the *Accounting Desk Book, Tenth Edition,* are identified by ADB, followed by the chapter number where the text can be found.

*Supplement* users will find the Index particularly helpful in locating all the major topics and minor subtopics that are covered in this *Supplement.*

*TMP*
*LRP*

## ACKNOWLEDGMENTS

We would like to acknowledge the invaluable editorial assistance of Christie Plank Ciraulo, our daughter, who recently celebrated her eleventh anniversary as the head of her own successful writing and graphic design firm in Los Angeles.

# Chapter 1

# Financial Accounting Standards Board Statements and Proposals

## ACCOUNTING AND REPORTING BY MUTUAL LIFE INSURANCE ENTERPRISES AND BY INSURANCE ENTERPRISES FOR CERTAIN LONG-DURATION PARTICIPATING CONTRACTS—FASB 120

FASB 120 is the result of considerable cooperation between the Financial Accounting Standards Board and the American Institute of CPAs to provide guidance in accounting, reporting, and disclosure procedures to mutual life insurance companies. Prior to the enactment of this standard and those rulings cited below, these companies reported financial information to their creditors and policyholders primarily following the statutory provisions of various state insurance regulatory bodies. The companies are now to report insurance and reinsurance activities according to GAAP.

The thrust of this Statement is to apply the provisions of FASB 60, *Accounting and Reporting by Insurance Enterprises*; FASB 97, *Accounting and Reporting by Insurance Enterprises for Certain Long-Duration Contracts and for Realized Gains and Losses from the Sale of Investments*, and FASB 113, *Accounting and Reporting for Reinsurance of Short-Duration and Long-Duration Contracts*, to mutual life insurance enterprises, assessment enterprises and to fraternal benefit societies. Certain participating life insurance contracts of those same enterprises have also been addressed in the AICPA's Statement of Position 95-1, *Accounting for Certain Activities of Mutual Life Insurance Enterprises*. Both become effective for financial statements for fiscal years beginning after December 15, 1995.

The three earlier FASB Statements had specifically exempted mutual life insurance enterprises from their requirements. FASB Interpretation 40, *Applicability of Generally Accepted Accounting Principles to Mutual Life*

1

*Insurance and Other Enterprises*, did not address or change the exemption of mutual life insurance companies from these Statements. Interpretation 40 had been scheduled to become effective earlier but the date was changed to permit simultaneous application with FASB 120 and SOP 95-1.

It was because there seemed to be little authoritative accounting guidance relative to the insurance and reinsurance activities of mutual life insurance enterprises that the FASB, along with the AICPA, decided to extend the requirements of the above mentioned standards to them. The AICPA's Statement of Position 95-1 sets guidelines for participating insurance contracts of mutual life insurance companies when:

1) They are long-duration participating contracts that are expected to pay dividends to policyholders based on the actual experience of the insurer.

2) The annual policyholder dividends are paid in a way that identifies divisible surplus, then distributes that surplus in approximately the same proportion that the contracts are estimated to have contributed to that surplus. Otherwise, accounting and reporting for these contracts are covered by the (now) four basic FASB insurance enterprise standards listed above.

The effect of initially applying FASB 120 is to be reported retroactively through restatement of all previously issued annual financial statements presented for comparative purposes for fiscal years beginning after December 15, 1992. Annual statements filed prior to that date may also be restated for any desired number of consecutive annual periods. The cumulative effect of adopting FASB 120 is to be included in the earliest year restated.

## ACCOUNTING FOR THE IMPAIRMENT OF LONG-LIVED ASSETS AND FOR LONG-LIVED ASSETS TO BE DISPOSED OF—FASB 121

FASB 121 sets up accounting standards for recording impairment of long-lived assets, certain identifiable intangibles, and goodwill applicable to assets which are to be held and used. In addition, it applies to those long-lived assets and certain identifiable intangibles which are to be disposed of. Statement 121 is effective for financial statements for fiscal years beginning after December 15, 1995, but the effects of the pronouncement have already become evident in companies that elected to comply with the provisions early and took major writedowns in the last quarter of 1995. Restatement of previously issued financial statements is not permitted.

FASB 121 does *not* apply to accounting for assets which are already covered by the following Statements:

1) FASB 50, *Financial Reporting in the Record and Music Industry,*
2) FASB 53, *Financial Reporting by Producers and Distributors of Motion Picture Films,*
3) FASB 63, *Financial Reporting by Broadcasters,*
4) FASB 86, *Accounting for the Costs of Computer Software to be Sold, Leased, or Otherwise Marketed,* and by
5) FASB 90, *Regulated Enterprises—Accounting for Abandonments and Disallowances of Plant Costs.*

Additionally, FASB 121 does not cover mortgage and related servicing rights, deferred tax assets, deferred policy acquisition costs, financial instruments, or certain long-term customer relations of financial institutions. The term *asset* within the scope of this Statement refers to assets grouped together at the lowest level at which cash flows can be identified and be relatively independent of the cash flows of other groups of assets.

## Impairment Review

The basic requirement is that the assets being held and used by an entity must be reviewed for impairment whenever there is any indication that the carrying amount of the particular asset might not be recoverable.

Events or changes which could signal the time for a review for impairment include the following:

1) Significant reduction in the usefulness of the asset.
2) Significant alteration in the way in which an asset is used to the detriment of its value.
3) Significant reduction in the market value of the asset.
4) Adverse change in the general business climate that could affect the value of an asset.
5) Adverse change in the laws or regulations relating to the asset.
6) Continued operating or cash flow loss.
7) Forecasted continuing losses or lack of long-term profitability related to a supposedly revenue-producing asset.
8) Costs exceeding those anticipated for the acquisition or construction of an asset.
9) Significant change in the physical condition of an asset.
10) Adverse legal or regulatory action against the asset.

As noted above, the basic tenet of this Statement is that assets should be reported at their recoverable amounts. If circumstances such as those listed above appear to have occurred to the extent that the carrying amount of a particular asset may, in fact, not be recoverable, a review for impairment is required. The thinking behind these provisions is that a tangible or intangible asset or group of assets, including goodwill, is impaired when the book value is not recoverable. Impairment is measured by the projected cumulative, undiscounted cash flow (excluding interest charges) related to the asset. If the resulting total amount for estimated future cash flows from the use of the asset and eventual disposition is less than the carrying amount, FASB 121 mandates that a new, lower cost basis for the asset be established. For those long-lived assets and identifiable intangibles an entity plans to hold and use, the new cost basis is to be set at fair value. The writedown is to be charged to income as an impairment loss.

For a depreciable asset, the new lower cost is to be depreciated over the remaining useful life of that asset. Whether there has actually been an impairment loss or not, when need for a review has been signaled, this might also be an appropriate time for a review of depreciation policies in line with APB 20, *Accounting Changes*.

The FASB decided that an impairment loss cannot be considered similar to an extraordinary item or a loss from discontinued operations. Thus, impairment losses are to be classified as components of earnings (losses) from continuing operations.

If an asset being assessed for possible impairment was acquired in a business combination and accounted for using the purchase method, any goodwill included must be considered in the asset grouping and prorated appropriately.

When goodwill *is* included as a portion of the impairment of a particular asset group, the carrying value of the goodwill must be eliminated prior to reducing the carrying value of impaired long-lived assets and other identifiable intangibles to the current fair value. As a result of this provision, it is probable that if a company appears to have overpaid for an acquisition because it is not producing the anticipated level of positive cash flow, the company will have decided to take a look down the road and write off the related goodwill.

This new Statement requires that the long-lived assets and certain identifiable intangibles which are being disposed of must be reported at the lower of carrying amount or fair value less the cost to sell the asset except when covered by APB-30, *Reporting the Results of Operations—Reporting the Effects of Disposal of a Segment of a Business, and Extraordinary, Unusual and Infrequently Occurring Events and Transactions.* These assets will still be reported at the carrying amount or net realizable value, less the cost to sell the asset, whichever is lower.

The Statement also requires that a rate-regulated entity must recognize an impairment when a regulator excludes all or a part of a cost from the entity's rate base.

The initial application of FASB 121 to assets being held at the time of adoption are to be reported as the cumulative effect of a change in accounting principle as prescribed in APB 20.

As stated above, in measuring for possible impairment, the use of the term *asset* here refers to assets grouped together at the lowest level at which cash flows can be identified and are relatively independent of cash flows of other groups of assets. Obviously, the formation of these groupings can lead to very subjective decisions. Differing businesses and industries operating under varying circumstances and conditions could conceivably justify disparate groupings. Decisions relating to grouping, as well as to estimating expected cash flow, must give due concern to possible outcomes and be founded on carefully considered facts, assumptions, and projections.

Unlike the accounting standards established in many countries and proposed by the International Accounting Standards Committee, this measure does not permit the write-back of impaired asset values from previous writedowns or writeoffs.

*Fair value* in the context of FASB 121 refers to the amount at which an asset could be exchanged in a current transaction between willing parties—not in a forced or liquidation sale. Determining the fair value of an asset is guided by several considerations:

1) The best indication would be the sales price or bid/asked price of that or a similar asset obtained from a securities exchange registered with the SEC; or an over-the-counter quotation if reported by NASDAQ or the National Quotation Bureau; or a foreign market price if that market is comparable to a U.S. exchange or market.

2) Otherwise, the estimate must be based on fundamental analysis employing whatever reliable information and valuation techniques are available: price of similar assets, appraisals, present value of estimated cash flows discounted for risk, option-pricing models, matrix pricing, and option-adjusted spread models, for example.

Impairment losses for assets being held and used in operations are to be reported as a component of income from continuing operations before income taxes in the income statement (for-profit entities) or in the statement of activities (not-for-profit organizations).

## Reporting and Disclosure

Disclosures to be made in the financial statements of the periods covering any impairment writedowns for assets to be held and used include the following:

**1)** A description of the impaired assets and the facts and circumstances leading up to recognition of impairment.

**2)** The extent of impairment and the methods used in determining the fair value.

**3)** The specific entry in the income statement or the statement of activities where the amount is reported, whether as a separate line item or part of an aggregated entry.

**4)** The segments affected, if applicable.

Financial statement reporting and disclosure requirements for assets to be disposed of include:

**1)** A description of the assets targeted for disposal, facts and circumstances leading up to the planned disposal, the expected disposal date, and the carrying amount of the targeted assets.

**2)** The business segment in which assets to be disposed of are located.

**3)** Any impairment loss resulting from the initial measurement made at the time of the decision to dispose of the asset.

**4)** Any gain or loss resulting from changes in the carrying amount of assets to be disposed of.

**5)** Identification of the entry in the income statement or statement of activities in which any gains or losses are aggregated if they were not presented as a separate entry or reported on the face of the statement.

**6)** The results of operations for those assets to the extent the results are included in the entity's results of operations for the period and are identifiable.

## Accounting for Real Estate

This standard is expected to have particular importance in bringing about accounting changes for companies with substantial real estate holdings. When these companies adopt the requirements, many will probably take significant writedowns whether their real estate assets are for rental to outsiders or for internal use. This group will include not only home builders who still hold high-priced land acquired during the 1980 boom years, but also owners of office buildings, shopping centers, apartment buildings, and hotels being carried at inflated prices.

FASB 121 could also cause substantial writedowns by companies with long-lived assets, which could impact the companies' earnings and share values. As mentioned elsewhere, however, the companies that take these writedowns could increase future earnings and also reduce future depreciation charges.

Accounting requirements previously had real estate companies carry for-sale real estate inventory at the lower of cost or net realizable value which places an asset at a value where it will break even in the future. Under the new standard, if a valuation adjustment is required, the asset is written down instead to fair value. This is usually a considerably more conservative measurement than net realizable value.

Accounting standards have been vague enough in the valuation of real estate held for use in the business that some companies have carried assets at depreciated cost with no writedowns even when returns on the assets were negative. Now assets held for use must be carried at the lower of their carrying values or fair value, but only if they fail an impairment test where the sum of the undiscounted cash flows before interest is less than the carrying amounts.

Real estate developers who issue financial statements will find specific instructions in FASB 121 for evaluating the impairment of real estate projects premised upon whether:

1) They are being held for and/or are in the process of development, or
2) They are substantially completed and ready for their intended use.

In effect, this new standard amends the impairment criteria established in FASB 67, *Accounting for Costs and Initial Rental Operations of Real Estate Projects.*

Projects held for development and sale are to be checked for impairment following the recognition and measurement provisions covering assets to be held and used. Thus, property that is being held for development, and property which is presently under development but not yet completed, should be checked for impairment only if events or changing circumstances signal possible impairment. If the estimated, undiscounted cash flows from the project fall short of the recorded cost, the property must be written down to fair value.

On the other hand, projects that are substantially completed and ready for sale or rental are to be accounted for as assets to be disposed of, and must be reported at the lower of carrying amount or fair value less cost to sell, except as mentioned above when covered by APB 30.

Specific indicators for real estate owners and developers that impairment may exist would include:

1) Expiration of material leases.
2) Insufficient rental demand for a project under development.
3) Deterioration of an area in which rental or sales property is located.

## Overall Effect

Insofar as company balance sheets are concerned, this Statement should result in the presentation of a more realistic picture of the value of an entity's assets. Since a company can no longer offset assets against each other, the impaired assets must be written off. Thus, current profit will be reduced when the one-time asset impairment charges are recorded. The financial picture after the writedown will show lower future costs resulting in higher future profits. Cash flow will not be affected by the writedown.

This improving financial picture may not necessarily mean that the future profit increases are the result of improving operations, only that "dead wood" has been trimmed from the balance sheet. On the other hand, the need to take a closer look at operations may very well lead to greater efficiency and improved capital allocation leading to increased economic value.

Part of the impetus for the adoption of this Statement was an attempt to increase the usefulness of financial reporting by making a comparison of entities with impairment losses more readily available. It is the belief of the majority of the FASB members that it will now be easier for financial statement users to compare one entity's response to economic or other outside forces to another entity's response to the same situation.

This Statement brings a greater degree of uniformity to financial reporting by providing accounting guidelines on when to test long-lived assets for impairment and how to go about the calculation. However, as in many prescribed situations, much is left to the discretion of management. The timing of the recognition of impairment, the measurement of the losses, the discount rate to use for similar levels of risk, and the composition of *asset groups* are examples of elements that may justifiably vary.

## ACCOUNTING FOR MORTGAGE SERVICING RIGHTS—FASB 122 (SUPERCEDED BY FASB 125 BELOW)

FASB 122 is an amendment to FASB 65, *Accounting for Certain Mortgage Banking Activities*. Mortgage servicing organizations often acquire the rights to service loans for others for a fee by purchasing or originating loans. They may then turn around and sell the loans, but keep the rights to service them.

FASB 65 made a distinction between loans originated by the servicer and those purchased. As a result, different accounting treatment was given to similar assets. To correct this situation, FASB 122 requires that mortgage service organizations recognize as separate assets the rights to service loans regardless of the manner in which they were acquired.

## Change of Direction

In effect, this means an about-face in GAAP from a prohibition against to a mandatory requirement to capitalize the cost of originating mortgage servicing rights when:

1) There is a definitive plan to sell or securitize the related mortgages.
2) The fair value of the mortgage and related servicing rights can be measured.

Accounting for the cost of mortgage servicing rights is to be handled in the following manner regardless of where and how the costs originated:

1) Cost of acquisition includes the cost of related mortgage servicing rights.
2) When a mortgage banking enterprise sells or securitizes a mortgage but retains servicing rights, total cost of the mortgage loan should be allocated to the mortgage servicing rights and the loans (minus the mortgage servicing rights) based on the fair values of each.
3) If there appears to be no practicable way to determine the fair values of each, the total cost of acquisition is to be allocated to the loan only with no cost being allocated to the servicing rights.
4) Any cost allocated to servicing rights constitutes a separate asset.
5) Mortgage servicing rights are to be amortized in proportion to and covering the period of their net servicing income.
6) Mortgage servicing rights are to be evaluated for impairment based on their fair value. In addition to the usual guidance provided for determining fair value (refer to discussion of FASB 121 above), other suggestions for determining fair value and measuring for impairment with specific attention to mortgage servicing rights are mentioned in the provisions in FASB 122.

## Precautions

Among the "flags" to keep in mind are:

1) Mortgage servicing rights are subject to devaluation resulting from prepayment of loans.
2) During an economic downturn, borrowers may find it necessary to default on loans.
3) When interest rates drop, borrowers will refinance to take advantage of the lower rates.

**4)** The predominant risk characteristics of different types of loans, such as various conventional or government guaranteed or insured mortgaged loans and adjustable-rate or fixed-rate loans, must be considered.

**5)** Factors relating to loan size, note rate, date of origination, term, and geographic location are relevant.

To put it succinctly, no matter how mortgage servicing rights were acquired, this new Statement requires mortgage servicers to recognize them as separate assets.

Sections of the Statement include background information, benefits and costs, recognition and measurement, recognition of gains on sales of mortgage loans, and other aspects of mortgage servicing.

FASB 122 applies prospectively beginning after December 15, 1995.

The costs associated with retained servicing rights generated internally must be capitalized. Growth companies that retain these rights may very well find that they benefit from FASB 122's provisions.

## ACCOUNTING FOR STOCK-BASED COMPENSATION—FASB 123

Passage of FASB 123 is not so much a compromise measure as an apparent agreement to get on to something else. In the final (for the time being) analysis, it offers an alternative approach to the present method of using APB Opinion 25, *Accounting for Stock Issued to Employees*, to account for stock options.

The new Statement sets forth a preferred method for accounting for stock-based employee compensation; however, companies are not required to follow the new guidelines, but may continue in their present accounting practice with only slight modification. The alternative approaches are:

**1)** The fair value method.

**2)** The intrinsic value method.

### Fair Value Method

In line with the current effort to bring a greater degree of uniformity and understanding to financial reporting, the FASB has premised the preferred method on fair value. Using this procedure, stock-based compensation cost is measured at the grant date based on the value of the award and is recognized over the employee's entire service period which is also normally the vesting period.

For stock options granted by a public entity, the fair value is determined using an option-pricing model that considers several factors present on the grant date—the exercise price and expected life of the option, the current price of the underlying stock and its expected volatility, expected dividends on the stock with specified exception, and the risk-free interest rate for the expected term of the option. The text suggests the Black-Scholes or a binomial model. When the fair value of the option has been determined at the grant date, it is not later adjusted for changes in the price of the underlying stock, its volatility, the life of the option, dividends on the stock or for the risk-free interest rate. For a nonpublic enterprise, the procedure is the same except that expected volatility need not be considered in estimating the option's fair value. Exclusion of the volatility factor in the estimation results in what is termed *minimum value.*

The Board feels that it should be possible to reach a reasonably accurate estimate of the fair value of most stock options and other equity instruments when they are granted. However, if there are complicated features which make this extremely difficult, even impossible, alternatives are suggested. If all else fails in finding a satisfactory estimate for the grant date, the Statement provides that the final measure of compensation cost is to be the value based on the stock price and any other pertinent information available on the first date that it is possible to reach a reasonable estimate of the value—generally, the date when the number of shares to which an employee is entitled and the exercise price are both determinable.

For nonvested or restricted stock awarded to an employee, the fair value is measured at the market price—or estimated market price if the stock is not publicly traded—of a share of nonrestricted stock at the grant date.

## Intrinsic Value Method

Stock-based compensation standards have heretofore been based on APB 25, and probably will continue to be so for most companies. Using the intrinsic value method, compensation cost is the excess, if there is any, of the quoted market price of the particular stock over the employee's exercise price at the grant date or at another specified measurement date—perhaps the service date.

There actually is no intrinsic value or excess of exercise price over market price of the stock at the grant date for most fixed stock option plans. Therefore, these current accounting requirements generally do not result in an expense charge for most options. Therefore, no compensation cost is recognized. On the other hand, normally a compensation cost is recognized for other types of stock compensation plans under the intrinsic value method. They are usually plans with variable, often performance-based features.

## Exceptions

Compensation costs need not be recognized for employee stock purchase plan discounts under the new Statement if the following three conditions exist:

1) The discount is relatively small.
2) Substantially all full-time employees participate on an equitable basis.
3) Provisions in the plan do not include any stock option features.

The compensation cost of stock awards required to be settled in cash is the amount of the change in the stock price in the periods in which the changes occur.

## Additional Requirements

While FASB 123 is effective for calendar year 1996 and information about options granted in 1995 must be included in the 1996 financial statements, the decade-long consideration of the controversial issue only "encourages" companies to account for stock compensation awards based on their fair value at the date the awards are granted with the compensation cost shown as an expense on the income statement.

Companies continuing to use the APB 25 intrinsic value method will be required to disclose, but only in a note to the financial statements, what the net income and earnings would have been had they followed the new accounting method.

## Controversy

The Board had long hoped to require full-scale fair value type measurement and accounting for employee stock compensation using a generally accepted options pricing model; however, those outside the Board were not ready to accept a mandate. After rather overwhelming pressure for more than a year from Congress, other politicians, other government agencies, businesses, and CPAs in public practice as well as those with commercial and industrial companies, a majority of the Board decided to emphasize improving disclosure rather than holding out for requiring an expense charge for all options. (See discussion on pp. 46-47.)

## ACCOUNTING FOR CERTAIN INVESTMENTS HELD BY NOT-FOR-PROFIT ORGANIZATIONS—FASB 124

FASB 124 is another step in the process of bringing reason, conformity, consistency, and comparability in accounting and financial reporting to the world of not-for-profit entities.

Earlier measures include:

1) FASB 93, *Recognition of Depreciation by Not-for-Profit Organizations.*
2) FASB 116, *Accounting for Contributions Received and Contributions Made.*
3) FASB 117, *Financial Statements of Not-for-Profit Organizations.* (See discussions in *ADB*, Chapter 13.)

This latest statement is reminiscent of FASB 115, *Accounting for Certain Investments in Debt and Equity Securities*, to the extent that it covers the same securities; however, accounting treatment for NPOs is markedly different from that applied to for-profit businesses.

## Fair Value Requirements

Statement 124 requires that certain equity securities and all investments in debt securities be reported at fair value. The specific equity securities are those with readily determined fair value which are not accounted for by the equity method or as investments in consolidated subsidiaries. Gains and losses are to be reported in the statement of activities. This Statement also requires specific disclosures about all investments, including the return on the investments.

*Readily determinable* fair value of an equity security is considered to have been met if one of the following criteria applies:

1) Sale prices or bid or asked quotations are available on an SEC registered exchange.
2) Sales prices or bid or asked prices on OTC markets if they are reported by NASDAQ or the National Quotation Bureau.
3) If the equity security is traded only on a foreign market, that market is comparable to one of those given above.
4) If a mutual fund investment, fair value per share or unit has been determined and published as the basis for ongoing transactions.

Although many NPOs have been reporting all of their investments at fair value, it has not been required; therefore, there has been a considerable degree of diversity in the various organizations' accounting and financial reporting. The FASB believes that fair value will give a truer picture of the resources available for the further growth of the program of a not-for-profit organization. In addition, not only the staff and administrators, but also the donors will have improved information to assist them in allocating their efforts and resources.

## Accounting Procedures

Application of this Statement may be made in either of two ways:

1) Restating of all financial statements presented for prior years.
2) Recognizing the cumulative effect of the change in the year of adoption.

Accounting and reporting for investments by various types of not-for-profit organizations has heretofore been provided by several AICPA guides. Any guidance in those sources which is inconsistent with the provisions of FASB 124 are superseded by these new requirements in this Statement.

In addition to the accounting principles set forth in this pronouncement, any additional disclosure and accounting requirements not discussed here but included in other Statements may apply to investments held by not-for-profit entities as well as to for-profit companies. They are:

1) FASB 107, *Disclosure about Fair Value of Financial Instruments* (amended).
2) FASB 133, *Accounting for Derivative Instruments and Hedging Activities.*

(FASB 107 is discussed in *ADB,* Chapter 10, and later in this chapter; FASB 133 is discussed at the end of this chapter.)

## Disclosure and Reporting

The Statement of Activities for each reporting period for an NPO must include the following specific items:

1) Investment income from dividends, interest, etc.
2) Net gains or losses on investments reported at other than fair value.
3) Net gains or losses on those reported at fair value.
4) Reconciliation of investment return if separated into operating and nonoperating amounts.
5) Description of the policy used to decide what items should be included in determining operating costs.
6) Discussion for so doing if there is a change in that policy.

The Statement of Financial Position for each reporting period for an NPO must include the following:

1) Aggregate carrying amount of investments by major type.

2) Basis on which carrying amounts were determined for investments other than equity securities with readily determinable fair value and all debt securities.

3) Procedures used in determining fair values of investments other than financial instruments if carried at fair value. (Financial instruments are covered by the same requirement in FASB 107.)

4) Aggregate amount of any deficiencies in donor-related funds in which fair value of the assets has fallen below the level necessary to abide by donor stipulation or legal requirements.

For the most recent period, a not-for-profit organization must disclose in the Statement of Financial Position the nature of and carrying amount of any investments that represent a significant concentration of market risk.

## ACCOUNTING FOR TRANSFERS AND SERVICING OF FINANCIAL ASSETS AND EXTINGUISHMENT OF LIABILITIES—FASB 125, AND DEFERRAL OF THE EFFECTIVE DATE OF CERTAIN PROVISIONS OF FASB STATEMENT 125—FASB 127

Before the requirements of FASB 125 could be put into effect, representatives from a wide variety of enterprises affected by the provisions raised serious objections to what they considered to be insufficient lead time. The new standard will change the accounting for many capital market transactions; therefore, many felt that the necessity to change both accounting and information systems with what they considered to be undue haste could lead to serious problems. Securities brokers and dealers were particularly concerned about the multitude of "dollar-rolls," repurchase agreements, securities lending and similar transactions that must be considered.

### Partial Deferral

After considerable debate concerning various approaches to meeting these objections, the Board decided that the effective date for *certain* parts of the standard would be *required* to be deferred for *all* entities. Those *certain* parts included the "dollar-rolls," etc. mentioned above as well as secured borrowings and collateral described in paragraph 15 of FASB 125. Those "parts" are deferred for one year to December 31, 1997. However, all other transactions involving transfer and servicing of financial assets and extinguishments of liabilities taking place after December 31, 1996 are not affected by FASB 127 and are covered by the provisions of FASB 125. With this partial deferral out of the way, it behooves us to discuss the provisions of the original Statement.

## Secured Borrowing or Sale?

FASB 125, *Accounting for Transfers and Servicing of Financial Assets and Extinguishments of Liabilities,* was promulgated in June 1996 to become effective for those transactions occurring after December 31, 1996. Its purpose is to provide accounting and reporting standards for transfers and servicing of financial assets and extinguishments of liabilities based on the consistent application of a financial components approach that focuses on control and the assumption that financial assets can be divided into a variety of component parts. Using that approach, after a transfer of financial assets, an entity:

1) Recognizes the financial and servicing assets it controls.
2) Recognizes the liabilities it has incurred.
3) Derecognizes financial assets when control has been surrendered.
4) Derecognizes liabilities when extinguished.

The Statement clarifies a long-standing dilemma concerning whether certain transactions should be accounted for as a pledge of collateral in a secured borrowing or as a sale. FASB 125 presents consistent standards for distinguishing between the two. A transfer of financial assets in which the transferor surrenders control over those assets is accounted for as a sale when consideration—other than beneficial interests in the transferred assets—has been received in exchange, and control of those assets has actually been relinquished by the transferor.

## Effective Transfer

The transferor has surrendered control over transferred assets only if all of the following conditions have been met:

1) The transferred assets have been isolated from the transferor; that is, the asset has presumably been placed beyond the reach of the transferor and any creditors, even in bankruptcy or other receivership situations.
2) One or the other of the following is true:
   a) each transferee obtains the right to pledge or exchange the transferred assets, free of conditions that could prevent it from taking advantage of that right, or

**b)** the transferee is a qualifying special-purpose entity and the holders of beneficial interests in that entity have the right to pledge or exchange those interests, free of any conditions that could prevent them from taking advantage of that right.

**3)** The transferor has not maintained effective control over the transferred assets through one of the following arrangements:

**a)** an agreement that both entitles and obligates the transferor to repurchase or redeem those assets before their maturity, or

**b)** an agreement that gives the transferor the right to repurchase or redeem transferred assets that are not readily obtainable.

The Statement further requires that liabilities and derivatives incurred or obtained by transferors as the result of a transfer of financial assets be initially measured at fair value, when practicable. Any gain or loss on the sale is to be recognized in income.

## Transferred Assets

In addition, the ruling requires that servicing assets and other retained interests in the transferred financial assets be measured by allocating the previous carrying amount between the assets sold and retained interests based on their relative fair values at the transfer date.

FASB 125 requires that after recognition of the transfer, the servicing assets and liabilities are to be measured by:

**1)** Amortization in proportion to and over the period of estimated net servicing income or loss, and

**2)** Assessment for asset impairment or increased obligation based on their fair values.

This Statement requires that debtors reclassify financial assets pledged as collateral and that secured parties recognize those assets and their obligation to return them in certain circumstances in which the secured party has taken control of those assets.

The Statement requires that a liability be derecognized if either:

**1)** The debtor pays the creditor and is relieved of obligation for the liability, or

**2)** The debtor is legally released from being the primary obligor under the liability either judicially or by the creditor.

In-substance defeasances fail to meet this second criterion and, therefore, are not considered to be an extinguishment of a liability under FASB 125.

It does provide implementation guidance for isolation of transferred assets and for accounting for transfers on the following transactions:

1) Servicing of mortgages and other financial assets.
2) Securitizations.
3) Transfers of sales-type and direct financing lease receivables.
4) Securities lending transactions.
5) Sales of partial interests in financial assets.
6) Repurchase agreements including "dollar rolls."
7) "Wash sales."
8) Pledges of collateral.
9) Loan syndications and participations.
10) Risk participations in banker's acceptances.
11) Factoring arrangements.
12) Transfers of receivables with recourse.
13) Extinguishments of liabilities.

## Organized Approach

Provisions contained in FASB 125 result in a more organized approach to numerous similar transactions which have previously been dealt with in haphazard fashion in different Statements—not always in a consistent manner. Further, FASB 125 adopts a practice of accounting for financial asset transfers in step with the widespread practice of the financial markets of disaggregating individual financial assets or pools of financial assets into component parts.

It supersedes FASB 76, *Extinguishment of Debt,* FASB 122, *Accounting for Mortgage Servicing Rights,* and FASB 77, *Reporting by Transferors for Transfers of Receivables with Recourse.* It amends FASB 115, *Accounting for Certain Investments in Debt and Equity Securities,* to clarify that debt securities, such as those that can contractually be prepaid, may not be classified as held-to-maturity if they can be prepaid; or settled in a manner in which the holder of the security would fail to recover substantially all of the recorded investment. Such securities must be classified as held-for-sale or trading securities.

As stated above, FASB 125 requires a company to recognize the financial and servicing assets it controls and the liabilities it incurs. For each servicing contract in existence before January 1, 1997, any previously recognized servicing rights and excess servicing receivables that do not exceed contractually specified servicing fees will be combined, net of any previously recognized servicing obligations under that contract, as a servicing asset or liability. Previously recognized servicing receivables that exceed contractually specified servicing fees will be reclassified as interest-only strips, and accounted for as either securities classified as available-for-sale or trading as set forth in FASB 115.

FASB 125 also amends and extends the existing accounting standards for mortgage servicing rights now in FASB 65, *Accounting for Certain Mortgage Banking Activities,* to all servicing assets and liabilities.

This Statement also supersedes Technical Bulletins No. 84–4, *In-Substance Defeasance of Debt,* No. 85–2, *Accounting for Collateralized Mortgage Obligations (CMOs),* and No. 87–3, *Accounting for Mortgage Servicing Fees and Rights.*

Accounting practice has treated most collateralized mortgage obligations (CMOs) as financing; however, under FASB 125 companies will be allowed to classify more of them as sales.

## Two Effective Dates

As indicated above, this Statement is effective for transfers and servicing of financial assets and extinguishments of liabilities occurring after December 31, 1996, with the exception of those transactions specified in FASB 127 which are deferred to December 31, 1997. The requirements must be applied prospectively. Earlier or retroactive application is not permitted.

## EXEMPTION FROM CERTAIN REQUIRED DISCLOSURES ABOUT FINANCIAL INSTRUMENTS FOR CERTAIN NONPUBLIC ENTITIES, AN AMENDMENT OF FASB 107—FASB 126

Statement 126, issued in December, 1996, amends FASB 107, *Disclosures about Fair Value of Financial Instruments,* to make the disclosures about fair value of financial instruments required in FASB 107 optional for entities that meet all of the following criteria:

1) It is a nonpublic entity.
2) Its total assets are less than $100 million on the date of the financial statements.
3) It has no instrument that, in whole or in part, is accounted for as a derivative instrument under FASB 133, *Accounting for Derivative Instruments and Hedging Activities,* during the reporting period.

## Nonpublic Entities

For use in this Statement, a "nonpublic entity" is defined in negative terms. It is *not* one that:

1) Has debt or equity securities traded in a public market, either on a domestic or foreign stock exchange or in the over-the-counter market, including securities quoted locally or regionally.

2) Makes a filing with a regulatory agency in preparation for the sale of any class of debt or equity securities in one of these public markets.

3) Is controlled by an entity answering to either of these two descriptions.

For entities that do not meet all three criteria for coverage by FASB 126, all provisions of FASB 107 *are* still in effect. Furthermore, the following *are* also still in effect for nonpublic entities. The requirements stipulated in:

1) FASB 115, *Accounting for Certain Investments in Debt and Equity Securities.*

2) FASB 124, *Accounting for Certain Investments Held by Not-for-Profit Organizations.*

This includes the disclosure in the Statement of Financial Position about financial instruments other than debt and equity securities that are measured at fair value.

## Immediate Effective Date

Unlike the FASB's usual procedure of setting the effective date of a new Statement several months in the future, this statement could be put to use immediately. Normally, the affected entities need time to adjust their accounting and reporting procedures to the new standard. In this instance, it was a matter of lessening the task which had been required under FASB 107. Thus, Statement 126 was made effective for fiscal years ending after December 15, 1996, but earlier application was permitted for financial statements that had not already been issued.

## EARNINGS PER SHARE—FASB 128

FASB 128 establishes new standards for computing and presenting earning per share (EPS) and applies to entities with publicly held common stock or potential common stock.

It simplifies the admittedly complicated methods used for computing earnings per share previously found in APB 15, *Earnings Per Share,* and makes the requirements comparable to new international EPS standards adopted recently. In doing this, FASB 128 replaces the presentation of primary EPS with a presentation of basic EPS. It also requires dual presentation of basic and diluted EPS on the face of the income statement for all entities with complex capital structures and requires a reconciliation of the numerator and denominator of the basic EPS computation to the numerator and denominator of the diluted EPS computation.

The oft interpreted, reinterpreted, and much maligned APB 15 had required that entities with simple capital structures present a single "earnings per common share" on the face of the income statement, whereas those with complex capital structures had to present both "primary" and "fully diluted" EPS. Primary EPS showed the amount of income attributed to each share of common stock if every common stock equivalent were converted into common stock. Fully diluted EPS considers common stock equivalents and all other securities that could be converted into common stock. The two EPS figures required under FASB 128 follow:

1) Basic Earnings Per Share is computed by dividing income available to stockholders by the weighted average number of common shares outstanding during the period. Shares issued during the period and shares reacquired during the period should be weighted for the portion of the period they were outstanding. The formula would be: (Net income minus preferred dividends) divided by common stock.

   Under the old rules, U.S. companies with complex capital structures could not present a basic earnings per share figure. (A company has a complex capital structure when it has issued securities convertible into common stock or has agreements to issue common stock at some future date.) The principal difference between basic and primary earnings per share is that the latter takes into account so-called common share equivalents. In nearly every country outside of the U.S. that requires an earnings per share disclosure, the requirement calls for a basic earnings per share presentation rather than a primary EPS figure. An entity's basic earnings per share will show higher earnings per share than primary earnings per share did, but this will mean no change as far as a company's actual equity valuation is concerned.

2) Diluted EPS reflects the potential dilution that could occur if securities or other contracts to issue common stock were exercised or converted into common stock or resulted in the issuance of common stock that would then share in the earnings of the entity. It is figured in a similar manner to basic EPS after adjusting the numerator and denominator for the possible dilution. Since it is, therefore, computed in a similar manner to fully diluted EPS under APB 15, it will produce a similar earnings per share figure.

## Equity Valuation Unchanged

The new standard will not change U.S. equity valuations because:

1) Even though basic earnings per share will show a higher figure than primary earnings per share, informed investors will not use basic

earnings per share anyway for companies with complex capital structures because it does not take into account the potential dilutive effect of convertibles, options, warrants, and the like.

**2)** Most entities' dilutive earnings per share will be substantially the same as their fully diluted earnings per share.

## Resulting Changes

Of course, the most important change introduced by the FASB's new standard is the elimination of the complicated calculations necessary to arrive at primary earnings per share and replace them with the simpler calculations necessary to obtain basic earnings per share for disclosure.

In addition, diluted EPS is somewhat different from "fully diluted earnings per share." Not only is "fully" dropped, but the calculation of the figure is changed in several ways:

**1)** Elimination of the provision that the diluted earnings per share need not be given if the potential dilution is less than three percent.

**2)** Elimination of the use of the end of period stock price in the treasury stock method calculation to determine maximum dilution.

**3)** Elimination of the modified treasury stock method that was used to calculate potential dilution in cases when an unusually large number of options or warrants were outstanding.

**4)** Use of the earnings from continuing operations as the "control figure" to determine if a security or contingent issuance is antidilutive in certain situations.

## Avoid Surprises, Recompute Now

To avoid possible surprises, company CFOs, accountants, analysts, and investors should recompute the earnings per share data currently reported for companies with complex capital structures. This will help determine *why* if, for some unexpected or unlikely reason, the new standard *does* materially change the earnings per share figures, even if not the true picture of a particular entity. This should be done as quickly as possible so that, if there is a noticeable difference, it can be examined and explained before any misunderstanding of the true impact of the differing figure's relevance can develop. Possible causes of a different figure could include:

**1)** Some companies that have *not* been reporting fully diluted earnings per share under the old rules may have to report diluted earnings per share under FASB 128.

**2)** Companies with an unusually large number of potentially dilutive common shares and/or shares that, because of the way they are written, could dilute earnings per share at some time in the distant future, may be required to report significantly different diluted EPS figures under the new standard.

3) The spread between basic and diluted earnings per share may be significantly different from the spread between the primary and fully diluted earnings per share figures that would have been disclosed under APB 15.

The new statement not only supersedes APB 15 and AICPA Accounting Interpretation 1–102 of APB 15, but it also supersedes or amends other accounting pronouncements scattered throughout accounting literature. The provisions in this Statement are substantially the same as those in International Accounting Standard 33, *Earnings per Share,* issued by the International Accounting Standards Committee at the same time.

## Effective Date

The effective date for the new U.S. earnings per share standard is 1998. To maintain comparability between earnings per share disclosures, the FASB decided to prohibit early adoption of the new standard; however, the Board permits disclosure in the notes of pro forma earnings per share data prepared using the new standard prior to the effective date. When FASB 128 goes into effect, companies are required to restate all prior period EPS figures presented in annual, interim, and summary financial presentations to conform to the new standard.

## Comparable to IAS 33

As mentioned in Chapter 3 on the International Accounting Standards Committee (IASC), the new EPS standard results from one of the earliest U.S.-IASC cooperative efforts to bring U.S. GAAP and international standards into a workable degree of coordination.

## DISCLOSURE OF INFORMATION ABOUT CAPITAL STRUCTURE—FASB 129

Statement 129 establishes standards for disclosing information about an entity's capital structure, and applies to all entities. The new standard does not countermand, but *continues* the requirements to disclose certain information about an entity's capital structure for those entities that were subject to the requirements found in:

1) APB 10, *Omnibus Opinion-1966.*
2) APB 15, *Earnings per Share.*
3) FASB 47, *Disclosure of Long-Term Obligations.*

The specific purpose for this Statement is to *eliminate* the *exemption* of nonpublic entities from certain disclosure requirements of APB 15 contained in FASB 21, *Suspension of the Reporting of Earnings per Share and Segment Information by Nonpublic Enterprises.* It supersedes specific disclosure requirements of APBs 10 and 15 and FASB 47 and consolidates them in this Statement to make it easier for nonpublic entities to know and be able to live up to the disclosures required of them.

## Two Are Better Than One

What began as one Statement has been divided into two: In January 1996, the Board issued an Exposure Draft on earnings per share, which included capital structure disclosure requirements for all entities. The Board decided to issue these latter disclosure requirements as a separate Statement since they are applicable to nonpublic entities and the earnings per share are not. Rationale behind issuing two separate standards was that the FASB did not want to include the capital structure disclosure requirements in a Statement on earnings per share which really did not apply to the nonpublic company. Why muddy the waters? In addition, they wanted to make it perfectly clear to these nonpublic companies that *all* companies are required to abide by FASB 129, whether they are public companies or not.

FASB 129 is effective for financial statements for periods ending after December 15, 1997. It contains no change in disclosure requirements for entities that were previously subject to the requirements of the Omnibus Opinion to consolidate existing disclosure requirements for ease of retrieval, nor a change in disclosure requirements for companies that were subject to the previously existing requirements.

## REPORTING COMPREHENSIVE INCOME—FASB 130

FASB 130 began in conjunction with the Exposure Draft (ED) on derivatives and hedging. However, since there is much less in it to cause prolonged controversy, this Standard was issued requiring reporting and display of comprehensive income effective in 1998, while the new derivatives standard will not be effective until June 15, 2000. Financial statements from previous periods used for comparison must be reclassified in line with the provisions of Statement 130.

At the time the EDs were issued, U.S. GAAP did not use a comprehensive income concept. The idea was to issue the two EDs simultaneously in anticipation of employing the concept in connection with the derivative and other future standards.

All of the items that are required to be recognized under accounting standards as components of comprehensive income must now be reported in a financial statement that is displayed with the same degree of prominence as other financial statements.

## Comprehensive Income Defined

Comprehensive income is defined in FASB Concepts Statement 6, *Elements of Financial Statements* as, ". . . the change in equity (net assets) of a business enterprise during a period from transactions and other events and circumstances from non-owner sources. It includes all changes in equity during a period except those resulting from investments by owners and distributions to owners."

FASB 130 considers that comprehensive income consists of two major components—net income and "other comprehensive income." The latter refers to revenues, expenses, gains and losses, that according to GAAP are included in comprehensive income, but excluded from net income. They are direct debits or credits to owners' equity that do not involve transactions with owners, such as foreign currency translation gains and losses, unrealized gains or losses on marketable securities classified as available-for-sale, and minimum pension liability adjustments. Thus, comprehensive income is the total of net income plus the revenue, expense, gain and loss changes in equity during a period which now is not included in net income.

## Equity Valuation Not Affected

This new display and related disclosures will not influence equity valuations, nor is any new or additional information disclosed. It merely repackages existing disclosed data in a new format. FASB 130 may not be of particular interest to sophisticated investors, creditors, and securities firms, but it should be of interest to accountants who have the task of implementing the new format. However, this should not be a particularly onerous job since it is largely a matter of displaying known financial data rather than calculating additional figures that would change recognition of income.

On the other hand, the FASB does appear to believe that, used in conjunction with related disclosures and other information in the financial statements, the comprehensive income information could help the knowledgeable user in assessing an entity's activities, and the timing and extent of future cash flows. Further, the Board emphasizes that while a total comprehensive income figure is useful, information about its components may give more insight into an enterprise's activities.

## Format for Presentation of Comprehensive Income

One aspect for the accountant to consider is the best way to use this new display to inform, but not confuse, the less sophisticated user of financial statements. Since the Statement does not require a specific financial statement format for the display of comprehensive income and its components, the accountant may be expected to make some choices.

1)  The requirement to report a new "income" figure for the quarter may be displayed as *either* a performance measurement or a change in equity. Which to choose?

2)  Companies are permitted to display total comprehensive income and its components in either an income statement type format or in a statement of changes in equity format. Would it be better to preserve the current income statement as a separate display and show a company's net income figure as the bottom line? Or not? (With the equity format, a statement of changes in equity must be displayed as a primary financial statement.)

3)  The Standard permits companies to report only a total for comprehensive income in condensed interim financial statements issued to shareholders. Would it be less confusing to show total comprehensive income as a part of a complete display of the calculations every time rather than as a single figure?

## Application of Requirements

FASB 130 applies to all companies that present a full set of general-purpose financial statements. Investment companies, defined benefit pension plans, and other employee benefit plans that are exempt from the requirement to provide a statement of cash flows by FASB 102, *Statement of Cash Flows—Exemption of Certain Enterprises and Certification of Cash Flows from Certain Securities Acquired for Resale,* are not exempt from requirements of FASB 130 if it applies in all other respects. However, it does not apply to organizations that have no items of comprehensive income in any period presented, or to not-for-profit organizations that are covered by FASB 117, *Financial Statements of Not-for-Profit Organizations.*

As mentioned above, the Statement suggests how to report and display comprehensive income and its components, but does not provide guidance on items that are to be included. For this guidance, the existing and future accounting standards mentioned earlier will need to be consulted.

## Components of Comprehensive Income

At this time, eight items qualify, according to GAAP, as components of other comprehensive income that, under prior standards, bypassed the income statement and had to be reported as a balance within a separate component of equity in a statement of financial position.

1) Foreign currency translation adjustments.

2) Gains and losses on foreign currency transactions that are designated as, and are effective as, economic hedges of a net investment in a foreign entity, commencing as of the designation date.

3) Gains and losses on intercompany foreign currency transactions that are of a long-term-investment nature (i.e., settlement is not planned or anticipated in the foreseeable future), when the entities to the transaction are consolidated, combined, or accounted for by the equity method in the reporting enterprise's financial statements.

4) A change in the market value of a futures contract that qualifies as a hedge of an asset reported at fair value according to FASB 115, *Accounting for Certain Investments in Debt and Equity Securities.*

5) A net loss recognized under FASB 87, *Employers' Accounting for Pensions,* as an additional pension liability not yet recognized as net periodic pension cost.

6) Unrealized holding gains and losses on available-for-sale securities.

7) Unrealized holding gains and losses that result from a debt security being transferred into the available-for-sale category from the held-to-maturity category.

8) Subsequent decreases (if not an other-than-temporary impairment) or increases in the fair value of available for-sale securities previously written down as impaired.

(This list will be expanded now that the derivatives and hedging standard is promulgated. Some gains and/or losses from those transactions will be included as part of other comprehensive income.)

## Terminology

The Statement does not require that the descriptive terms "comprehensive income," "total comprehensive income," or "other comprehensive income" be used in financial statements. It permits companies to use equivalent terms, such as "total non-owner changes in equity," "comprehensive loss" or other appropriate descriptive labels. It may be that most entities will choose to use alternative terms since "comprehensive income" still has a rather hollow ring to it.

## Cash Flow and Equity Valuation Not Affected

Inasmuch as all of the items included in other comprehensive income are noncash items, the FASB decided that indirect-method cash flow statement presentation would continue to begin with net income as required by FASB 95, *Statement of Cash Flows.*

FASB 130 should clarify the extent to which revenue, expense, gain and loss items are being taken directly to owners' equity, but, as mentioned above, the display of comprehensive income and its components will not affect equity valuation. Unlike the requirements in FASB 131, *Disclosures About Segments of an Enterprise and Related Information,* which calls for greatly expanded reporting on segments, the requirements of FASB 130 call for no new data. Since informed investors have always examined owners' equity to evaluate the material now collected under the other comprehensive income items, the new display should have little impact on the public's conception of a company's financial condition.

## DISCLOSURES ABOUT SEGMENTS OF AN ENTERPRISE AND RELATED INFORMATION—FASB 131

Continuing the newfound path of developing Standards with other standard-setting bodies, the FASB issued Statement 131, *Disclosures About Segments of an Enterprise and Related Information* in conjunction with the Accounting Standards Board (AcSB) of the Canadian Institute of Chartered Accountants. Simultaneously, the two bodies published almost identical statements to become effective in 1998. FASB 131 supersedes FASB 14, *Financial Reporting for Segments of a Business Enterprise.*

At the same time as the U.S. and Canadian groups were working together, the International Accounting Standards Committee (IASC) was also working closely with them to revise International Accounting Standard (IAS)14, *Reporting Financial Information by Segment.* However, after the many discussions to minimize differences that effectively reduced the gap, the international organization still decided to publish its own standard. That group declined to go as far in requiring increased disclosure in IAS 14 (rev.), *Segment Reporting,* as the U.S. and Canadian pronouncements required.

## Reporting Requirements

FASB 131 sets forth stricter requirements than previously for the way a business reports financial and related information about reportable operating segments in annual and interim reports. The Statement does not apply to nonpublic business enterprises or to not-for-profit organizations.

The requirements go into effect for the first annual statement after December 15, 1997, but quarterly interim statements are not due until *after* the first annual disclosure. Thus, the interim statements will not begin until 1999. Then, comparative information for interim periods in the first year is to be reported in financial statements for the second year.

FASB 131 establishes new standards for related financial and other disclosures in relation to:

1) Products and services.
2) Geographical areas.
3) Major customers.

This information is to be reported whether the business actually uses it in making operating decisions or not—unless preparing information that is not used internally would be impracticable. The enterprise must also:

1) Provide background information about the manner in which the operating segments were established.
2) Describe the particular products and/or services provided by each segment.
3) Explain any differences between the measurements used in reporting segment information and those used in their general-purpose financial statements.
4) Explain any changes in the measurement of segments from one reporting period to another.

## Objectives of the Standard

It would appear that the FASB considers this a refinement of the general principles of good general-purpose financial reporting. The Board apparently feels that providing the required segment information will better the financial statement user's ability to:

1) Understand the enterprise's performance.
2) Estimate the enterprise's prospects relating to future cash flows.
3) Arrive at better informed judgments about the enterprise as a whole.

## Information from Within

Generally, this new standard requires that the information be reported on the same basis as the enterprise uses *internally* for evaluating segment performance and deciding how to allocate resources to segments.

This will lead to new data being disclosed by companies and should be useful to investment analysts and informed investors. They will become privy to much of the operations information that goes to upper management to assist them in their decision making.

Reporting financial information under FASB 131 is based on the *management approach* in contrast to the *industry approach* that has been used in FASB 14. While this standard has required reporting of information about major customers, and some data was provided on related product and service groups, it was felt that the industry approach was too subjective. So much discretion was left to the reporting company in the application of FASB 14 that unfavorable earnings figures could be hidden (by switching industry groupings around, for example).

## Management Approach

The management approach is based on the way management organizes the segments within a company for making operating decisions and assessing performance. Because of this, the segments should be evident from the structure of the company's organization. Therefore, financial statement preparers should be able to provide the additional required information without a great amount of additional time and effort.

The management approach should result in consistent descriptions of a company in its annual report since it focuses on financial information that an enterprise's decision makers have been using to make their decisions regarding company operations. The components that management establishes for that purpose are referred to in FASB 131 as operating segments.

According to the FASB, if management were to change the internal structure of their organization to the extent that the operating segment lines were altered, the changed reporting may be handled in one of two ways.

1)  By restating segment information for earlier periods, including interim periods.
2)  By disclosing segment information for the current period under both the old and the new bases of segmentation unless it is impracticable to do so.

## Operating Segments Defined

FASB 131 defines an operating segment as a component of an enterprise:

1)  That engages in business activities from which it may earn revenues and incur expenses.

2) Whose operating results are regularly reviewed by the enterprise's chief operating decision maker regarding decisions about resources to be allocated to the segment and to assess its performance.

3) For which discrete financial information is available.

## No More Secrets

As with other recent exposure drafts and standards, there was a storm of protest raised about the requirements. Most of the complaints were leveled at the increased disclosure requirements that respondents felt would result in competitive harm. They felt that the specificity of the required reporting would place them at a disadvantage by giving competitors and suppliers sufficient information to figure out their profit margin on particular products.

## Segment Quantitative Thresholds

A company must report separately information about an operating segment that meets any of the following quantitative thresholds:

1) Its reported revenue, including both sales to external customers and intersegment sales or transfers, is 10% or more of the combined revenue, internal and external, of all reported operating segments.

2) The absolute amount of its reported profit or loss is 10% or more of the greater, in absolute amount, of one of the following:
   a) The combined reported profit of all operating segments that *did not* report a loss.
   b) The combined reported loss of all operating segments that *did* report a loss.

3) Its assets are 10% or more of the combined assets of all operating segments.

Information about operating segments that do not meet any of the quantitative thresholds may be disclosed separately.

FASB 131 permits the combination of information about operating segments that do not meet the quantitative thresholds with information about other operating segments that do not meet the quantitative thresholds to produce a reportable segment only if the operating segments have similar economic characteristics and share a majority of the following aggregation criteria:

1) The nature of the products and services.
2) The nature of the production process.

3) The type or class of customers for their products and services.

4) The methods used to distribute their products or provide their services.

5) If applicable, the nature of the regulatory environment (banking, insurance, or public utilities, for example).

If the total of external revenue reported by operating segments is less than 75% of the enterprise's total consolidated revenue, additional operating segments must be identified as reportable segments. This must be done even if the segments do not meet the quantitative threshold criteria until at least 75% of total consolidated revenue is included in reportable segments.

Finally, an "all other" category is to be set up for disclosure about other business activities and operating segments that are not reportable under the previously mentioned quantitative threshold criteria. Sources of the revenue included in this category must be revealed.

## Rules for Single Segment Entities

FASB 131 includes disaggregated disclosure requirements for companies that have a single reportable segment, and whose business activities are not organized on the basis of differences in related products and services, or differences in geographical areas of operations. Disclosures about products and services, geographical areas, and major customers are required of these companies. As a result:

1) The expanded disclosure of operating segment income statements and asset data will enhance investors' understanding of an operating segment's performance, cash flows, and investment requirements.

2) The operating segment data presentation will be more consistent with other parts of a company's annual report.

## This and That

Under FASB 131:

1) Disclosures about different parts of a business are required, but the basic income statement and balance sheet are not changed.

2) Entities may no longer claim that their business consists of only one segment if, in fact, it does not.

3) Operating segment data will be reported quarterly.

4) Reporting geographic operating data by countries should aid in the evaluation of performance and risk resulting from the global nature

of present day business and commerce. The cultural, economic, political, and social data resulting from this disclosure and reporting should better serve top management as well as creditors and investors in evaluating a company as a whole—not just particular segments.

5) The FASB has taken the first big step in its consolidations projects. Consolidations policy and procedure, and unconsolidated entities are still to come.

In the final analysis, FASB 131 attempts to provide information for the user of financial statements about the different types of business activity in which a company engages, the different environments in which it operates, and the nature of its client base.

## EMPLOYERS' DISCLOSURES ABOUT PENSIONS AND OTHER POSTRETIREMENT BENEFITS—FASB STATEMENT 132

This new standard revises and improves the effectiveness of current note disclosure requirements for employers' pensions and other postretirement employee benefits (OPEBs), but does not alter the retiree benefit accounting rules. It does not deal with recognition or measurement issues, but provides additional information to facilitate financial analysis and eliminates some disclosures that are no longer useful.

### Less May Be Better

In direct response to analysts' requests for additional pertinent data, more information is required on cash flows including contributions and benefits paid. To a considerable extent, it standardizes disclosure for retiree benefits.

The disclosure requirements are intended to be easier to read and understand, and to eliminate certain previously mandated items which were seldom, if ever, used and resulted in needless "clutter" on a financial statement. The standard includes reduced disclosure requirements for nonpublic entities and participants in multiemployer plans. The new Statement allows aggregation of plans for both public and private companies. Private companies will find that disclosure requirements are considerably reduced while public companies will see less reduction in quantity, but the quality of reporting should be effectively increased.

Public companies must make a full set of the revised disclosures. A sensitivity analysis is required to disclose the effects of a 1% increase and a 1% decrease in the long-term health care trend rate on pension benefit costs.

## Response to Jenkins Committee Report

FASB 132 results from the 1994 report of the Jenkins Committee on improving business reporting in which concerns were expressed about existing disclosure requirements. One of the most important results of this committee is the emphasis placed on updating the system by identifying user-based suggestions for improvement. (This report of the special AICPA committee was titled, "Improving Business Reporting—A Customer Focus." Its chairman was Edmund L. Jenkins, who assumed chairmanship of the FASB for a five-year term on July 1, 1997.)

The objective of this particular project was not only to improve retiree benefit disclosures, but to determine whether the steps taken here might apply to the admitted need to improve financial reporting and the effectiveness of present disclosure requirements relating to a number of other accounting topics. Consideration is being given to similar projects in the areas of leases and income taxes.

At this juncture, both preparers and users of the affected financial statements appear to agree that this measure will lead to simpler, more effective reporting. The Statement is to be used for fiscal years beginning after December 15, 1997.

(In Canada, the Accounting Standards Board (AcSB) has issued a proposed standard on retiree benefits which would make it closer to U.S. standards.)

## ACCOUNTING FOR DERIVATIVE INSTRUMENTS AND HEDGING ACTIVITIES—FASB 133

The derivatives standard was adopted by a unanimous vote on June 1, 1998, after more than 10 years of painstaking effort by the FASB. Unquestionably, this Standard will be one of the most far-reaching accounting standards yet produced. It will also be the one that has raised the most hue and cry in every segment of the economy.

The FASB repeatedly made it clear that they would not back down on certain requirements, regardless of "special interest" objections. The Board pointed out that trillions of dollars' worth of derivative transactions are occurring in the marketplace and they believe "investors have little, if any, information about them." They believe that the new Standard will give the investor further information about an entity so that they can make more knowledgeable decisions.

The U.S. Senate, the House of Representatives, the Federal Reserve, the American Bankers Association, and assorted others entered the fray over derivatives with very little success. On the other hand, the

Board had modified some of the earlier positions in response to user requests, as in the Chicago Board of Trade's concern about some of the provisions relating to hedging.

One of the most important concessions was to the projected timing of the effective date. The Standard was to have become effective June 15, 1999. This meant that for calendar-year companies it would be effective January 1, 2000. Many segments had complained that the extra time and money being expended on trying to solve Y2K problems, coping with a new derivatives Standard of such proposed magnitude by December 15, 1998, was expecting too much. (Now another postponement; see p. 48.)

The FASB has also appointed a special task force to aid with implementation issues on derivatives. Among the comments received from users were many related to the complicated provisions of the proposed Standard—admittedly covering very complicated financial instruments. The Board agreed with the constituents that it should be prepared to provide assistance and guidance on a timely basis: thus, the task force. It will help in identifying implementation issues and recommending conclusions to the Board.

## ED Modified Somewhat, Not Substantially

Regardless of objections, the Standard retains most of the provisions that were issued in the September 1997 recap of salient points. All derivatives are to be reported as assets or liabilities in financial statements at their fair value. New approaches to hedge accounting are outlined. As a result, more detailed, useful disclosures of derivatives, hedging activities, and related accounting practices should furnish the investor, creditor, and user with a better picture of an entity's true financial condition. In effect, the new derivative accounting practices should then reveal the economic realities of derivative transactions to the financial statement reader.

The requirements to record all derivatives on the face of the balance sheet at fair value, and some of the new hedge accounting requirements, may very well increase the assets reported by some companies and change their return on assets. On the other hand, the result may be an increase of the liabilities reported by some companies, resulting in a change in their liabilities-to-owners' equity ratio.

## Hedge Accounting

Under certain conditions, the new derivative Standard will permit management to designate a derivative as one of the following hedges—a fair value, cash flow, or foreign exchange hedge.

1) A *fair value hedge* is a hedge of the exposure to changes in the fair value of an asset or liability recognized on the balance sheet or of a firm commitment. The exposure to change must be attributable to a specific risk.

   For this type of hedge, the gain or loss is recognized in current income. This amount is offset by the gain or loss in the fair value of the hedged item. The carrying amount is adjusted to reflect the fair value gain or loss. If the hedge is working as it is intended, the adjustment to the carrying amount of the hedged item recognized in income will equal the offsetting gain or loss on the hedging derivative and there will be no net effect on earnings. If the hedge, on the other hand, is not operating as it should, earnings will be affected to the extent that the hedge is ineffective. Assessment of effectiveness is required.

2) A *cash flow hedge* is a hedge of an exposure to variability in the cash flows of an asset or liability recognized on the balance sheet, or of a forecasted transaction, that is attributable to a particular risk. Forecasted transactions include forecasted sales and purchases for which no firm commitment has been made, and interest payments on variable rate debt reported as a liability.

   The effective part of a gain or loss on a derivative designated as a cash flow hedge is initially recognized in owners' equity as part of other comprehensive income and then in earnings in the same period in which the hedged forecasted transaction affects earnings. The ineffective aspect of the gain or loss is recognized in earnings.

3) A *foreign currency exposure hedge* is a hedge of the foreign currency exposure of:

   a) A firm commitment which is a foreign currency fair value hedge.

   b) An available-for-sale debt security, a foreign currency fair value hedge.

   c) A foreign currency-denominated forecasted transaction which is a foreign currency cash flow hedge.

   d) A net investment in a foreign operation.

   The gain or loss on a derivative or nonderivative financial instrument designated as a foreign currency hedge is accounted for depending upon its designations as a fair value or cash flow hedge in the same way as outlined above for those types of hedges.

   Thus, the gain or loss on a derivative financial instrument designated and qualifying as a foreign currency hedging instrument is to be accounted for as follows:

   a) The gain or loss on the hedging instrument in a hedge of a firm commitment is to be recognized in current earnings along with the loss or gain on the hedged firm commitment.

**b)** The gain or loss on the hedging derivative in a hedge of an available-for-sale security is to be recognized in current earnings along with the loss or gain on the hedged available-for-sale security.

**c)** In general, the effective aspect of the gain or loss on the hedging instrument in a hedge of a foreign-currency denominated forecasted transaction is to be reported as a component of other comprehensive income, outside of earnings. It is to be recognized in earnings in the same period or periods during which the hedged forecasted transaction affects earnings. The ineffective aspect of the gain or loss on the hedging instrument and any other remaining gain or loss on the hedging instrument is to be recognized in current earnings.

**d)** The foreign currency transaction gain or loss on the hedging instrument in a hedge of a net investment in a foreign operation is to be reported in other comprehensive income as part of the cumulative translation adjustment. The remainder of the gain or loss on the hedging instrument is to be recognized in current earnings.

## Lest We Forget—Derivatives

A derivative is a financial instrument or other contract with several distinguishing characteristics:

**1)** It has one or more *underlyings* and one or more *notional amounts* or payment provisions or both. Those terms determine the amount of the settlement or settlements, and in some cases, whether or not a settlement is required.

**2)** It requires no initial net investment or one that is smaller than would be required for other types of contracts expected to have a similar response to changes in market factors.

**3)** The terms require or permit net settlement; it can readily be settled net by a means outside the contract, or it provides for delivery of an asset that puts the recipient in a position not substantially different from net settlement.

An "underlying" may be one of a number of variables that is applied to the notional amount to determine the cash flows or other exchanges required by the contract—a commodity price, a per-share price, an interest rate, a foreign exchange rate, or some other variable.

"Notional amount" refers to an amount of money, a number of shares, a number of bushels, pounds, or whatever can be dreamed up to create a more exotic derivative. A contract with these characteristics is a derivative instrument according to the Statement if, by the terms at its inception or upon the occurrence of a specified event, the entire contract meets the conditions delineated above.

FASB 133 specifically states that the following transactions do not constitute derivatives for the purpose of this Statement:

1) Regular security trades.
2) Normal purchases and sales.
3) Contingent consideration from a business combination.
4) Traditional life insurance contracts.
5) Traditional property and casualty contracts.
6) Most financial guarantee contracts.

The new Statement also points out that some contracts may be accounted for as derivatives by the holder but not by the user. These would include:

1) Contracts that are both indexed to the entity's own stock and classified in stockholders' equity on their balance sheets.
2) Contracts issued in connection with stock-based compensation arrangements covered in FASB 123, *Accounting for Stock-Based Compensation.*

## ACCOUNTING FOR MORTGAGE-BACKED SECURITIES RETAINED AFTER THE SECURITIZATION OF MORTGAGE LOANS HELD FOR SALE BY A MORTGAGE BANKING ENTERPRISE—FASB 134

FASB 134 is an amendment of FASB 65, *Accounting for Certain Mortgage Banking Activities*, which established accounting and reporting standards for certain activities of mortgage banking enterprises and other enterprises that conduct operations which are substantially similar to the primary operations of a mortgage banking enterprise.

FASB 65, which had previously been amended by FASB 115, *Accounting for Certain Investments in Debt and Equity Securities*, and FASB 125, *Accounting for Transfers and Servicing of Financial Assets and Extinguishments of Liabilities*, requires that after the securitization of a mortgage loan held for sale, an entity engaged in mortgage banking activities classify the resulting mortgage-backed security as a trading security.

This Statement further amends FASB 65 to require that after the securitization of mortgage loans held for sale, an entity engaged in mortgage banking activities classify the resulting mortgage-backed securities or other retained interests based on its ability and intent to sell or hold those investments. This Statement conforms to subsequent accounting for securities retained after the securitization of mortgage loans by a mortgage banking enterprise with the subsequent accounting for securities retained after the securitization of other types of assets by a nonmortgage banking enterprise.

The Statement became effective for the first fiscal quarter beginning after December 15, 1998. On the date of its initial application, an enterprise could reclassify mortgage-backed securities and other beneficial interests retained after the securitization of mortgage loans held for sale from the trading category, except for those with sales commitments in place. Those securities and other interests could be classified based on the entity's ability and intent on the date of initial application, to hold those investments.

Unlike most EDs leading to new Statements, the FASB exposed its proposed mortgage amendment for only 45 days. The board decided that the accounting for securities retained after the securitization of mortgage loans should be the same as the accounting for securities retained after the securitization of other types of assets.

This Standard makes it possible for a mortgage banking enterprise to utilize FASB 115 to determine a classification: a) trading, b) available for sale or c) held to maturity. The only added requirement is that if a sales commitment has been agreed to, the classification must be "trading."

Thus, FASB 134 accounting is more consistent with other accounting treatment. The change also affected retained nonsecurity interests. To be consistent, the board eliminated the trading requirement for those that are held for sale. The portions of FASB 65 relating to nonsecurity interests were not amended. The Board believed it would have been inconsistent to require a trading classification for retained nonsecurity interests intended to be sold if it no longer required one for retained security interests intended to be sold.

## Rescission of Statement 75 and Technical Corrections—FASB 135

In 1980, the FASB issued Statement 35, *Accounting and Reporting by Defined Benefit Pension Plans*, which applied to the private sector and—as there was no GASB then—to state and local governments as well. Two years later, however, the FASB deferred the statement's applicability to state and local governments. And in 1983, Statement 75, *Deferral of the Effective Date of Certain Accounting Requirements for Pension Plans of State and Local Governmental Units*, made that postponement indefinite and retroactive to December 15, 1980.

By the early 1980s, GASB was already in the planning stages. In preparation, the National Council on Governmental Accounting (NCGA) was also considering deferral of its own pension guidance, which differed from FASB 35. So, in issuing Statement 75, FASB said "mutual deferral of both Statement 35 and NCGA Statement 6 is appropriate while discussions relating to the formation and operation of the GASB are in progress." In the following years, GASB published its own guidance on pension accounting for state and local governments.

In February 1999, the FASB realized that deferral of Statement 35 was no longer necessary. It issued Statement 135, *Rescission of FASB Statement 75 and Technical Corrections*, which clarifies that GASB guidance applies to state and local governments and also makes several purely technical changes to some existing FASB standards. It became effective for financial statements for fiscal years ending after February 15, 1999, with earlier application encouraged.

## CONSOLIDATED FINANCIAL STATEMENTS

In February 1999, the FASB issued an Exposure Draft proposing that businesses and not-for-profit organizations that control other entities include those subsidiaries in their consolidated financial statements. The deadline for written comment was May 24, 1999.

Control is defined as the ability to direct the ongoing policies and management that guide the activities of another entity so as to increase the benefits and limit losses from directing those activities, and this decision-making ability is not shared with others.

The proposed Statement would require a controlling entity to consolidate all entities that it controls unless control is temporary when acquired. The current rule is that 50% plus owned entities be fully consolidated unless control is temporary. Full consolidation results—after adjusting for intercompany activities—in combining all of the controlled entity's assets, liabilities, revenues, expenses, gains and losses, and cash flows into the reporting entity's consolidated financial statements.

Business enterprises and not-for-profit organizations often carry out and finance a significant part of their economic activity through subsidiaries, joint ventures and complex strategic arrangements. The Board believes that this Statement fills a significant need by providing a framework for assessing and determining whether a particular relationship between two entities involves control of one entity by the other entity or not.

### Who Controls Whom?

The proposed Statement provides the basis for resolving several issues not addressed by FASB 94, *Consolidation of All Majority-Owned Sub-*

*sidiaries*. It eliminated certain exceptions to consolidation that existed prior to 1987, but did not resolve:

1) When control exists through means other than a majority voting interest.
2) When control does not rest with the owner of a majority voting interest.
3) When control is temporary.

As presently written, when and if this rule is adopted, it could be expected that it would result in full consolidation of entities where the reporting company can be said to have:

1) A majority voting interest in the election of a corporation's governing body.
2) A right to appoint a majority of its governing body.
3) If not a majority, a large minority voting interest in the election of a corporation's governing body. (And no other minority group has a significant voting interest.)
4) A unilateral ability to *obtain* a majority voting interest in the election of a corporation's governing body.
5) A unilateral ability to *obtain a right to appoint* a majority of the corporation's governing body through the present ownership of convertible securities or other rights that are currently exercisable at the option of the holder.

It is expected that the proposed standard would result in a number of now unconsolidated controlled entities being included in the controlling entity's consolidated statements on a fully consolidated basis. The result should be that financial statements would provide a better understanding of some companies' business and financing risks and a clearer understanding of their actual net income.

## Lessening the Gap

This proposal moves U.S. consolidation policy closer to that of many other countries that have also adopted similar objectives, similar definitions of control, and other requirements relating to consolidated financial statements. However, one rather important difference does exist.

Many other countries base their consolidation accounting on the *entity* approach. The consolidated financial statements are prepared from the *consolidated entity's point of view*. Minority interest is included in consolidated owners' equity and consolidated net income. The FASB's proposal continues the U.S. practice of basing consolidation accounting on the *parent company point of view*. Minority interest is shown outside of consolidated owners' equity and is deducted in the measurement of consolidated net income.

The proposed Statement would be effective for financial statements for annual periods beginning after December 15, 1999, and all interim periods in the year of adoption. Earlier application would be encouraged.

## FASB Issues Invitation to Comment on Business Combinations

In December 1998, the FASB, and the G4+1 (standard setters from Australia, Canada, New Zealand, United Kingdom and the United States) and the International Accounting Standards Committee (IASC), published an Invitation to Comment on certain issues that it expects to deliberate in its project on business combinations. The content of the document reflects the conclusions of the *individuals* participating in its development, not the standard-setting bodies themselves. It states that one method of accounting should be used for all business combinations and that *the purchase method, rather than the pooling of interests or fresh start methods*, is the appropriate method.

The FASB felt that the comments received on the Invitation to Comment would be helpful to the Board in deliberating the issues in its own project on business combinations. They emphasized the point that this is the first time this international group has issued a joint position paper. Since there are currently significant differences internationally in the accounting standards on this important and controversial issue, the FASB hopes to reach convergence among the countries involved and the IASC so that the accounting standards, and the resulting financial reporting, are similar. (Where these standard setters go, the rest of the accounting world is very apt to follow.)

Here again, this is not a sudden decision by the Board; it has been researching business combinations issues since 1996. The issues surrounding the project are particularly important because the increasing growth of mergers has brought greater attention to perceived flaws and deficiencies in existing accounting standards. The rapidly accelerating movement of capital flows globally continues to point up the need for standards to be comparable internationally. Evidently the comments resulting from this invitation left little doubt about the demerits of "pooling."

## Elimination of Pooling of Interests Accounting

Given the lackluster nature of the last two FASB Standards, it is probably not an overstatement to say that the most important news to originate with the FASB since adoption of the Standard on derivatives occurred in April 1999 when the Board announced that it would eliminate pooling of interests as a method of accounting for business combinations. In a unanimous vote, the Board decided that using the purchase method is preferable to allowing more than one method to be used when businesses combine. The change will be effective for business combinations initiated after the FASB issues a final Standard on the issues.

The Board expects to issue for comment a formal proposal on business combination issues sometime early in the third quarter of 1999. The new Standard would be effective after the expected issuance of the final Standard in late 2000.

## Merits of Purchase Method Accounting

The Board has been working on the business combinations issues for several years. They had come to the conclusion that it is difficult for investors to make sound decisions about combining companies when two different accounting treatments exist for what is essentially the same transaction. They decided that the *purchase method* of accounting gives investors a better idea of the initial cost of a transaction and the investment's performance over time than does the pooling of interests method.

With the *purchase method*, one company is identified as the buyer and records the company being acquired at the price it actually paid. With the *pooling of interests method*, the two companies just add together the old book values of their net assets. As a result, the shareholders and investors have a difficult time trying to figure out just what did occur in the transaction.

Using the purchase method in a business combination is consistent with how other acquired assets are accounted for because all assets, whether a piece of inventory, a building, or a whole company, are recorded on the balance sheet at their cost (the current market value at that date) when they are initially acquired.

Under this method, the excess of the purchase price over the fair market value of the acquired company's net assets is known as *goodwill*. Goodwill is charged to the buyer's earnings over time. The Board intends to reconsider its prior (most recent) tentative decisions about goodwill before issuing its proposal on business combination issues.

Widespread use of the pooling of interests method is largely an American phenomenon. The U.S. not only is out of step with other countries on the pooling versus purchase issue, but domestically the accounting treatment shows a *great deal of diversity in practice as well*. Pooling of interests is the exception almost everywhere else in the world, and some countries, including Australia, actually ban its use altogether; New Zealand is planning to eliminate its use.

The Board's decisions to date do not affect combinations of companies under control or not-for-profit organizations.

### More Merger Mania?

This latest decision, along with an earlier FASB decision to issue a new Standard requiring capitalization of acquired in process research and development (R&D) for transactions initiated after the adoption of such a Standard, probably in late 1999, could result in some interesting maneuvers:

1) Some companies in an acquisitive mode may be spurred to action if they perceive advantages in acquiring other companies *before* they can neither use the pooling of interests method nor avoid capitalizing acquired in process research and development.

2) Companies that might be less attractive acquisitions if they had to be accounted for as a purchase could include pharmaceutical, financial and service enterprises, as well as the frequently sought-after software, high-tech, and internet companies.

3) Acquirers may be tempted to overpay to obtain targeted acquisitions "right now" in order to use the old accounting methods. The "signing bonus" could be kept out of future operating earnings by using pooling of interests accounting or the one-time write-off of acquired in process research and development (IPR&D).

4) Those companies willing to be or wanting to be acquired may also be motivated to accelerate their plans to be acquired. Their attitude might result from a desire to capture any beat-the-deadline premium for their shareholders, and avoid the adverse earnings effects of goodwill and the proposed capitalized R&D accounting for the combined acquirer and acquiree company.

Regardless of the reasoning of the acquirers and the acquirees, the FASB's proposals are expected to accelerate corporate takeovers as companies race to find partners before the accounting changes can take effect. As an indication of the popularity of the pooling of interest accounting method, 9 of the 10 largest acquisitions in 1998 were accounted for in this manner.

### MORE PROJECTS IN THE WORKS

The decision to eliminate pooling of interests accounting is one of a number of decisions the FASB has made as part of its *business combination and intangible assets* agenda. The FASB's other related announcements include a whole new approach to goodwill to get more in step with the recently adopted IASs and the rest of the accounting world; however, at this point the Board appears to be waffling to some extent, particularly in regard to cutting the life span of goodwill. Other purchased intangible assets and R&D are also under scrutiny.

## Goodwill

1) When allocating the cost of an acquired entity to the assets acquired and liabilities assumed, every effort should be made to recognize all of the net assets acquired (including intangible assets) and measure them at their fair values.

2) If the fair value of the acquired net assets exceeds the fair value of the purchase consideration (negative goodwill), an extraordinary gain should be recognized and measured at the amount of that difference. (Current accounting requires the excess to be used to reduce the values assigned to the acquiree's noncurrent assets, except marketable securities. If any remains after reducing these values to zero, the residual is amortized systematically as a credit to income over a period not to exceed 40 years.)

3) If the fair value of the purchase consideration exceeds the fair value of the net assets acquired (positive goodwill), purchased goodwill should be recognized as an asset and measured initially at the amount of the difference.

4) Purchased goodwill should be amortized on a straight-line basis over its useful (finite) life.

5) The amortization expense for goodwill should be displayed as a separate line item within income from continuing operations in the income statement.

6) The useful life of goodwill should be presumed to be 10 years or less and should never exceed 20 years. (The FASB has indicated that it will review this decision. It may eliminate the 10-year requirement and extend the 20-year maximum period to a longer period. The present rule is that goodwill should be amortized over a period not to exceed 40 years.)

7) A review of goodwill for impairment should be required no later than two years after the acquisition date if certain indicators are present. (There is no such requirement now.)

## Other Purchased Intangible Assets

1) Intangible assets that are reliably measurable should be recognized separately as assets. Intangible assets should be presumed to have a useful economic life of 20 years or less and generally should be amortized over their useful economic lives—the existing rule permits a maximum amortization period of 40 years.

**2)** Intangible assets that are separable or potentially exchangeable and that have a) either an observable market value, or b) are based on rights conveyed by law or contract that extend beyond 20 years may be amortized over longer periods. They may not be amortized at all if they have indefinite lives. If this is the case, they should be reviewed for impairment on a fair value basis.

**3)** All purchased R&D, whether a) purchased singly, b) as part of a group of assets, or c) business combination that is accounted for by the purchase method, should be recognized as an intangible asset and amortized over its useful economic life.

## General Provisions

**1)** Goodwill and intangible assets should be displayed as a separate line item in the balance sheet.

**2)** The provisions of the proposed standard related to goodwill and other purchased intangibles would be effective for transactions initiated after the issuance of the final standard.

### PROPOSED INTERPRETATION ON STOCK COMPENSATION

The FASB released a proposal late in March 1999 for public comment that would resolve practice issues raised when accounting for stock options. The deadline set for written comment was June 30, 1999.

APB Opinion 25, *Accounting for Stock Issued to Employees*, was issued in 1972. Since that time, questions have been raised concerning its application as differing practices have developed. The Board's broad reconsideration of the stock compensation issue culminated in the issuance of FASB Statement 123, *Accounting for Stock-Based Compensation*, in 1995. (See page 10.)

Because there was so much controversy surrounding this issue, the FASB finally gave in to a compromise measure—but very reluctantly and not happily. As a result, FASB 123 permits the continued application of APB 25. However, questions remain about the proper application of APB 25 in a number of circumstances. This proposed Interpretation would clarify how to apply APB 25 in certain situations.

The proposed Interpretation includes the following conclusions:

**1)** Once an option is repriced that option must be accounted for as a variable plan from the time it is repriced to the time it is exercised.

**2)** Employees would be defined as they are under common law for purposes of applying APB 25.

**3)** APB 25 does not apply to outside directors because, by definition, an outside director cannot be an employee.

Since APB 25 was issued in 1972, the terms of many "Section 423" plans have changed from those in existence at the time. Many of those plans now provide that employees can purchase an employer's stock at the lesser of 85% of the stock price at the date of grant or 85% of the price at the date of exercise. This provision is referred to as a "look-back" option. The Board decided that plans with a look-back option do not, in and of themselves, create a compensatory plan.

A subsidiary may account for parent company stock issued to its employees under APB 25 in their separately issued financial statements, provided the subsidiary is part of the parent's consolidated financial statements.

The proposed Interpretation does not address issues related to the application of FASB 123 and all issues are addressed and resolved by applying the requirements of APB 25. It would be effective upon issuance, which is expected in September 1999, but generally would cover events that occur after December 15, 1998. (See discussion on pp. 10-12.)

## USING CASH FLOW INFORMATION AND PRESENT VALUE IN ACCOUNTING MEASUREMENT

The FASB released a proposal at the end of March 1999 for public comment that would provide a framework for using future cash flows as the basis for an accounting measurement. The deadline for written comment was set for August 1, 1999.

The proposed Concepts Statement would provide general principles governing the use of present value, especially when the amount of future cash flows, their timing, or both are uncertain. It also would provide a common understanding of the objectives of present value in accounting measurements.

The Board first issued an ED on this project in June 1997. This 1999 proposal is the culmination of redeliberation and consideration of issues raised in comment letters received following the issuance of that ED. Most of the changes made were in response to requests for clarification of or suggestions about *how* the proposed Concepts Statement could be improved

The 1997 proposal described two objectives for present value measurements of assets—fair value and entity-specific measurement. After redeliberation, the Board decided to remove the option of entity-specific measurement from the 1999 proposal because it *attempts* to capture the value of an asset or liability in the context of a particular measurement.

Thus, it differs from fair value by substituting the entity's assumptions for those that marketplace participants would make.

The 1997 proposal described three objectives for present value of liabilities. The current proposal eliminates entity-specific measurement of liabilities and clarifies that the most relevant measure of a liability should always reflect the credit standing of the entity obligated to pay.

## LATE UPDATE: TWO NEW FASBs

### Transfer of Assets to a Not-for-Profit or Charitable Trust That Raises or Holds Contributions for Others—FASB 136

The Statement requires a recipient organization to recognize an asset and a liability rather than contribution revenue if it accepts cash or other financial assets from a donor and agrees to disburse them, the return from investing them, or both, to the specified beneficiary. The latter reports its interest in the assets held by the recipient organization as an asset and contribution revenue.

The Statement also covers situations in which the transfer is not a contribution because it is recvocable or reciprocal. It is effective for financial statements for calendar-year 2000.

### Accounting for Derivative Instruments and Hedging Activities: Deferral of Effective Date of FASB 133—FASB 137

This Statement delays for a year the required application of FASB 133 to June 15, 2000; however, entities that have already issued interim or annual financial statements according to the requirements of Statement 133 *may not* return to their previous method of accounting for derivatives or hedging activities.

FASB 137 does not change any of the requirements; it merely postpones the inevitable to give the issuers additional time to cope with Y2K considerations and digest the ramifications of the new requirements.

# Chapter 2

## International Accounting Standards Committee

After a very slow start in 1973 when it was established by professional accountancy bodies (including the AICPA) from nine countries—to attempt to bring some degree of order, uniformity and reliability to accounting practices and procedures in developing market countries—the International Accounting Standards Committee (IASC) has now delivered to the International Organization of Securities Commissions (IOSCO) the set of 30 core accounting standards suitable for use in cross-border listings.

That original group has now increased to 142 accounting organizations in 103 countries representing 2,000,000 accountants worldwide.

In December 1998, the Board approved an International Accounting Standard, *Financial Instruments: Recognition and Measurement* completing the core set of Standards, identified in an agreement with the International Organization of Securities Commissions (IOSCO) in 1993. For the first time, IASC feels confident in saying that it has a comprehensive set of Standards covering all the major areas of importance to general businesses. At the same time, they concede there is still much to be accomplished.

## A CHANGING WORLD ECONOMY

The position of accounting standard setters has changed enormously since IASC's formation. Not the least important of these positions is the attitude toward IASC. The tide has certainly turned from a rather grudging tolerance of its activities to a realization that you'd better get your input in or you may find the rest of the accounting world leaving you behind.

At the time of its inception, many countries, including some with highly developed economies, had no official accounting standards or only rudimentary ones. But, as the IASC points out, the explosion of demand for accounting standards had been set in motion. The investing public had been made aware, by headline events in the financial newspapers, of the enormous flexibility in measuring a company's results or assets and liabilities under rules existing at the time.

These problems have not *all* been fully resolved nor are they likely to be as long as there is anyone capable of painting a corporate picture in a rosier hue that it deserves. But it's up to the standard makers—nationally and internationally—to keep trying.

In a 1998 landmark speech (according to the IASC), the Chairman of the Securities and Exchange Commission criticized U.S. business managers for continuing to use means available to them to disguise the pattern of income or profits over time, from what it would be with unbiased measurement, to produce the appearance of a smoother trend.

The international organization reasons that accounting standards can limit the opportunities for earnings management and they believe the Standards finalized by IASC during 1998 do so, along with those of the many national standard setters. However, they realize that strong and independent behavior by auditors and regulators can also contribute to resolving this problem to limit the degree of judgment in applying accounting Standards. Their focus is likely to shift towards enforcement activities.

Evidently, they believe the SEC Chairman's concern will have a beneficial effect upon progress in standard setting and enforcement by reminding one and all that these problems continue *even in the most financially sophisticated countries of the world.*

## Two Basic Needs

The need for global accounting standards, or at a minimum for less diversity in national standards, became painfully evident in 1998—in some quarters, at least. The economic difficulties that began in Asia and spread to other regions of the world rather graphically demonstrated the interdependencies of different nations in the modern global economy. It has been suggested that part of the blame should be placed on "accounting"—or lack of it. The IASC felt that international investors possibly lacked confidence in the accounting of the countries where the difficulties originated. They felt that the lack of confidence made capital more expensive than it needed to be and added to the threat of serious worldwide economic recession.

As a result, the IASC appears to have become as committed as the

SEC and the FASB to the belief that "comparability" and "transparency" are key words in healthy financial markets. They acknowledge that:

1) An important emphasis in the demand for global accounting standards has been *comparability* among businesses in different countries to serve the demands of international capital markets, and

2) Accounting standards are needed to bring about greater *transparency* and openness in financial reporting by individual countries and their business corporations and financial institutions.

## European Union

Another important current development in the demand for International Accounting Standards is taking place in Europe. A key current objective of the European Union (EU) is the development of a single economic market. The introduction of the euro on January 1,1999 was an important step in that direction. The single economic market would almost necessitate a single capital market with companies from the different countries competing for capital on equal terms.

This, in turn, suggests that those putting up the capital must be able to assess the performance of different companies with full comparability. Said comparability is not attainable if different accounting standards are used by different companies—even if they are reporting in a common currency. Ergo, IASs to the rescue.

From the beginning, rather than establish a separate European Accounting Standards Board, the European Commission (EC) planned to work with the IASC to standardize accounting practices for multinational companies within the European Union. Now the EC has decided that its preferred option for the future development of accounting in the EU is to "oblige" listed companies to follow International Accounting Standards. Other companies would follow national codes within the framework of the European directives.

According to IASC, several EU countries—Austria, Belgium, France Germany, Italy, and possibly Spain—have issued laws or regulations permitting companies to use IAS in lieu of domestic law. Denmark, Finland and Sweden are said to be considering similar measures. There are various conditions: notably, the countries are not authorized under EU law to permit inconsistencies with EU law.

In some countries, the permission to use IASs is restricted to consolidated financial statements, particularly of companies with cross-border listings. The European Commission is said to be considering making a proposal to require *all* listed EU companies to use IAS.

An April 1999 report published by the European Commission concludes that there are no significant conflicts between the EC Accounting Directives and those International Accounting Standards and interpretations of the Standing Interpretations Committee (SIC) that are applicable to accounting periods beginning before July 1, 1998.

## COMPLETING THE CORE STANDARDS

The main focus of IASC's technical work recently has been the completion of the core set of Standards agreed upon with IOSCO. The work program to complete the core Standards was comprised of 40 topics classified into twelve major projects:

1) By the end of 1997, five of those had been completed.
2) Two more, the Standards on *Interim Financial Reporting* and *Employee Benefits*, were adopted in January 1998.
3) The Standards on *Discontinuing Operations and Impairment of Assets*, and an Exposure Draft on Financial Instruments were adopted at the April 1998 Board meeting.
4) At the July meeting, Standards on *Provisions, Contingent Liabilities and Contingent Assets* and also on *Intangible Assets*, together with agreement on associated amendments to the existing Standard on *Business Combinations* were approved.
5) At a special extra meeting in December, agreement was reached on the last of the twelve major projects—the Standard on *Recognition and Measurement of Financial Instruments*.
6) Two minor additional tasks in the IOSCO work program were completed in 1999:
   a) Revisions to parts of IAS 10 to prescribe procedure for handling events after the balance sheet date which was accomplished in March.
   b) Investment properties for which an Exposure Draft was prepared for consideration at the June-July Board meeting.

## STANDING INTERPRETATIONS COMMITTEE

In 1997, faced with an ever-growing list of standards to be revised, adopted, applied, interpreted, the IASC Board decided to set up a Standing Interpretations Committee (SIC) to consider, on a timely basis, accounting issues that are likely to receive divergent or unacceptable treatment in the absence of authoritative guidance. The SIC reviews accounting issues within the context of existing International Accounting Standards and the IASC framework. In developing Interpretations, the SIC works closely with similar national committees. It also seeks public input before reaching a final consensus. When consensus is reached, the SIC publishes authoritative pronouncements on the application of IAS and recommends solutions for situations not covered by existing standards. Its function is similar to that of the FASB's Emerging Issues Task Force (EITF).

Standard setting obviously requires some type of committee to provide guidance on the application of Standards. IASC understandably considers it vital that this task be undertaken at the international level rather than being left to national groups that could undoubtedly develop conclusions that differed from country to country—even when exemplary translations are available.

As an indication of the area covered by this committee, the three initial interpretations focused on the following topics:

1) SIC-1. A company should use the same cost formula for all inventories having similar nature and use. Different cost formulas may be justified for inventories with different nature and use but, for example, a difference in geographic location of inventories, in itself, should not be construed to justify the use of a different cost formula.

2) SIC-2. A company capitalizing borrowing costs directly attributable to the acquisition, construction, or production of qualifying assets, should apply that policy consistently for all qualifying assets and periods.

3) SIC-3. Unrealized gains and losses from transactions between an investor and associates should be eliminated in consolidated financial statements to the extent of the investor's interest in the associate. Unrealized losses should not be eliminated to the extent that the transaction provides evidence of an impairment.

SIC *Draft* interpretations have dealt with numerous topics. Under 20 have been ratified thus far.

## NOW IT'S IOSCO'S MOVE

The July 1995 Agreement stated that IOSCO would consider endorsement of International Accounting Standards once the core Standards had been completed. IOSCO has been working with IASC, providing comments on published proposals and, since mid-1996, participating in Board meetings as an observer member. Through this, it has already undertaken much of the preliminary work needed for its consideration of endorsement. The IASC reports that in September 1998, IOSCO approved "Disclosure Standards to Facilitate Cross-Border Offerings and Listings of Multinational Issuers." They are now considering the acceptability of the entire group of Standards.

Many of the members of IOSCO (including the SEC) will also have to undertake their own review process before accepting financial reports prepared in accordance with International Accounting Standards for cross-border listings in their own countries, at least where they are not already accepted. Most members are in an advanced stage of the evaluation process.

## NEW PROJECTS

It is anticipated that IASC work will continue at its recent high level even though its first big goal has been reached. While IOSCO is reviewing, viewing, and discussing and the national bodies are doing the same, the IASC will be working on:

1)  Specialized industry accounting to complete work on Standards on agriculture, insurance, and the extractive industries. These are obviously areas of extreme importance worldwide—and particularly in some of the emerging economies. (An Exposure Draft on agriculture was drawn up for deliberation at the Board's 1999 summer meeting.)

2)  A project on discounting, in recognition of its importance to many aspects of existing Standards and the need to have consistent approaches in these different Standards.

3)  A review of the existing Standard on business combinations, as regards the relative roles of "purchase accounting" and "pooling accounting."

## MERGER ACCOUNTING DIFFERENCES

Existing Standards of IASC and national standard setters contain wide differences on merger accounting with very important consequences for the comparability of financial statements. The G4+1 group of standard setters (the national standard setters of Australia, Canada, New Zealand, the United Kingdom and the United States, together with IASC) have agreed to work on a project to eliminate existing differences in members' standards on merger accounting. The Group supported a paper put forward by the U.S. FASB proposing the elimination of "pooling accounting." IASC, along with the members of G4+1, has published this proposal as a consultative paper. IASC strongly supports the objective of eliminating existing differences in merger accounting. (For information on the FASB proposed elimination of "pooling of interests," see Chapter 1.)

## ACCOUNTING FOR DEVELOPING ECONOMIES AND EMERGING MARKETS

Increasingly, emerging market countries and their regulatory authorities have adopted, indicated their intention to adopt, and/or based their own standards on IAS. Among these are China, the Confederation of Independent States (CIS), Singapore, Malaysia, Hong Kong, Indonesia, Viet Nam, Cambodia, Turkey, Lebanon, Trinidad and Tobago, Barbados, Uganda, Malta, and Zimbabwe.

The rules and regulations committee of the Federation of Euro-Asian Stock Exchanges (FEAS ) has also recommended that all members require listed companies to use IAS. FEAS is made up of 20 member exchanges from 18 countries in central and south Asia, the Middle East and Europe outside of the European Union and EFTA

During 1998, the Board began a project on accounting in developing countries and countries with emerging markets. This project emphasizes IASC's commitment to help these countries with the development of their accounting standards. In many of the countries, International Accounting Standards are already used as national standards. The project is considering whether some extra Standards are needed in developing countries and whether modifications and/or additional guidance may be needed to assist in applying International Accounting Standards in countries which are only now developing market economies.

When one considers that U.S. GAAP is based upon almost 140 FASB Standards, well over 300 opinions by the FASB's Emerging Issues Task Force, APB Opinions, SEC accounting and financial reporting requirements, AICPA Position Papers and Industry Accounting Guides, plus assorted other documents—39 IAS Standards and fewer than 20 SICs might provide rather thin coverage for international accounting regulation. (It's somewhat like comparing an anatomical skeleton to a living, breathing body.)

An IASC Steering Committee has been formed to consider the issues raised and make recommendations to the Board as to what detailed work needs to be done.

It would appear to be apparent that U.S. and non-U.S. investors, exchanges, accountants, corporate managers, CEOs, CFOs, and others in international business should become knowledgeable about the IAS and the activities of the IASC because sooner rather than later they are going to play a very important part in capital formation and financial accounting worldwide.

## AUTHORIZED TRANSLATIONS

The official language of IASC is English. It is the only language in which International Accounting Standards are approved by the Board, but they are aware that it is imperative to have reliable translations available in other languages. It is quite reasonable to assume that accounting standards will not receive effective application if they are not understood. To assure the quality of any translation, IASC has developed processes for making high quality "authorized" translations of its Standards. After all, a poor translation could nullify the benefits of the very carefully worded original English language standard. The first two translations, German and Russian, were published during 1998; a Spanish translation was scheduled for 1999. Other widely used languages will follow.

## GROWING ACCEPTANCE OF INTERNATIONAL STANDARDS

As mentioned above, many countries base their standards to a great extent directly on IASs as their national standards or develop national standards based primarily upon them. In some cases, the national standards indicate the relationship or comparison between the national standard and the relevant IAS.

In fewer than one dozen countries national standards are developed with little reliance upon IASs. A number of these countries (highly developed economic powers) have moved toward meshing their national standards with the IASC Standards.

Examples include:

1)  The FASB-IASC development of the Earnings per Share standard.
2)  IASC revision of the standard on Segment Reporting to harmonize with the standards developed jointly by FASB and Canadian standard setters.
3)  The UK-IASC cooperation on their standards on Impairment of Assets and also on Provisions, Contingent Liabilities and Contingent Assets.
4)  The current joining of forces by the G4+1 and the IASC to work on merger accounting.

If all of this sounds too quick and easy, it may just be. In the first place, the IOSCO approval requires a unanimous vote of its members to approve the core standards. Even then, this is only a recommendation and the individual securities commissions have the prerogative of making their own decision whether or not to support the international standards.

Many foreign companies appear willing to adopt IAS Standards while still being loath to abide by U.S. GAAP. On the other hand, now that many of the international standards have been tightened and more of the U.S. requirements have been adjusted to move closer to other national standards and the IASs, the more obvious advantages to complying only with the international standards may disappear.

What originally concerned much of the regulatory hierarchy in the U.S. might be dubbed the "either/or" mentality of the IASC in its attempt to provide something for everyone. (Some have suggested that this occurred primarily because of the attempt to keep both the U.S. and the U.K. happy—when their Standards were often at odds.) But subsequently the differences in these accounting systems have been reduced.

What about the attitude of various interested groups and organizations in the U.S.?

## NYSE AND SECURITIES DEALERS

The New York Stock Exchange and securities dealers are in favor of permitting foreign corporations that have adopted the international standards to be listed on U.S. exchanges even if this means having to educate the investor on discrepancies between GAAP and IAS. A large majority of the largest 500 corporations worldwide are not listed here principally because of what the companies have considered the too onerous U.S. GAAP requirements. Listing all of those foreign corporations would result in much greater volume—even adding two or three dozen of the largest foreign firms to the NYSE listings could certainly result in a marked increase in its market capitalization.

## FASB ATTITUDE

The FASB's growing involvement with the IASC (after a very tentative, if not altogether hostile, appraisal of this outside influence) will certainly smooth the way toward the time when both IAS and U.S. GAAP will be regarded as being acceptable and practicable global accounting standards. Understandably, the FASB is zealously guarding its power over U.S. accounting standards. It appears that the group realizes the inevitability of compromise and cooperation inasmuch as many U.S. firms and institutions had become disenchanted with some of the gyrations necessary to meet existing or proposed requirements relating to earnings per share, derivatives, hedging.

The FASB's and the IASC's efforts toward a common goal really appear to have begun with the earnings per share and segment standards. That this cooperation became a two-way street was made easier since even the FASB admitted that the IASC's—and much of the rest of the world's—approach to figuring EPS was superior to and far less convoluted than previous U.S. requirements.

Close cooperation between the two bodies has moved IAS closer to U.S. GAAP and, at the same time, U.S. GAAP is closing the gap with international accounting standards. All along, the FASB has undoubtedly had reservations about the breadth and depth of the IASC representation actively engaged in the standard setting process. They may have worried that what could turn out to be good enough for a foreign firm would fall short of being good enough for a U.S. firm to file in the U.S.

At least this had been the perception—that the U.S. would protect GAAP regardless. Not so. The FASB has taken steps to change or nullify several of the more divergent provisions to bring them closer to IAS requirements. Now the FASB has come out explicitly in favor of the IASC's aim of establishing a single set of Standards.

At the same time, the FASB is extremely concerned about the makeup of the revised format that the IASC has outlined for its new structure, functions and image.

## FUTURE STRATEGY

IASC's Strategy Working Party continued in 1998 with its deliberations which had begun in 1997. It published a document towards the end of 1998 setting out proposals for a restructuring of IASC and requesting comments from interested parties.

The proposals are based on their view that world capital markets want financial reports that comply with a high-quality body of global accounting standards applied consistently by international and large national organizations—all businesses with stock market listings among others. IASC agrees that the core set of Standards is not sufficient to meet the needs of the capital markets fully. Significant differences continue to exist between *international standards* and *national standards*. This, in turn, still leads to a lack of comparability across political boundaries.

A key element of the proposals of the Strategy Working Party is to bring national standard setters into membership of IASC. They hope it may be possible to eliminate the differences between national standards and international standards if the major standard setters concerned agree to work together with that aim in mind.

The Working Party has proposed the model for that new structure. It has taken the view that a small sovereign board such as is found in national standard setters in the U. S. or the UK is unlikely to be a complete solution at the international level. A board of this size could be part of the solution because of its advantages in efficient study of the technical issues and its ability to achieve a high level of independence. At the same time, the IASC structure must provide full representation of a large number of countries with more and more countries becoming interested in being involved in its work.

And at this stage in the development, there must also be a reasonable representation of users of accounts, preparers, auditors, academics and others.

They feel that the continuation of an organization like the present board is needed to meet this requirement for representation. Thus, some general features of the required restructuring may seem clear. But much work remains to be done to decide the details that will obtain the agreement of IASC's present members and the key national standard setters.

The IASC agrees that maintaining the status quo is not a viable way forward. They realize that the differences between national standards and international standards cannot be eliminated without the actual participation of national standard setters in an international body and, if IASC cannot adopt an acceptable structure for this, the likelihood is that some other organization will do so.

The Commission acknowledges that it has been suggested that a new organization could be promoted, if necessary, by a strong national standard setter such as the FASB or a group such as G4+1. They believe, of course, that a restructuring of IASC is a preferable way. They point to their established body of international standards as providing a starting point, an established international due process, broad and balanced international support, and international connections of the kind that are needed. (They also have a rather "neutral" coloration although they are headquartered in London.)


## CLOSER ALLIANCE WITH NATIONAL STANDARD SETTERS

The changes in IASC's status mean, in the Working Party's view, that structural changes are needed so that IASC can anticipate the new challenges facing it and meet those challenges effectively. The Working Party has identified the following key issues that must be addressed: "IASC should enter into a partnership with national standard setters so that IASC can work together with them to accelerate convergence between national standards and International Accounting Standards around solutions requiring high-quality, transparent and comparable information that will help participants in capital markets and others to make economic decisions."

Among their recommendations to achieve this partnership, they suggest the following:

1) Steering Committees would be replaced by a Standards Development Committee, on which national standard setters would play a major role in developing International Accounting Standards for approval by the IASC Board.

2) The Standards Development Committee would be supported by a Standards Development Advisory Committee, which would act as a channel of communication with those national standard setters who

are unable to participate directly in the Standards Development Committee because of its limited size.

3) Wider participation within the IASC Board; the IASC Board should be expanded from sixteen countries and organizations to twenty-five countries and organizations, without diluting the quality of the Board's work.

4) The current Advisory Council would be replaced by twelve Trustees (three appointed by the International Federation of Accountants, three by other international organizations and six by the Trustees to represent the world "at large"). The Trustees would appoint members of the Standards Development Committee, the Board, and the Standing Interpretations Committee. The Trustees would also have responsibility for monitoring IASC's effectiveness and for finance.

The IASC points out that the Strategy Working Party's recommendations cover a number of other areas, including the objectives of IASC, IASC's due process, implementation, education and enforcement and funding.

By early June of 1999, the Working Party has received 81 Letters of Comment on it proposals. After due consideration of these comments, they hope to submit final recommendations to the IASC Board by the end of the year.

## FASB AND FAF QUESTION STRUCTURE OF "NEW" IASC

In a March 1999 comment letter, the FASB complained that the IASC proposal to change its structure so that its accounting standards could become more acceptable globally does not go far enough. The FASB agrees with the objectives of working toward a single set of high-quality accounting standards for companies to use for cross-border filings. However, they believe that the proposed new structure will not accomplish that goal. They feel the proposal does not go far enough in creating a high-quality, *independent* standard setter that would be acceptable worldwide.

The Financial Accounting Foundation (FAF), which oversees the FASB, has also for some time joined the latter in supporting the goal of a single set of high-quality accounting standards. Both groups believe that a single set of high-quality international standards is desirable and would improve international comparability; reduce costs to financial statement users, preparers, auditors, and others; and ultimately, optimize the efficiency of the world's capital markets.

Their reservations are not so much a problem with the core set of standards that has now been developed, but with the hierarchy that has been proposed to carry on the work. The FASB and the FAF feel the IASC needs to make several improvements to its proposed structure before it could be acceptable.

A letter to the IASC detailed the FASB and FAF's concerns over the proposal, including:

1) The proposed Standards Development Committee (SDC) should be independent of other organizations. It should have the final authority to set its own agenda and to issue proposals and standards, rather than giving that power to the IASC Board.

2) The proposal that the IASC Board should have veto power over standards developed and approved by the SDC would undermine the autonomy and efficiency of the SDC and the resulting quality of the standards.

3) The proposed Board of Trustees should be independent and have the ultimate authority to oversee the IASC structure and process.

4) The Trustees should be responsible for selecting the individuals to serve on the SDC and the IASC Board.

5) They question why the proposal calls for the Trustees to select the individuals on the SDC but allows the member countries of the IASC Board to select their own delegates.

6) Fundraising should be explicitly and exclusively the province of the Board of Trustees. (The fact or appearance that votes could be influenced by the source or amount of contributions to the process must be avoided.)

It was also pointed out that there are other issues in the IASC proposal that the FASB does not agree with or that are not addressed adequately. They believe that the IASC still needs to strengthen and improve such areas as the composition of the SDC and criteria for membership; rotating versus permanent seats on the SDC, IASC Board, and Board of Trustees; coordinating national and international due process; its budget; who retains the authority to approve interpretations of the SDC's standards; the size of the IASC staff.

The FASB and FAF have stated that they feel that if these improvements are accepted, it would indicate that sufficient progress has been made to support their future endeavors. However, the IASC must continue to work toward the goal of being a truly independent body with standards of the highest quality before it can be totally accepted worldwide, they believe.

## SEC's CAUTIOUS APPRAISAL

From the very beginning, the Securities and Exchange Commission displayed cautious interest in the IASC, and as a member of IOSCO supported development of international standards. But, of course, the SEC's stated purpose is to safeguard the U.S. investor—whether naive or sophisticated, but particularly the former.

The more sophisticated investor and his advisor will be aware of the fact that a foreign stock or bond may not be the bargain it appears to be if insufficient data has been reported to permit an intelligent analysis of the offering. Therefore, the market will drive the price of the securities down and the issuing company will discover that raising capital may be more costly than necessary if management attempts to be coy about revealing the full picture of the financial status of the company. (And, of course, formal adoption of the IASs will not guarantee that an entity is actually following them.)

This truth was made abundantly clear when a member of the staff of the SEC reported at a conference, "The staff (of the SEC) has become aware of situations where a registrant prepares its financial statements in accordance with home country GAAP and in its footnotes asserts that the financial statements 'comply in all material respects with' or 'are consistent with' International Accounting Standards. In some of these situations, the registrant may have applied only certain International Accounting Standards or omitted certain information without giving any explanation of why the information was excluded. The staff has challenged these assertions and will continue to do so. Where the assertion cannot be sustained, the staff will require either changes to the financial statements to conform with International Accounting Standards, or removal of the assertion of compliance with International Accounting Standards."

The SEC is certainly taking its oversight position seriously, but at the same time it is willing to adjust to the conditions of a global market as is evidenced by the following announcement: "The Securities and Exchange Commission (the "Commission") is proposing to improve the comparability of information provided to investors and securities markets by issuers offering or listing securities in multiple markets. To achieve this goal, we are proposing to revise our disclosure requirements for foreign private issuers to conform to the international disclosure standards endorsed by the International Organization of Securities Commissions in September 1998. Under this proposal, the international disclosure standards would replace most of the nonfinancial statement disclosure requirements of Form 20-F, the basic disclosure document for foreign private issuers. We would make conforming changes to the registration statements used by foreign private issuers under the Securities Act of 1933, to reflect the changes in Form 20-F. We also are taking this opportunity to propose changes in the definition of 'foreign private issuer' to give clearer guidance on how foreign companies should determine whether their shareholders are U.S. residents."

The above is the "Summary" of a proposed rule published by the SEC in February 1999 for comment by April 12. Note that this is for the *nonfinancial statement portion* of a disclosure document.

Even those U.S. groups and organizations that are interested in expanding cross-border listing are concerned that too much pressure may be exerted to allow foreign issuers to list their stock under standards that are too lenient, open to varying interpretations and not properly enforced. They tend to agree with SEC officials who point out that at least part of the reason for the strong U.S. capital markets is the strong oversight which focuses on full disclosure. Therefore, the Commission has emphasized that acceptance of the IASC standards is not a foregone conclusion—that they must provide full disclosure, they must be "transparent." (And the SEC could still retain the right to impose requirements beyond or in addition to international standards as it does with FASBs.)

## CURRENT IASC STANDARDS

Following is a list of the IASC standards covering what is considered to be the core group of international standards necessary for cross-border filings. Some of the core group have been rather extensively revised; some have just recently been written; others may be considered for slight modification. A few are not actually a part of the "core."

| | |
|---|---|
| IAS 1 (rev.) | Presentation of Financial Statements |
| IAS 2 | Inventories |
| IAS 3 | Replaced by IAS 27 |
| IAS 4 | Depreciation |
| IAS 5 | Superseded by IAS 1 (rev.) |
| IAS 6 | Replaced by IAS 15 |
| IAS 7 | Cash Flow Statements |
| IAS 8 | Net Profit or Loss for the Period, Fundamental Errors and Changes in Accounting Policies |
| IAS 9 | Superseded by IAS 1 (rev.) |
| IAS 10 (rev.) | Contingencies and Events Occurring After the Balance Sheet Date (partly superseded by IAS 37) |
| IAS 11 | Construction Contracts |
| IAS 12 (rev.) | Income Taxes |
| IAS 13 | Superseded by IAS 1 (rev.) |
| IAS 14 (rev.) | Segment Reporting |
| IAS 15 | Information Reflecting the Effects of Changing Prices (not a core IAS) |
| IAS 16 | Property, Plant and Equipment (not mandatory; impairment provisions revised in IAS 36) |

IAS 17 (rev.) Accounting for Leases

IAS 18         Revenue

IAS 19 (rev.) Employee Benefits

IAS 20         Accounting for Government Grants and Disclosure of
               Government Assistance

IAS 21         The Effects of Changes in Foreign Exchange Rates

IAS 22 (rev.) Business Combinations

IAS 23         Borrowing Costs

IAS 24         Related Party Disclosures

IAS 25         Accounting for Investments

IAS 26         Accounting and Reporting by Retirement Benefit
               Plans (not a core IAS)

IAS 27         Consolidated Financial Statements and Accounting for
               Investments in Subsidiaries

IAS 28         Accounting for Investments in Associates

IAS 29         Financial Reporting in Hyperinflationary Economies

IAS 30         Disclosures in the Financial Statement of Banks and
               Similar Financial Institutions (not a core IAS)

IAS 31         Financial Reporting of Interests in Joint Ventures

IAS 32         Financial Instruments: Disclosures and Presentation

IAS 33         Earnings Per Share

IAS 34         Interim Financial Reporting

IAS 35         Discontinuing Operations

IAS 36         Impairment of Assets

IAS 37         Provisions, Contingent Liabilities and Contingent Assets

IAS 38         Intangible Assets

IAS 39         Financial Instruments: Recognition and Measurement

# Chapter 3

## Recently Adopted or Revised International Accounting Standards

### DISCONTINUING OPERATIONS, IAS 35

This new Standard's objectives are to establish a basis for segregating information about a major operation that an enterprise is discontinuing from information about its continuing operations and to specify minimum disclosures about a discontinuing operation. It is effective for financial reporting periods beginning January 1, 1999.

IAS 35 is a presentation and disclosure Standard that focuses on how to present a discontinuing operation in an enterprise's financial statements and what information to disclose. It does not establish any new principles for deciding when and how to recognize and measure the income, expenses, cash flows, and changes to assets and liabilities relating to a discontinuing operation. Instead, it requires that enterprises follow the recognition and measurement principles in other International Accounting Standards.

### Definition of Discontinuing Operation

A discontinuing operation is considered in IAS 35 to be a component of an enterprise:

1) That the enterprise, pursuant to a single plan, is:
   a) disposing of substantially in its entirety,
   b) disposing of piecemeal, or
   c) terminating through abandonment.

2) That represents a separate major line of business or geographical area of operations.

3) That can be distinguished operationally and for financial reporting purposes.

Thus, a discontinuing operation is a relatively large component of an enterprise—such as a business or geographical segment under IAS 14, *Segment Reporting*—that the enterprise, pursuant to a single plan, is disposing of substantially in its entirety or is terminating through abandonment or piecemeal sale.

The new Standard requires that disclosures about a discontinuing operation begin earlier, after the *earlier* of the following:

1) An enterprise has entered into an agreement to sell substantially all of the assets of the discontinuing operation.

2) The board of directors or other similar governing body has both approved and announced a detailed plan for discontinuance.

## Disclosure Requirements

Required disclosures include:

1) Description of the discontinuing operation.

2) The business or geographical segment(s) in which it is reported in accordance with IAS 14, *Segment Reporting*.

3) The date that the plan for discontinuance was announced.

4) The timing of expected completion (date or period), if known or determinable.

5) The carrying amounts of the total assets and the total liabilities to be disposed of.

6) The amounts of revenue, expenses, and pretax profit or loss from ordinary activities attributable to the discontinuing operation during that specific reporting period, and the related income tax expense.

7) The amount of any gain or loss that is recognized on the disposal of assets or settlement of liabilities attributable to the discontinuing operation, and related income tax expense.

8) The net cash flows attributable to the operating, investing, and financing activities of the discontinuing operation.

9) The net selling prices received or expected from the sale of those net assets for which the enterprise has entered into one or more binding sale agreements, and the expected timing thereof, and the carrying amounts of those net assets.

## Further Considerations

Financial statements for periods after initial disclosure must update those disclosures, including a description of any significant changes in the amount or timing of cash flows relating to the assets and liabilities to be disposed of or settled and the causes of those changes.

The disclosures would be made if a plan for disposal is approved and publicly announced after the end of an enterprise's financial reporting period but before the financial statements for that period are approved. The disclosures continue until completion of the disposal.

To improve the ability of users of financial statements to make projections, comparative information for prior periods presented in financial statements prepared after initial disclosure must be restated to segregate the continuing and discontinuing assets, liabilities, income, expenses, and cash flows.

## Comparison to U.S. GAAP

IAS 35 brings another of IASC's accounting standards closer to U.S. GAAP in that the IASC's standards now actually include a discontinuing operation standard—similar in many respects to the comparable U.S. GAAP standard, Accounting Principles Board Opinion 30 (APB 30).

However, as in most instances, this standard does vary slightly from GAAP. Two examples follow:

1) APB 30 requires the results of discontinuing operations to be reported on the face of the financial statements while IAS 35 only recommends this approach to disclosure.

2) While IASC emphasizes the timeliness of its required initial disclosure event, APB's requirement would very probably occur earlier than IAS 35's requirement. The initial disclosure event specified in IAS 35 is a *binding sales agreement* or board of director's approval of a *detailed discontinuing operations plan* and a formal announcement of that plan. On the other hand, APB 30 specifies that the initial disclosure event is the date on which management having authority to approve the discontinuance commits to a formal plan to dispose of a segment of the business.

## More Uniform Approach

Since many developing economies (as well as other more advanced ones) do not have specific guidance relating to discontinuing operations accounting, it is probable that the issuance of IAS 35 will inspire a number of them to adopt it outright or to develop their own national standard which will closely follow the requirements of IAS 35. Regardless, a more uniform approach to reporting discontinuing operations should result. As an additional inducement to use the principles of this Standard, appendices to IAS 35 provide illustrative disclosures and guidance on how prior period information should be restated to conform to the presentation requirements of IAS 35.

## IMPAIRMENT OF ASSETS, IAS 36

In June 1998, the IASC issued International Accounting Standard 36, Impairment of Assets, prescribing the accounting and disclosure requirements specifically for impairment of:

1) Goodwill.
2) Intangible assets and property.
3) Plant and equipment.

The Standard includes requirements for identifying an impaired asset, measuring its recoverable amount, recognizing or reversing any resulting impairment loss, and disclosing information on impairment losses or reversals of impairment losses.

It prescribes how an enterprise should test its assets for impairment, that is:

1) The procedures that an enterprise should apply to ensure that its assets are not overstated in the financial statements.
2) How an enterprise should assess the amount to be recovered from an asset (the "recoverable amount").
3) When an enterprise should account for an impairment loss identified by this assessment.

The Standard does *not* cover accounting and disclosure requirements for:

1) Inventories.
2) Deferred tax assets.
3) Assets arising from construction contracts.
4) Assets arising from employee benefits.
5) Most financial assets.

The Standard is effective for accounting periods beginning on and after July 1, 1999.

## Requirements of IAS 36

According to this IAS, an impairment loss should be recognized whenever the recoverable amount of an asset is less than its carrying amount (sometimes called "book value"). The new standard spells out in detail the procedures to follow when this occurs:

1) The recoverable amount of an asset is defined as the higher of:
   a) Net selling price as measured by the amount obtainable from the sale of the asset in an arm's length transaction between knowledgeable, willing parties, less the cost of disposal.
   b) Value in use as measured by the present value of the asset's estimated future cash flows including disposable cash flows, if any, expected to arise from its continuing use and eventual disposal. The discount rate should be a pretax rate that reflects current market assessments of the time value of money and the risks specific to the asset.

2) An impairment loss should be recognized as an expense in the income statement for assets carried at cost and treated as a revaluation decrease for assets carried at revalued amount.

3) An impairment loss should be reversed and income recognized when there has been a *change* in the estimates used to determine an asset's recoverable amount after the last impairment loss was recognized.

4) The recoverable amount of an asset should be estimated whenever there is an indication that the asset may be impaired. IAS 36 includes a list of indicators of impairment to be considered at each balance sheet date. In some cases, the IAS applicable to an asset may include requirements for additional reviews.

5) In determining value in use, an enterprise should use:
   a) Cash flow projections based on reasonable and supportable assumptions that reflect the asset in its current condition and represent management's best estimate of the set of economic conditions that will exist over the remaining useful life of the asset.
   b) Estimates of future cash flows should include all estimated future cash inflows and cash outflows except for cash flows from financing activities and income tax receipts and payments.
   c) A pretax discount rate that reflects current market assessments of the time value of money and the risks specific to the asset. The dis-

count rate should not reflect risks for which the future cash flows have been adjusted.

6) If an asset does not generate cash inflows that are largely independent from the cash inflows from other assets, an enterprise should determine the recoverable amount of the cash-generating unit to which the asset belongs. IAS 36 provides explicit directions concerning these cash-generating units:

   **a)** "Cash-generating unit" refers to the smallest identifiable group of assets that generates cash inflows which are largely independent of the cash inflows from other assets or group of assets.

   **b)** The requirements for recognizing and reversing impairment losses for a cash-generating unit are the same as those for an individual asset.

   **c)** The concept of cash-generating units should often be used in testing assets for impairment because, in many cases, assets work together rather than in isolation.

   **d)** In addition, IAS 36 provides information on how to identify the cash-generating unit to which an asset belongs and further requirements on how to measure an impairment loss for a cash-generating unit and then allocate the loss between the assets of the unit.

7) Reversal of impairment losses also comes in for extensive consideration:

   **a)** An impairment loss recognized in prior years should be reversed if, and only if, there has been a change in the estimates used to determine recoverable amount since the last impairment loss was recognized.

   **b)** An impairment loss should only be reversed to the extent the reversal does not increase the carrying amount of the asset above the carrying amount that would have been determined for the asset (net of amortization or depreciation) had no impairment loss been recognized.

   **c)** An impairment loss for *goodwill* should be reversed only if the specific external event that caused the recognition of the impairment loss reverses.

   **d)** A reversal of an impairment loss should be recognized as income in the income statement for assets carried at cost and treated as a revaluation increase for assets carried at revalued amount.

8) When impairment losses are recognized or reversed, an enterprise should disclose certain information by *class of assets* and by *reportable segments*. Further disclosure is required if impairment losses recognized or reversed are *material* to the financial statements of the reporting enterprise as a whole.

Upon first adoption of IAS 36, its requirements should be applied *prospectively* only; that is, prior periods will *not* be restated.

## IASC-UK Cooperation

IAS 36 differs materially in a number of instances from U.S. Generally Accepted Accounting Principles (U.S. GAAP) and the asset impairment rules of a number of other countries. On the other hand, there are aspects of the international standard that are closer to the provisions of other established national standards.

For example, in developing IAS 36, proposals of the Accounting Standard Board (ASB) in the United Kingdom for a Financial Reporting Standard (FRS) on impairment of assets were closely monitored by the international body. The ASB and the IASC shared the same objectives for their project, and many of their views regarding requirements coincided. Therefore, the resulting standards are very similar.

Furthermore, IAS 36 provides a standard approach to the recognition, measurement, and disclosure of asset impairments by non-U.S. companies that use IAS in financial statements and also furnishes a model for the many developing economies which have not yet adopted an asset impairment standard of their own, but look often to IASC for guidance.

The IASC considers this an important step forward from the requirements and guidance for impairment losses that were previously included in their Standards. They point out that it provides more details on how to perform an impairment test and it eliminates certain alternatives, such as the option not to use discounting in measuring recoverable amount. (The "options" in many of the older IASs have been particularly worrisome to the SEC, the FASB and other standard-setting bodies.)

## Differences from GAAP

As mentioned above there is a number of significant differences between IAS 36 and U.S. GAAP specified in *Accounting for the Impairment of Long-Lived Assets and for Long-Lived Assets to Be Disposed Of*, FASB 121. (For a review of the requirements of FASB 121, see Chapter 1.)

Differences between the two Standards include:

1) Probably most significantly, FASB 121 *does not permit reversal* of asset impairment losses as does IAS 36—along with much of the rest of the accounting world. (It might be pointed out here that there seems to be little global consensus yet about how to account for asset impairment. Some countries have rulings similar to GAAP, others to the new IAS, others to the old IAS. Still others have standards relating to assessment of recoverability, not valuation; many have no stan-

dard at all on impairment. On the other hand, many of the emerging nations will undoubtedly adopt IAS 36.)

2) GAAP requires a *quantitative test* of asset impairment before the measurement and recognition of an asset impairment loss is necessitated. This involves figuring the expected cumulative net cash flows from continuing use of the asset, not including interest and not to be discounted less than the asset's carrying amount. IAS 36 does not include this type of test.

3) IAS 36 does not distinguish between assets to be held and used and assets to be disposed of when measuring impairment loss; FASB 121 has different impairment loss measurement approaches for the two categories.

   a) FASB 121's measurement of the impairment loss of an asset *to be used* is the difference between the asset's carrying amount and its fair value.

   b) FASB 121 measurement of the impairment loss of an asset *to be disposed of* is the asset's carrying amount less its net realizable value.

   c) IAS 36's measurement of *either* impairment loss is the asset's carrying amount less the higher of its value in use or its net realizable value (fair value minus disposal costs).

4) FASB 121 relies on *management judgment* to determine the appropriate future cash flow period and cash flows to determine the equivalent of IAS 36's value in use. Unless management can justify otherwise, IAS 36 limits the maximum future cash flow period to five years and specifies the growth rate in cash flows.

## PROVISIONS, CONTINGENT LIABILITIES AND CONTINGENT ASSETS, IAS 37

IAS 37, *Provisions, Contingent Liabilities and Contingent Assets* issued in September 1998 is effective for annual financial statements issued on and after July 1, 1999.

This Standard requires that:

1) Provisions should be recognized in the balance sheet only when:

   a) An enterprise has a present obligation (either legal or constructive) as a result of a past event;

   b) More likely than not a transfer of economic benefits will be required to settle the obligation;

   c) The amount of the obligation can be measured reliably.

**2)**   Provisions should be measured in the balance sheet at the best estimate of the expenditure required to settle the present obligation at the balance sheet date. This is the amount that an enterprise would rationally pay to settle the obligation, or to transfer it to a third party, at that date. When measuring provisions, an enterprise should take into account any risks and uncertainties. However, uncertainty does not justify the creation of excessive provisions or a deliberate overstatement of liabilities—in other words, the "big bath."

An enterprise should discount a provision where the effect of the time value of money is material and should take future events, such as changes in the law and technological changes, into account where there is sufficient objective evidence that they will occur.

**3)**   The amount of a provision should not be reduced by gains from the expected disposal of assets (even if the expected disposal is closely linked to the event giving rise to the provision) or by expected reimbursements—from insurance contracts, indemnity clauses, suppliers' warranties and the like. When it is virtually certain the reimbursement will be received if the enterprise settles the obligation, the reimbursement should be recognized as a separate asset.

**4)**   A provision should be used only for expenditures for which the provision was originally recognized and should be reversed if an outflow of resources is no longer probable.

IAS 37 sets out three specific applications of these general requirements:

**1)**   A provision *should not be recognized* for future operating losses.

**2)**   A provision *should be recognized* for an onerous contract in which the unavoidable costs of meeting the obligations under the contract are greater than the expected economic benefits.

**3)**   A provision for restructuring costs *should be recognized only* when an enterprise has a detailed formal plan for the restructuring and has raised a valid expectation in those affected that it will carry out the restructuring by starting to implement that plan or announcing its main features to those affected by it; for this purpose, a management or board decision is not enough.

A restructuring provision should exclude costs—such as retraining or relocating continuing staff, marketing or investment in new systems and distribution networks—that are not necessarily entailed by the restructuring or that are not associated with the enterprise's ongoing activities.

IAS 37 replaces part of IAS 10, *Contingencies and Events Occurring After the Balance Sheet Date*. It prohibits the recognition of contingent liabilities and contingent assets. An enterprise should disclose a contingent liability, unless the possibility of an outflow of resources embodying economic benefits is remote, and disclose a contingent asset if an inflow of economic benefits is probable.

## UK-IASC Cooperative Effort

Here again, the IASC and the UK's Accounting Standards Board worked in close conjunction to develop virtually identical accounting standards. Their aim is to eliminate many of the questionable accounting practices that have been developing.

One of the most obvious is the "big bath" mentioned above and included in the "hocus pocus" practices that SEC Chairman Arthur Levitt feels has been sullying the financial reporting process here—as well as globally. (The ploy is to report excessive liabilities currently to make future profits look even rosier at the time the liabilities are actually being incurred.)

## Global Aspects

On the global front, the new standards should help to lessen the diversity of provision recognition and measurement practices that have evolved along with varying accounting regulations and tax treatment of provisions. Not only do these standards cut down on the welter of provisions that were previously provided for in financial statements prepared according to UK and IAS principles, but they also move much closer to U.S. GAAP (contained in FASB 5, *Accounting for Contingencies*).

Some technical differences between GAAP and the two standards are slight enough that they should pose no problem in doing comparative valuations of U.S. and non-U.S. companies. Since provisions can significantly affect a company's balance sheet and net income, reducing the divergence in the handling of "provisions" should be considered an important step in harmonization of global accounting practices, particularly when considering the fact that many countries that have no established procedure for handling provisions and contingencies—or very haphazard ones—will now adopt IAS 37.

## EFFECT OF IAS 36, 37 AND 22 ON OTHER IASs

In October 1998, after the June introduction of IASC 36, the September introduction of IAS 37, and the revision of IAS 22, *Business Combinations*, the International Accounting Standards Committee published limited revisions to IAS 16, *Property, Plant and Equipment*, and revisions to certain paragraphs of IAS 28, *Accounting for Investments in Associates*, and IAS 31, *Financial Reporting of Interests in Joint Ventures*. The revisions to IAS 16, IAS 28 and IAS 31 are limited and made for consistency with the Standards described above:

**1)** Instead of including separate specific requirements, IAS 16 and IAS 28 now refer to IAS 36 for impairment testing of property, plant and equipment, and of investments in subsidiaries, associates, and joint ventures which are accounted for under the equity method. IAS 31 is amended to clarify the recognition of an impairment loss on an asset when traded at a loss between a joint venture and a venturer.

**2)** IAS 16 now references IAS 37 for guidance on recognizing a provision for the costs of dismantling and removing an item of property, plant and equipment.

**3)** Guidance in IAS 16 on determining the fair value of an item of property, plant and equipment which has been revalued has been made consistent with the guidance in IAS 22 (revised 1998) on determining the fair value of an item of property, plant and equipment acquired in a business combination. Guidance in both Standards no longer refers to the existing use of the asset. (Fair value is defined as the amount for which an asset could be exchanged, or a liability settled, between knowledgeable, willing parties in an arm's length transaction.)

## INTANGIBLE ASSETS, IAS 38

IAS 38 is effective for accounting periods beginning on or after July 1,1999. At the time it is adopted, IAS 22 (rev.), *Business Combinations*, and IAS 36, *Impairment of Assets*, must also be adopted since they have direct bearing upon this new standard.

### Scope of IAS 38

IAS 38 applies to all intangible assets that are not specifically handled in other IASs. Included in the lists of things it does deal with are the accounting for expenditures on advertising, training, start-up activities, research and development activities (R&D), mortgage servicing rights, customer lists, licensing agreements, motion picture patents, and copyrights. It also covers expenditures for computer software that is an integral part of a tangible asset.

The Standard does *not* apply to intangible assets covered by other IASs; financial instruments; mineral rights and expenditures for the exploration, development, and extraction of minerals, oil, natural gas—nonregenerative resources; insurance contracts.

Among those intangible assets covered by another IAS are deferred tax assets, intangible assets held for sale in the ordinary course of business, leases, employee benefits, and goodwill arising from a business transaction.

IAS 38 includes transitional provisions that clarify when the Standard should be applied retrospectively and when it should be applied prospectively.

## Requirements of IAS 38

The basic features of IAS 38 include:

1) An intangible asset should be recognized initially, at cost, in the financial statement whether it has been acquired externally or generated internally, if, and only if:
   a) it is probable that the future economic benefits attributable to the asset will flow to the enterprise;
   b) cost of the asset can be measured reliably;
   c) the asset falls within the classification of an *intangible* asset; that is, it is *an identifiable nonmonetary asset without physical substance held for use in the production or supply of goods or services, for rental to others, or for administrative purposes.*

2) If an intangible item does not meet both the definition and the criteria for the recognition of an intangible asset, IAS 38 requires the expenditure on this item to be recognized as an *expense* when it is incurred. An enterprise is not permitted to include this expenditure in the cost of an intangible asset at a later date.

3) Therefore, it becomes evident from the recognition criteria that all expenditures on research should be recognized as an expense. The same treatment applies to start-up costs, training costs, and advertising costs. IAS 38 also specifically prohibits the recognition as assets of internally generated goodwill, brands, mastheads, publishing titles, customer lists and such. However, as mentioned above, occasionally developmental expenditure may result in the recognition of an intangible asset—some internally developed computer software, for example.

4) In accounting for a business combination that is an acquisition, IAS 38 works in combination with the above mentioned IAS 22, *Business Combinations.* This reinforces the stipulation that if an intangible item does not meet both the *definition* and the *criteria* for the recognition as an intangible asset, the expenditure for this item which was included in the cost of acquisition should form part of the amount attributed to goodwill at the date of acquisition.

Therefore, according to this Standard, purchased R&D-in-process should not be recognized as an expense immediately at the date of acquisition, but it should be recognized as part of the goodwill recognized at the date of acquisition and amortized under IAS 22 (rev.), unless it meets the criteria for separate recognition as an intangible asset.

IAS 22 (rev.) provides that if there is sufficient evidence that the useful life of goodwill will exceed 20 years, an enterprise should amortize the goodwill over its estimated useful life and:

a) Test goodwill for impairment at least annually in accordance with IAS 36, *Impairment of Assets.*

b) Disclose the reasoning behind the presumption in the initial recognition that the useful life of goodwill would not exceed 20 years, and specify the factor(s) that were significant later in determining the useful life of goodwill.

IAS 22 (rev.) does not permit an enterprise to assign an infinite useful life to goodwill.

5) Requires that after initial recognition in the financial statement, an intangible asset be measured under either the *benchmark treatment* or the allowed *alternative treatment.*

a) The benchmark treatment is historical cost less any amortization and impairment losses. It is consistent with the GAAP approach.

b) The allowed alternative treatment is the revalued amount based on fair value minus any subsequent amortization and impairment losses. However, this treatment is permitted if, and only if, fair value can be determined by reference to an active market for the intangible asset—which is fairly unlikely for *intangible* assets.

The Standard defines fair value of an asset as the amount for which that asset could be exchanged between knowledgeable, willing parties in an arm's-length transaction.

## Comparison to GAAP

IAS 38 and the comparable GAAP are similar in many respects. There are some major differences, but even here the FASB and the SEC are looking into possible revisions in some areas. Current differences include:

1) Here again, an international standard differs from U.S. GAAP on the revaluation issue: IAS 38 permits revaluation; GAAP does not.

2) GAAP requires that an intangible asset's amortization period not exceed forty years. IAS 38 specifies a maximum twenty-year amortization period. This is rebuttable if a longer amortization period can be justified. (The FASB has now voted to cut to twenty years the write-off time for goodwill from an acquisition.)

3)  GAAP does not require an active market-based valuation for internally generated intangible assets; IAS does.

4)  Except for computer software development, GAAP does not permit capitalization of development costs. On the other hand, IAS 38 requires capitalization of development costs in certain cases.

## FINANCIAL INSTRUMENTS: RECOGNITION AND MEASUREMENT, IAS 39

In March 1999, IASC announced that it had published a comprehensive standard on accounting for financial instruments after nine years' effort and four public comment documents. This new Standard, IAS 39, *Financial Instruments: Recognition and Measurement*, will take effect for annual financial statements covering periods beginning on or after January 1, 2001. Earlier application is permitted as of the beginning of a fiscal year that ends after March 15,1999. Retrospective application is not permitted.

Financial instruments include conventional financial assets and liabilities, such as cash, trade receivables and payables, investments in debt and equity securities, and notes, bonds, and loans payable. Financial instruments also include derivatives such as futures, forwards, swaps, and option contracts.

### Background

IAS 39 has been in development by IASC since 1989. Its "final" form was preceded by exposure drafts in 1991, 1994, and 1998 and by a steering committee discussion paper in 1997. In 1996, IASC adopted *Financial Instruments: Disclosure and Presentation* (IAS 32) pending completion of a standard on recognition and measurement. IAS 39 expands those disclosures and resolves the accounting questions, including the important area of accounting for hedging transactions. (At one point, it looked as though the international body would adopt the provisions of the newly adopted FASB 133; however, differing views among the board members temporarily postponed the decision on a final version of IAS 39.)

Publication of this Standard was particularly gratifying to IASC because it finalized the basic requirement of IASC's commitment to the International Organization of Securities Commissions (IOSCO) to produce a comprehensive core set of accounting standards. The agreement is that now this body will review the standards to determine whether they will endorse them for adoption for cross-border listing and trading.

IASC officials emphasized their belief that IAS 39 fills the biggest void in global accounting standards. They pointed out that of their 103 member countries only the United States has adopted a truly comprehensive standard on recognition and measurement of financial instruments and hedge accounting (FASB 133).

## Need for Greater Uniformity

With the phenomenal growth of global trading (and the equally amazing growth of imaginative derivatives which are often not recognized in the financial statements), IASC suggests that investors sometimes get very unwelcome surprises when losses surface.

The IASC is aware that current accounting practices for financial instruments vary widely around the world, with the result being noncomparability and investor confusion. Even when financial assets such as investments have been recognized on the balance sheet, some companies have measured them at cost, others at lower of cost or market, and still others at fair value.

Further, in the absence of hedge accounting standards, companies often have postponed recognizing any changes in the fair values of financial instruments or, if recognized, companies have deferred the profit-or-loss effects of such changes in the balance sheet. IAS 39 addresses these and other shortcomings of current practice.

Many developing economies are adopting the International Accounting Standards outright or using them as a basis for developing their own national standards. It is probable that not only they, but also many of the developed economies, will progress to more comprehensive accounting standards for financial instruments, including derivatives. After all, both the FASB and the IASC have spent years going over the ground trying to find an effective solution to satisfy all segments of the business and financial world.

IAS 39 does not go as far in accounting for certain financial instruments as U.S. GAAP, but it does move the international standards closer. It should also reduce the global diversity of financial instrument accounting practices, particularly those dealing with debt and equity security instruments, derivatives, and hedges.

## Principal Requirements

IAS 39 requires that all financial assets and all financial liabilities, including all derivatives, be recognized on the balance sheet. This means that derivatives can no longer be off-balance-sheet items.

Initially, financial assets and liabilities will be measured at cost, including transaction costs. After initial recognition, most financial assets must be remeasured at fair value; however, the following will be carried at amortized cost subject to a test for impairment:

1) Loans and receivables originated by the enterprise and not held for trading.

2) Other fixed maturity investments, such as debt securities and mandatorily redeemable preferred shares, that the enterprise intends and is able to hold to maturity.

3) Financial assets whose fair value cannot be reliably measured (limited to some equity instruments with no quoted market price and some derivatives that are linked to and must be settled by delivery of such unquoted equity instruments).

After acquisition, most liabilities will be measured at original recorded amount less principal repayments and amortization. Only derivatives and liabilities held for trading (such as short sales of securities) will be remeasured to fair value.

To record the complete amount of periodic unrealized fair value changes an enterprise will have a single, enterprise-wide option to either:

1) Recognize the entire amount in income; or

2) Recognize in income only those changes in fair value relating to financial assets and liabilities held for trading, with the value changes for nontrading instruments reported in equity until the financial asset is sold, at which time the realized gain or loss is reported in net profit or loss. For this purpose, derivatives are always deemed held for trading unless they are part of a hedging relationship that qualifies for hedge accounting.

## Hedge Accounting

The IASC considers hedging, for accounting purposes, as designating the change in value of a derivative, or in limited circumstances a nonderivative financial instrument, as an offset, in whole or in part, to the change in fair value or cash flows of a hedged item. A hedged item can be an asset, liability, firm commitment, or forecasted future transaction that is exposed to risk of change in value or changes in future cash flows. Hedge accounting recognizes the offsetting effects on net profit or loss symmetrically.

Thus, hedge accounting is permitted under IAS 39 in certain circumstances, provided that the hedging relationship is *clearly defined, measurable, and actually effective.*

IAS 39, like FASB 133, recognizes and defines three types of hedges although they are not identical.

1) Fair value hedge: a hedge of the exposure to changes in the fair value of a recognized asset or liability (such as a hedge of exposure to changes in the fair value of fixed rate debt as a result of changes in in-

terest rates). To the extent that the hedge is effective, the gain or loss from remeasuring the hedging instrument at fair value is recognized immediately in net profit or loss.

At the same time, the gain or loss on the hedged item adjusts the carrying amount of the hedged item and is recognized immediately in net profit or loss.

2) Cash flow hedge: a hedge of the exposure to variability in cash flows attributable to a recognized asset or liability (such as all or some future interest payments on variable rate debt) or a forecasted transaction (such as an anticipated purchase or sale). A hedge of an unrecognized firm commitment to buy or sell an asset at a fixed price in the enterprise's reporting currency is accounted for as a cash flow hedge even though it has a fair value exposure. To the extent that the gain or loss on the effective portion of the hedging instrument is recognized initially, it is recorded directly in equity. Subsequently, that amount is included in net profit or loss in the same period or periods during which the hedged item affects net profit or loss (for example, through cost of sales, depreciation, or amortization). For hedges of forecasted transactions, the gain or loss on the hedging instrument will adjust the basis (carrying amount) of the acquired asset or liability.

3) A hedge of a net investment in a foreign entity (as defined in IAS 21, *The Effects of Changes in Foreign Exchange Rates*): These are accounted for as cash flow hedges.

As we have seen above, hedge accounting is permitted when the hedging relationship is clearly defined, measurable, and actually effective. The enterprise must designate a specific hedging instrument as a hedge of a change in value or cash flow of a specific hedged item, rather than as a hedge of an overall net balance sheet position. However, the approximate income statement effect of hedge accounting for an overall net position can be achieved, in some cases, by designating part of one of the underlying items as the hedged position.

## Derecognition

In addition, IAS 39 establishes conditions for determining when control over a financial asset or liability has been transferred to another party. For financial assets a transfer normally would be accounted for as a sale (derecognized) when:

1) The transferee has the right to sell or pledge the asset.
2) The transferor does not have the right to reacquire the transferred assets unless either the asset is readily obtainable in the market or the reacquisition price is fair value at the time of reacquisition.

With respect to derecognition of liabilities, the debtor must be legally released from primary responsibility for all or part of the liability either judicially or by the creditor. If part of a financial asset or liability is sold or extinguished, the carrying amount is split based on relative fair values. If fair values are not determinable, a cost recovery approach to profit recognition is taken.

## Additional Disclosure Requirements

IAS 39 moves international requirements a big step in the direction of greater transparency. The principal disclosure requirements for financial instruments include:

1) Description of methods and assumptions used in estimating fair values.

2) Disclosure of whether purchases of financial assets are accounted for at trade date or settlement date.

3) Description of the enterprise's financial risk management objectives and policies.

4) For each category of hedge: a description of the hedge; which financial instruments are designated as hedging instruments; and the nature of the risks being hedged.

5) Disclosure of significant items of income and expense and gains and losses resulting from financial assets and financial liabilities, and whether they are included in net profit or loss or as a separate component of equity and, if in equity, a reconciliation of movements in and out of equity;

6) Explanation of details of securitization and repurchase agreements.

7) Description of the nature, effect, and reasons for reclassifications of financial assets from amortized cost to fair value.

8) Explanation of the nature and amount of any impairment loss or reversal of an impairment loss.

## A Stop-Gap Solution

Even though IAS 39 goes a long way toward fair value accounting, the IASC considers it only a partial step. The Board decided not to require fair value measurement for the originated loans and receivables or for held-to-maturity investments at this time for a number of reasons:

1) Too drastic a change from current practice would be required in many jurisdictions.

2) The existence of portfolio linkage of those assets, in many industries, to liabilities that, under IAS 39, will continue to be measured at their amortized original amount. Banks, for example, say that they manage their depositor liabilities in tandem with their portfolios of mortgage and commercial loans.

3) Some question the relevance of fair values for financial assets intended to be held until maturity, particularly if fair value changes enter into measuring net profit or loss.

The resulting standard should probably be considered a stop-gap measure published to meet the deadline the IASC had set to submit the core set of standards to IOSCO. As noted, it also serves, at least to a certain extent, to answer the urgent need in many countries for a comprehensive financial instruments standard. While it is similar in many respects to U.S. GAAP, IAS 39 needs more work to raise it to the level of quality the IASC seeks in its standards. (As a matter of fact, there is still considerable debate about whether FASB 133 is the final word on financial instrument accounting and disclosure in this country.)

## Joint Working Group

At the suggestion of IASC, when it became fairly obvious by 1997 that problems relating to a standard on financial instruments, fair values, and so on, were not going to be easily solved, a committee was formed. The Joint Working Group (JWG) was established to explore the feasibility of moving to comprehensive fair value accounting requirements for Financial Instruments over the medium term. The Joint Working Group is chaired by the IASC representative and has members representing 13 national standard setters or other national administrations. The group was formed because several standard setters felt that fair value measurement would be the only satisfactory long-term solution for all financial instruments.

They also recognized, however, that more work was needed to confirm or refute this point of view and to deal with the many practical difficulties that must be resolved before any such requirement could be introduced. At present, the members of the JWG consider it imperative to decide whether or not further development and refinement of an integrated and harmonized financial instruments accounting standard is practicable.

Whether and how fair value can be reliably estimated for the unquoted equities also is under study by that group. Depending on the outcome of those studies, the group may recommend that its members pursue greater use of fair values than IAS 39 requires.

Possibly too idealistically, early on, the group hoped to develop proposals for a further standard on recognition and measurement for financial instruments that could be adopted by all the national standard setters as well as by the IASC. Their stated goal is to produce an Exposure Draft by mid-1999 and a final standard by mid-2000.

## EVENTS AFTER THE BALANCE SHEET DATE, IAS 10 (REV.)

IAS 10 was revised (based on E 63) in March 1999 to cover only events after the balance sheet date. In 1998, the portion of IAS 10 dealing with contingencies was replaced by IAS 37, *Provisions, Contingent Liabilities and Contingent Assets.*

The revised Standard becomes effective for annual financial statements covering periods beginning on or after January 1, 2000.

Major provisions of the statement include:

1) An enterprise should adjust its financial statements for events after the balance sheet date that provide further evidence of conditions that existed at the balance sheet.

2) An enterprise should not adjust its financial statements for events after the balance sheet date that are indicative of conditions that arose after the balance sheet date.

3) If dividends to holders of equity instruments are proposed or declared after the balance sheet date, an enterprise should not recognize those dividends as a liability.

4) An enterprise may give the disclosure of proposed dividends (required by IAS 1, *Presentation of Financial Statements*) either on the face of the balance sheet as an appropriation within equity or in the notes to the financial statements.

5) An enterprise should not prepare its financial statements on a going concern basis if management determines after the balance sheet date either that it intends to liquidate the enterprise, or to cease trading, or that it has no realistic alternative but to do so. (The existing IAS 10 contains a similar requirement.)

6) There should no longer be a requirement to adjust the financial statements where an event after the balance sheet date indicates that the going concern assumption is not appropriate for part of an enterprise.

7) An enterprise should disclose the date when the financial statements were authorized for issue and who gave the authorization. If the enterprise's owners or others have the power to amend the financial statements after issuance, the enterprise should disclose that fact.

8) An enterprise should update disclosures that relate to conditions that existed at the balance sheet date in the light of any new information that it receives after the balance sheet date about those conditions.

## EARNINGS PER SHARE, IAS 33

The objective of the FASB and IASC earnings per share standards is to prescribe principles for the determination and presentation of earnings per share that will lead to global harmonization of earnings per share measurements and disclosures. To this end, both standard setters have concluded where appropriate two earnings per share figures should be presented, namely,

1) Basic Earnings Per Share, which is computed by dividing income available to stockholders by the weighted average number of common shares outstanding during the period. Shares issued during the period and shares reacquired during the period should be weighted for the portion of the period they were outstanding.

2) Diluted Earnings Per Share, which is computed in a similar manner to basic earnings per share after adjusting the numerator and denominator of the calculation for the effects of all potential dilutive common shares that were outstanding during the period. It is effective for financial statements issued on or after January 1, 1998. Earlier application is encouraged. One difference between FASB 128, *Earnings per Share*, and IAS 33 is a matter of degree. FASB 128 requires disclosure of per-share figures for income from continuing operations on the face of the income statement and for extraordinary items, accounting changes and discontinued operations. The international standard requires only net profit per-share amounts on the face of the income statement but also encourages other disclosures.

The IASC and FASB also differ in their view of the objective of a diluted earnings per share presentation. The IASC views the figures as an early warning to investors of possible reductions in the value of EPS while the FASB sees it as a measure of performance rather than an indicator of the future. However, except for some language differences, the basic provisions of IAS 33 are substantially the same as those of FASB 128. (These provisions are discussed more fully in connection with FASB 128 in Chapter 1 in this Supplement.)

### Global Adoption

It is anticipated that IAS 33 will be adopted by:

1) Many countries as a national standard.
2) Stock exchanges for listing purposes.
3) Corporations with a global stock ownership.

These adoptions will be a significant contribution to facilitating global investing in common stocks.

## INTERIM FINANCIAL REPORTING, IAS 34

This standard was issued in February 1998 to become effective for financial reporting periods beginning January 1, 1999.

IAS 34 *Interim Financial Reporting* requires that companies that prepare interim reports apply the same accounting recognition and measurement principles used in their last annual statements. This requirement will tend to make interim earnings more volatile for non-U.S. companies that heretofore had followed U.S.-style interim reporting rules. U.S. rulings permit some interim income smoothing recognition and measurement practices. The statement also specifies that measurements in interim financial statements should be made on a financial year-to-date basis.

It does not mandate that interim reports be published in the first place, who should publish them, how often they should be prepared, or how soon they should appear after the end of an interim reporting period, if they are prepared. The IASC decided these matters were better left to the discretion of the national governments, securities regulators, stock exchanges, and accounting organizations. At present, in at least 30 countries, the securities regulators and stock exchanges do, in fact, require interim reporting. Interim reports are used by investors and creditors to check for any signs of weakness—or strength, for that matter.

IAS 34 applies to recognizing, measuring, and disclosing assets, liabilities, income, and expenses for quarterly, biannual, or any other type of interim report.

The United Kingdom's Accounting Standards Board (ASB) recently issued a nonmandatory "best practice" statement on interim reporting that is almost identical to the IASC standard. Both use the discrete method for interim reporting. Under this method, as amplified below, the interim period is treated as an accounting period distinct from the annual period. Incomplete transactions are reported, using the same principles that are used for the annual reports.

This new statement will get close scrutiny from many sources including U.S. investors and creditors with worldwide interests. Interim financial reports issued by foreign companies do not conform to APB 28, *Interim Financial Reporting*. This new standard also differs in a number of significant areas from U.S. GAAP. However, U.S. accountants, investors, and financial advisors are already aware of the fact that the accounting used for interim financial reporting purposes in many countries outside of the U.S. is considerably different from U.S. GAAP. The foreign standards are similar in many respects to IAS 34.

Below is a comparison of a few of the provisions to U.S. GAAP governing interim financial reports included in Accounting Principles Board APB 28. (A discussion of other information relating to U.S. GAAP can be found in Appendix D of the ADB.)

## Independent Theory

IAS 34 for the most part adopts the independent theory of interim reporting. This approach regards each interim period as a discrete or "stand-alone" reporting period. That is, the events and transactions within each accounting period are to be reported in the accounting period, regardless of its length. Under the independent view, the results of operations for each interim period should be determined basically in the same manner as if the interim period were an annual accounting period. Under this approach, deferrals, accruals, and estimations at the end of each interim period are determined by following basically the same approach as in the annual reports. Thus, if an expenditure is expensed in the annual statement, it should be expensed in any interim report, regardless of the amount of the expenditure and the relationship to the annual amount or the revenues of other interim periods for that year.

## Dependent Approach

APB 28 generally follows the dependent theory of interim period reporting. This approach regards each interim period as an integral part of the annual period. According to the dependent view, interim financial data are an integral part of the annual period, and it is essential to provide investors with timely information on the progress the entity is making in realizing its annual results of operations. Therefore, the usefulness of interim data rests on the predictive relationship that it has to the annual report. Thus, each interim period should be regarded as an integral part of the annual period rather than a discrete period standing on its own.

Under this approach, deferrals, accruals, and estimations at the end of each interim period are affected by predictions about the results of operations for the remainder of the year. Thus, for example, a portion of an estimated annual expenditure that might be expensed for the entire annual period might be accrued or deferred at the end of an interim period as management allocates the estimated annual expense between interim periods on a basis that reflects time, sales volume, or production activity.

## Other Differences

If fully aware of the important differences between the two alternative interim financial reporting approaches, the user of the financial reports should be able to make an intelligent analysis of the information presented. Some of those differences are presented below:

*Dependent/independent.*    Because the dependent approach gives accounting flexibility in managing interim earnings to minimize any possibility that the figures might give a misleading picture of the company's current and future performance, company management probably prefers it.

Some users believe that the dependent approach properly applied gives a better indication of a company's annual results, earnings volatility, and risks when the company is geared to such things as seasonal ups and downs of irregular sales, income and expenses. Here the independent approach may result in interim financial reports that overstate the level of risk and volatility associated with the company's actual annual earnings picture.

On the other hand, there are others who are quite sure that the independent approach produces a clearer and more timely picture of coming events in a company's financial prospects.

*Mandated/suggested.*    The new Statement does not require companies complying with IAS in their annual reports to publish interim financial reports. The IASC, however, has indicated that it intends to strongly encourage governments, security regulators, stock exchanges, international bodies, and accounting standard setters to require companies whose debt or equity securities are publicly traded to provide interim financial reports that conform to IAS 34 principles. The IASC will also encourage publicly traded companies to provide interim reports complying with the Statement's principles at least at the end of the first six months of their financial year.

U.S. GAAP does not mandate publication of interim financial reports; however, the Securities and Exchange Commission and the stock exchanges do require listed companies to publish them for the first three quarters of the fiscal year.

When interim financial reports are published, both IAS 34 and U.S. practice require that they include:

1)  Condensed balance sheet.
2)  Condensed income statement.
3)  Condensed cash flow statement.
4)  Footnote disclosures focusing on changes since the last annual report in accounting principles or estimates, unusual events, trends, and turning points.

*Costs.*    According to APB 28, costs and expenses that are not allocated or associated directly with product and service revenues may be expensed as incurred or allocated among interim periods based on an estimate of time expired, benefit received, or other activity associated with the period.

IAS 34 requires costs that are incurred unevenly during a company's financial year be anticipated or deferred for interim reporting only if it is appropriate to anticipate or defer those costs at the end of the financial year. An example of costs that often fall into this category are periodic major maintenance or retooling projects.

*Comparability.*   In the final analysis, even though the interim financial statements may look alike, the operating results for the period under the IASC proposal of a discrete approach and the U.S. GAAP integral approach will not be comparable because of the different concepts. At the same time, comparison of operating results among U.S. companies is not always possible because of discretionary accounting differences permitted for certain items under APB 28.

## PRESENTATION OF FINANCIAL STATEMENTS, IAS 1 (REV.)

IAS 1 (rev.) supersedes IAS 1, *Disclosure of Accounting Policies;* IAS 5, *Information to Be Disclosed in Financial Statements;* and IAS 13, *Presentation of Current Assets and Current Liabilities.* It is effective for accounting periods beginning after July 1, 1998.

IAS 1 (rev.) requires all companies, including banks and insurance companies, that state their financial statements comply with IAS to do so with each applicable Standard, including all disclosure requirements. It also provides guidance on the structure of financial statements.

According to IASC, the revised IAS 1 is designed to improve the quality of statements by:

1) Ensuring financial statements comply with *each* applicable IAS standard. Departures from IAS requirements will be limited to a few exceptions. The IASC will monitor instances of noncompliance and will issue new guidance when appropriate.

2) Providing guidance on the overall financial statements, including minimum requirements for each primary statement, accounting policies, and notes and illustrative appendices.

3) Establishing practical requirements on issues such as materiality, going concerns, offsetting, accrual basis of accounting, the selection of accounting policies when no standard exists, and the presentation of comparative information.

The revised standard prescribes the minimum structure and content, including certain information required on the face of the financial statements. The four basic financial statements are required:

1) Balance sheet (current/noncurrent distinction not required, but defined in the standard).

2) Income statement (operating/nonoperating separation); must also show revenue, results of operating activities, finance costs, income from associates and joint ventures, taxes, profit or loss from ordinary activities, extraordinary items, minority interest, net profit or loss.

3) Cash flow statement.

4) Statement showing changes in equity (various formats allowed).

There is also a new requirement for a primary financial statement that shows gains and losses not presented in the income statement. This revision is in response to users' requests that performance information be measured more comprehensively than previously. The new statement may be shown either as a traditional equity reconciliation or as a statement of performance on its own.

## ACCOUNTING FOR INCOME TAXES, IAS 12 (REV.)

The International Accounting Standards Committee has revised International Accounting Standard (IAS) 12, *Income Taxes*, effective for financial statements beginning in January 1998. The revisions are extensive and adopt a single approach to accounting for deferred taxes. The revision results in bringing the IAS and U.S. GAAP closer together since both:

1) Require the liability method to account for deferred taxes.

2) Have similar rules for accounting for deferred taxes.

3) Handle deferred taxes arising from business combinations in basically the same manner.

IAS 12 (rev.) requires recognition of a deferred tax asset or liability for all temporary differences, regardless of when the temporary difference is expected to reverse. Thus it adopts a comprehensive approach to deferred tax accounting in most instances, not the alternative partial approach used in many countries. This latter method recognizes deferred tax assets and liabilities if there are reasonable grounds to believe that a tax asset or liability will materialize in the near future, usually considered to be within three years. On the other hand, this comprehensive tax allocation approach requires recognition of all tax effects resulting from differences between the tax base and balance sheet amounts of a company's assets and liabilities which in the future will have tax consequences.

## Differences from Original IAS 12

The revision differs in several important respects from the original standard. Many of the previous requirements were quite contrary to U.S. GAAP, which is based on FASB 109, *Accounting for Income Taxes*. There are still differences, but as mentioned above, this revision does lessen the gap. A sampling of important provisions is listed below:

1) One of the big objections to international standards has been that alternative methods were permitted in accounting approaches. For example, under the old rule companies were permitted to account for deferred taxes using either the deferral or liability method. Now the liability method is required. This means that deferred tax liabilities/ assets computations are based on the differences between tax and financial accounting practices that result in differences between an entities balance sheet account and their tax basis.

2) As noted above, the new ruling requires the comprehensive tax allocation approach in most instances.

3) IAS 12 (rev.) requires that deferred tax assets be recognized when it is probable that taxable profits will be available against which the deferred tax asset can be utilized.

4) IAS 12 (rev.) requires the recognition of deferred tax assets and liabilities related to temporary differences between the fair value of the acquiree's assets and liabilities and their tax basis arising from business combination fair value adjustments. (The tax base of an asset or liability is the amount attributable to that asset or liability for tax purpose.)

5) Formerly, no guidance was provided on the measurement of deferred tax assets and liabilities in cases where the tax rate differed in relation to the manner of recovery or settlement. IAS 12 (rev.) requires that the measurement of deferred tax assets and liabilities be based on the tax consequences that follow from the manner in which the company expects to recover or settle the carrying amount of its assets and liabilities.

## Effect of Revision

After pointing out some of the differences between the revision and the original standard of IAS 12, we find that companies preparing financial statements using IAS will note the following impact in their accounting for income taxes:

1) Higher tax expense for companies that used the partial tax allocation approach for determining deferred taxes. Deferred tax assets and liabilities are only recognized to the extent that it is a probability that a

tax asset or liability will materialize in the near future (usually in the next three years).

2) More deferred tax assets will be recognized with offsetting credits to deferred tax expense.

3) Different working capital levels and ratios will result for companies that classified deferred taxes as current items.

4) Companies will be able to recognize one-time deferred tax charges or credits to income when statutory tax rate changes are made.

5) Different deferred tax items will be recorded for companies that used the deferral method to compute deferred taxes. This is an approach to deferred tax expense/income accounting that computes deferred taxes based on the differences between tax and financial statement accounting practices that results in differences between a company's taxable income and financial statement pretax profits.

6) A deferred tax liability related to asset revaluations can be recorded by companies that now do not record a deferred tax liability on revaluations.

7) Deferred tax assets and liabilities will be recorded on business combinations.

## SEGMENT REPORTING, IAS 14 (REV.)

A revised version of IAS 14 has been approved by the IASC. The release of the new standard was delayed while efforts were made to harmonize the IAS standard with the new segment disclosure standards being jointly developed by the FASB and Canadian standard setters. This standard amends the original IAS 14 to bring it into line with the common disaggregated disclosure requirements agreed upon by the IASC and the FASB, and embodied in FASB 131, *Disclosure About Segments of an Enterprise and Related Information*. (See Chapter 1 in this Supplement.)

The new IAS and the FASB/Canadian measures all adopt the management approach to segment disclosure; that is, a company's internal structure and its system of internal financial reporting to senior management should normally be the basis for the purpose of identifying reportable segments and, thus, for its segment disclosures. After the many discussions to minimize differences that did effectively reduce the gap, the IASC still decided to publish its own standard. They declined to go as far in requiring increased disclosure in IAS 14 (rev.), *Segment Reporting*, as the U.S. and Canadian pronouncements require.

Unlike the two North American standards, IAS 14 (rev.) does allow management under some circumstances to depart from the management approach. It also differs from them in another respect. The IASC standard requires that segment data disclosures be prepared using the accounting policies adopted for the company's consolidated financial statements. In contrast, FASB 131 requires the same accounting as management uses internally to be used in its segment data disclosures.

## ACCOUNTING FOR LEASES, IAS 17 (REV.)

The International Accounting Standards Committee (IASC) has issued a new lease accounting standard IAS 17 (rev.) effective January 1, 1999. It replaces IAS 17, *Accounting for Leases,* which will remain in effect until that date. IAS 17 (rev.) retains the original basic premise that the classification of a lease depends on the extent to which risks and rewards incident to ownership of a leased asset lie with the lessee or lessor.

IAS 17 (rev.) defines a lease as an agreement whereby the lessor conveys to the lessee in return for a payment or series of payments the right to use an asset for an agreed period of time. The IASC term "finance (or financing) lease" encompasses both the finance lease and capital lease concepts referred to in FASB Statement 13, *Accounting for Leases.*

Below is a listing of some of the salient features of international accounting for leases:

1)  Finance leases are those that transfer substantially all risks and rewards to the lessee.

2)  Lessee should capitalize a finance lease at the lower of the fair value and the present value of the minimum lease payments.

3)  Lessee should calculate depreciation on leased assets using useful life, unless there is no reasonable certainty of eventual ownership. In the latter case, the shorter of useful life and lease term should be used.

4)  Lessee should expense operating lease payments.

5)  IAS 17 (rev.) requires enhanced disclosures by lessees, including disclosure of rental expenses, sublease rentals, and a description of leasing arrangements.

6)  IAS 17 (rev.) requires enhanced disclosures by lessors, such as disclosure about future minimum rentals and amounts of contingent rentals included in net profit or loss.

7)  For lessors, finance leases should be recorded as receivables. Lease income should be recognized on the basis of a constant periodic rate of return.

8)  IAS 17 (rev.) requires that a lessor should use the net investment method to allocate finance income. The net cash investment method is no longer permitted.

9)  Rental payments should be split into:

**a)** A reduction of liability.

**b)** A finance charge designed to reduce in line with the liability.

**10)** For a sale and leaseback that results in a finance lease, any excess of proceeds over carrying amount should be deferred and amortized over the lease term.

Organizations following IAS 17 (rev.) closely should increase the frequency of leases being treated as *financing* leases rather than *operating* leases by those companies that have adopted IAS. Currently, many companies treat leases as *operating* leases.

Finance lease accounting increases an entity's financial leverage—debt-to-equity ratio—and lowers its return on assets. IAS 17 (rev.) should also reduce the frequency of front-end-loading profits in sales-type leases. Sales-type leases arise when dealers or manufacturers use leasing as a means of marketing their products. A dealer or manufacturer recognizes profit on the *sale* and *finance income* on the lease.

## Operating and Financing Leases

Typically, under IAS 17 (rev.), leases are classified as either operating or financing leases. In the case of operating leases, lessees account for lease payments as a lease expense. Lessors account for these payments as lease income. In the case of finance leases, lessees account for the lease agreement as if the lessee had purchased the leased asset and financed it with debt; that is, the lessee records a depreciation and interest expense. Lessors record a lease payment receivable and recognize finance income.

## Finance Lease Classification

IAS 17 (rev.) expands the list of situations that *could* lead to a lease being classified as a finance lease. Thus, it should result in more finance-type leases being recognized as such for financial reporting purposes but, when using the financial statements of non-U.S. companies that have leased assets, it may be that finance-type leases will still be classified as operating leases for financial reporting purposes.

Examples of the expanded list include the following:

**1)** The lease transfers ownership of the asset to the lessee by the end of the lease term.

**2)** The lessee has the option to purchase the asset at a price expected to be sufficiently lower than the fair value at the date the option becomes exercisable such that, at the inception of the lease, it is reasonably certain that the option will be exercised.

3)  The lease term is for the major term of the economic life of the asset even if title is not transferred.

4)  If the lessee can cancel the lease, any losses associated with the cancellation are borne by the lessee.

5)  The lessee has the ability to continue the lease for a secondary period at a rent substantially lower than the market rent.

6)  The leased assets are of a specialized nature such that only the lessee can use them without major modifications being made.

Under IAS 17 (rev.), any lease not classified as a financing lease is classified as an operating lease.

## EMPLOYEE BENEFITS, IAS 19 (REV.)

The IASC has also approved IAS 19, *Employee Benefits.* This standard is consistent in many respects with U.S. GAAP. It adopts a market-based approach and requires a single accrued benefit method, the projected credit method, to measure retiree benefit costs and obligations. Plan assets are measured at fair value. It was originally titled *Economic Benefits,* and in some contexts is referred to as *Post-Employment Benefits Including Pensions,* but it's all the same standard (revised) however it's labeled.

The standard outlines the manner in which retirement benefit costs should be handled on the balance sheet. It states that a company is to recognize the aggregate of the following amounts as a defined benefit-type employee benefit expense or income:

1)  Current service cost.

2)  Interest cost.

3)  The expected return on any plan assets.

4)  Actuarial gains and losses, to the extent that they fall outside the 10% "corridor."

5)  Past service cost should be recognized over the average period until the amended benefits become vested.

6)  The effect of termination, curtailment, or settlement should be recognized when the event occurs.

In the case of defined contribution-type employee benefits, the expense is the contribution payable for the period.

Other points include replacing projected valuation methods with a single accrued benefit method and measuring defined benefit obligation for each balance sheet date. Also, discount rates for both funded and unfunded obligations would be measured at the balance sheet date at the market yield for high quality, fixed-rate bonds of maturity comparable to plan obligations. If measuring in economies where this type of bond is seldom used, the yield should be matched to government bonds.

If the net cumulative unrecognized actuarial gains and losses exceed the greater of 10% of the present value of the plan obligation, and 10% of the fair value of plan assets, that excess must be amortized over a period not longer than the estimated average remaining working lives of employees participating in the plan.

Faster amortization, including immediate income recognition for all actuarial gains and losses, is permitted if an enterprise follows a consistent and systematic policy.

# Chapter 4
## Plain English Disclosure Rule

The Securities and Exchange Commission has adopted a Plain English Disclosure rule incorporating changes made as a result of comments received and the lessons learned from participants in the plain English pilot program. The rule requires issuers to write the *cover page, summary*, and *risk factors section* of prospectuses in plain English. The previous requirements for those sections have been changed to the extent they conflicted with the plain English rule. In conjunction with this rule, the SEC also provides issuers more specific guidance on how to make the entire prospectus clear, concise, and understandable.

The Commission believes that using plain English in prospectuses will lead to a better informed securities market in which investors can more easily understand the disclosure required by the federal securities laws. The rule became effective on October 1, 1998, with the compliance date being the same.

## INVESTOR PROTECTION

Obviously, the intended purpose of financial reporting should be full and fair disclosure. In fact this is one of the cornerstones of investor protection under federal securities laws. The SEC points out that if a prospectus fails to communicate information clearly, investors do not receive the basic protection intended.

Yet prospectuses have often employed complex, legalistic language, confounding all but the most erudite lawyers, accountants or financial ex-

perts. The Commission emphasizes that the proliferation of complex transactions and securities (including all manner of derivatives) has only magni-
fied this problem. A major challenge facing the securities industry and its
regulators is the assurance that financial and business information reaches
investors in a form they can read *and understand*.

The SEC anticipates, and many public comment letters concur, that
implementation of the plain English rule will:

1) Allow investors to make better-informed assessments of the risks and
   rewards of investment opportunities.
2) Reduce the likelihood that investors make investment mistakes because of incomprehensible disclosure documents.
3) Reduce investors' costs of investing by lowering the time required to
   read and understand information.
4) Increase consumers' interest in investing by giving them greater confidence in their understanding of investments.
5) Reduce the number of costly legal disputes because investors are
   more likely to understand disclosure documents better.
6) Lower offering costs because investors will ask issuers fewer questions about the offering.

All well and good, but how is all of this expected to happen?

## PROSPECTUS SIMPLIFICATION

The Commission stated that the new rules will change the face of every
prospectus used in registered public offerings of securities. They expect
these prospectuses will be simpler, clearer, more useful, and hopefully,
more widely read and understood when clarity prevails:

1) The new rules require issuers to write and design the cover page, summary, and risk factors section of their prospectuses in plain English. Issuers will also have to design these sections to make them inviting to
   the reader. The new rules will *not* require issuers to limit the length of
   the summary, limit the number of risk factors, or prioritize risk factors.
2) The SEC is also providing guidance to issuers on how to comply with
   the current rule that requires the entire prospectus to be clear, concise, and understandable. The goal is to dispense with legalese and
   repetitions that tend to blur the pertinent information (and facts) that
   investors actually need in making informed decisions.

With that in mind, the Office of Investor Education and Assistance produced a handbook with practical tips on document presentation. A *Plain English Handbook: How to Create Clear SEC Disclosure Documents*, outlining methods and techniques on how to apply plain English principles to the disclosure documents, is the resulting publication.

## PLAIN ENGLISH PILOT PROGRAM

To test plain English in disclosure documents, the Division of Corporation Finance experimented with a pilot program in 1996 for public companies willing to file plain English documents under either the Securities Act of 1933 or the Securities Exchange Act of 1934. More than 75 companies volunteered to participate in the pilot program. Many participants got into the spirit of the project to the extent that they even prepared disclosure documents that are not subject to the plain English rule: proxy statements, footnotes to financial statements, management's discussion and analysis of financial condition and results of operations.

Assessment of the results of the pilot program affirmed the SEC's belief that preparing documents in plain English increases investors' understanding and helps them make informed investment decisions. Thus, the package of rules adopted, as well as the handbook, should enable issuers to improve dramatically the clarity of their disclosure documents.

## RULE 421(D), THE PLAIN ENGLISH RULE

Basic rules outline how prospectuses must be prepared. This new ruling requires preparation of the front portion of the prospectus in plain English. The plain English principles apply to the organization, language, and design of the front and back cover pages, the summary, and the risk factors section. Also, when drafting the language in these front parts of the prospectus, the preparer must comply substantially with six basic principles:

1) Short sentences.
2) Definite, concrete, everyday language.
3) Active voice.
4) Tabular presentation or bulleted lists for complex material, whenever possible.
5) No legal jargon or highly technical business terms.
6) No multiple negatives.

Does this all sound very reminiscent of your high school English teacher preparing you to write term papers? It should. And it does seem strange that it takes a Final Rule of the Securities and Exchange Commission to remind prospectus preparers of these basic rules for written communication. (Unless obfuscation is their objective.)

A number of comment letters noted that the rule *dictates* how to write the front of the prospectus. The SEC observed marked improvement in the clarity of disclosure when pilot participants used these recognized, basic principles of clear writing. They decided that the benefits to investors supported *mandating* the use of the principles for the front of the prospectus.

In addition, the cover page, summary, and risk factors section must be easy to read. The text and design of the document must highlight important information for investors. The rule permits the issuer to use pictures, charts, graphics, and other design features to make the prospectus easier to understand.

## Rule 421(b), Clear, Concise, Understandable Prospectuses

This ruling currently requires that the entire prospectus be clear, concise, and understandable. These stipulations are in addition to the plain English rule, which applies only to the front of the prospectus.

Amendments to Rule 421(b) also provide guidance on how to prepare a prospectus that is actually clear, concise, and understandable. The amendments set out four general writing techniques and list four conventions to *avoid* when drafting the prospectus. In effect, these amendments codify earlier interpretive advice.

Amended Rule 421(b) requires use of the the following techniques when writing the entire prospectus:

1) Presentation of information in clear, concise sections, paragraphs, and sentences. Whenever possible, the use of short explanatory sentences and bullet lists.

2) Use of descriptive headings and subheadings.

3) Avoidance of frequent reliance on glossaries or defined terms as the primary means of explaining information in the prospectus. Definition of terms in a glossary or other section of the document only if the meaning is unclear from the context. Use of a glossary only if it facilitates understanding of the disclosure.

4) Avoidance of legal and highly technical business terminology.

## How to Comply

The new note to Rule 421(b) provides further guidance on how to comply with the rule's general requirements. Because they make the document harder to read, the note lists the following tactics to *avoid*:

1) Legalistic or overly complex presentations that make the substance of the disclosure difficult to understand.
2) Vague boilerplate explanations that are readily subject to differing interpretations.
3) Complex information copied directly from legal documents without any clear and concise explanation or interpretation of the provision(s).
4) Repetitive disclosure that increases the bulk of the document, but fails to further clarify the information.

## Technical Terminology

Several comment letters stated that the SEC should permit public companies to use legal and technical business terminology. The argument was that high tech companies must use technical terms to distinguish their products or services from others in the industry. The Commission agreed that certain business terms may be necessary to describe operations properly, but cautioned against using excessive technical jargon that only competitors or industry specialists could understand.

The focus of the Plain English Rule is that the disclosure in the prospectus is for the benefit of the *investors*. When too many highly technical terms are employed, the investor soon becomes bogged down in a welter of verbiage and little if anything is "disclosed." If technical terms are unavoidable, the preparer must attempt to make their meaning perfectly clear at the onset.

## Legal Documents

Several comment letters noted that some investors, particularly institutional investors, want to read the specific terms of contracts or of the securities offered. For example, the SEC concedes an investor may want to read the specific language of a loan agreement's financial covenants or an indenture's default provisions.

The current rule permits summarizing an exhibit's key provisions in the prospectus. The issuer is also required to file material contracts and any instruments that define the rights of security holders. The SEC believes this approach generally serves the needs of all investors in the market.

If the language from an exhibit in the prospectus cannot be summarized adequately, then the explicit language may be included, but it must be presented clearly and its meaning to the investor explained precisely.

## REVISIONS TO REGULATIONS S-K AND S-B

The following revisions to Regulation S-K and S-B, covering requirements applicable to nonfinancial portions of the registration statements, annual and interim reports to stockholders, proxy, and other information statements, are addresses to specific sections of the narrative portions of the disclosure documents. Evidently the SEC hopes that prospective customers and stockholders will be given a better opportunity to understand the written portions of a prospectus and other relevant documents whether they really grasp the financial import of the documents or not. (Regulation S-B applies specifically to "small" businesses.)

### Item 501—Forepart of Registration Statement and Outside Front Cover Page of Prospectus

The formal design requirements for the prospectus cover page have been eliminated but the issuer is required to limit the front cover of the prospectus to one page. It is expected that the revisions will result in a cover page written and designed to focus investors on *key information* about the offering and encourage them to read the important information in the prospectus. The SEC also expects the amendments to give the flexibility needed to design a cover page tailored to the specific company and the offering.

Under the revised disclosure item, the issuer is free to use pictures, graphs, charts, and other designs that accurately depict the company, business products, and financial condition; however, design features and font types that make the disclosure difficult to read or understand are taboo.

The formalized requirements on how to present the mandatory legends on the cover page have been amended. The only restrictions on presentation of these legends are:

1) The legends must be prominent.
2) The print type must be easy to read.

The Commission has amended Item 501 to provide two plain English examples of the legend that state the Commission has not approved the offering. The item also provides a plain English example of the legend that states the prospectus is not yet complete. It is commonly printed in red ink and referred to as the "red herring" legend.

The Commission has amended the requirements detailing information that must always be included on the prospectus cover page. The goal is to have the cover page focus only on *key information* about the offering. The issuing company is cautioned to avoid moving unnecessary information to this page.

Original plans were to eliminate the requirement to refer to the risk factors on the cover page; however, comment letters suggested the mandate be retained. Therefore, the cover page must now not only reference the risk factors section but must also cite the page number on which the risk factors begin.

## Cover Page Format

*Retained* on the cover page from previous requirements are:

1) Company name.
2) Title, amount, and description of securities offered.
3) Selling securities holder's offering.
4) Bona fide estimate of range of maximum offering price, and numbers of securities.
5) If price not set, indication of how price will be determined.
6) State-required legends.
7) Date of prospectus.

Adopted changes to Regulation S-K—Item 501 to the prospectus cover page include:

1) Cross reference to risk factors *must include page number.*
2) Bullet list or other design that highlights the information showing *price, underwriting commission, and proceeds of the offering* replaces formatted distribution table.
3) Bullet list or other design that highlights the *best efforts disclosure* replaces the formatted distribution table.
4) Commission legend retained in plain English. Reference to *state securities commissions* to be included.
5) Information concerning *underwriters' over-allotment option and the number of shares* retained on the cover page. Expenses of the offering, the number of shares, commissions paid by others, and other non-cash consideration and finder's fees *moved* to the plan of distribution section.
6) Identification of market for securities, trading symbol, underwriters, and type of underwriting arrangements.

**7)** Prospectus "Subject to Completion" legend retained in plain English.

**8)** Cover limited to one page.

## Limited Partnership Offerings Risk

Several comment letters suggested that the plain English rule and the revised disclosure requirements should replace earlier interpretive advice on cover page disclosure for *limited partnership* offerings.

The SEC acknowledges that under existing advice, the cover page must list the offering's key risks, resulting in repetitious disclosure of those risks. However, they feel that the unique nature of limited partnership offerings and the risks they present to investors warrant requiring the issuer to highlight these risks on the cover page. Of course, the cover page, summary, and risk factors section must otherwise comply with the plain English rule and the revised disclosure requirements being adopted.

## Item 502—Inside Front and Outside Back Cover Pages

Item 502's amended requirements for the inside front cover page and outside back cover page of the prospectus now significantly limit the information required on these pages. The hope is that this will give further freedom to the issuer to arrange the information in the prospectus from the *investor's viewpoint.*

The Commission prefers that the required table of contents immediately follow the cover page, but the ruling permits the preparer to have the flexibility to include it on either the inside front or outside back cover page of the prospectus. However, if a prospectus is delivered to investors electronically, the table of contents must come immediately after the cover page so that investors need not scroll to the end of the prospectus to see how it is organized.

Although some comment letters recommended elimination of the requirement to disclose the dealer's prospectus delivery obligations, the SEC decided to retain this disclosure on the outside back cover page. They suggest this disclosure is helpful to dealers in reminding them of their legal obligation to deliver the prospectus

Following are disclosures *previously required* on the inside front or outside back cover pages and their *new location* adopted under Regulation S-K—Item 502:

**1)** Availability of Exchange Act reports generally—moved to description of business section or, for short-form registration statements, to the incorporation by reference disclosure.

**2)** Identification of market for securities—moved to cover page.

3) Availability of annual reports to shareholders with financial statements for foreign issuers and others not subject to proxy rules— moved to description of business section.

4) Availability of Exchange Act reports incorporated by reference in short-form registration statements—moved to incorporation by reference disclosure.

5) Stabilization legend—moved to plan of distribution section.

6) Passive market-making activities legend—deleted. Disclosure retained in plan of distribution section.

7) Dealer prospectus delivery page—retained on outside back cover as noted above.

8) Enforceability of civil liability provisions of federal securities laws against foreign persons—moved to description of business section.

9) As mentioned above, the table of contents may still be located on either the inside front cover or the outside back cover unless it is sent electronically. Then it must be on the inside front cover.

In line with other changes, Forms S-2, S-3, S-4, F-2, F-3, and F-4 are also being amended.

Along with the list of reports incorporated by reference, the issuer must include information on:

1) How investors may obtain a copy of these reports.

2) How investors may obtain copies of the other reports filed with the SEC.

## Item 503—Summary Information, Risk Factors, and Ratio of Earnings to Fixed Charges

*Summary Information.* If a summary is included, it must be brief and in plain English. Further, if a summary description of the company's business operations or financial condition is included, the information must be written in plain English even if not identified as a "summary."

Length of the summary is not mandated, but the SEC emphasizes that this section should *highlight the most important features* of the offering. It *should not* include a lengthy description of the company's business and business strategy. They suggest this detailed information is better included in the disclosure in the body of the prospectus.

Although there is no list of items that must be in a summary (if there is one), since the financial statements are an important part of the disclosures made by public companies, the SEC believes the issuer should continue to *highlight financial information* in the summary in a manner readily understood by the user.

***Risk Factors.*** When a risk factors section is included in the prospectus, the risk factors must be detailed in plain English avoiding trite "boilerplate" risk factors. Any risk factors must be explained in context so investors can understand the specific risk applicable to that particular company and its operations.

***Ratio of Earnings to Fixed Charges.*** Where a summary or similar section is included in the prospectus, amended Item 503 requires showing the ratio of earnings to fixed charges as part of the summarized financial data.

Issuers offering debt securities must show a *ratio of earnings to fixed charges*. Those registering preference equity securities must show the *ratio of combined fixed charges and preference dividends to earnings*. The issuer must present the ratio for each of the last five fiscal years and the latest interim period for which financial statements are presented in the document.

If the proceeds from the sale of debt or preference securities are used to repay any outstanding debt or to retire other securities, and the change in the ratio would be ten percent or greater, a ratio showing the application of the proceeds, the *pro forma ratio*, must be used. If a ratio indicates less than one-to-one coverage, the dollar amount of the deficiency is to be disclosed. The pro forma ratio may be shown only for the most recent fiscal year and the latest interim period. The net change in interest or dividends from the refinancing should be used to calculate the pro forma ratio.

## COMMENTS ON THE PLAIN ENGLISH REQUIREMENTS

Forty-five comment letters on the plain English proposals generally favored requiring plain English for the front of prospectuses—the cover page, summary, and risk factors section—to ensure that investors receive clear information. They believe that requiring plain English will focus all parties involved in the offering process—issuers, underwriters, trustees, and counsel—on clear and readable disclosure.

Other comment letters raised the following general concerns about the rule:

1) Will the plain English rule increase a registrant's liability?
2) How will the staff review and comment on plain English filings?
3) Will the Commission deny acceleration of a filing if it does not comply with the plain English rule?

After studying these questions, the SEC has concluded that issuers really have little, if any cause, for concern: *following the new rulings* should not alter established procedures and practices for handling relevant matters.

## Cost Factors

While project participants who responded to benefit-cost questions had incurred some additional document preparation costs, the majority estimated them to be low and predicted that they would fall over time. The participants anticipated little added, and perhaps even lower, overall cost. Some even predicted they might save money on printing and distribution costs and on the amount of time spent on answering investors' questions. Based on the experiences of pilot program participants, the SEC believes that the substantial benefits to investors of plain English—and the probable ongoing cost savings to issuers—justify the short-term cost to public companies of learning to prepare documents in plain English.

# Chapter 5

## Mutual Fund "Profile" Disclosure Option

The Securities and Exchange Commission has adopted a new Rule that permits an open-end management investment company (mutual fund) to offer investors a new disclosure document called a "profile." This document summarizes key information about the fund, including the fund's investment strategies, risks, performance, and fees, in a concise, standardized format.

A fund that offers a profile will be able to give investors a choice of the amount of information that they wish to consider before making a decision about investing in the fund; investors will have the option of purchasing the fund's shares after reviewing the information in the profile or after requesting and reviewing the fund's prospectus (and other information). An investor deciding to purchase fund shares based on the information in a profile will receive the fund's prospectus with the confirmation of purchase.

The SEC also adopted amendments to Rule 497 under the Securities Act to require a fund to file a profile with the Commission at least 30 days prior to the profile's first use. At the same time, they adopted revisions to the prospectus disclosure requirements in Form N-1A, the registration statement used by funds. The revisions should *minimize* prospectus disclosure about technical, legal, and operational matters that generally are common to all funds and thus *focus prospectus disclosure on essential information* about a particular fund. The reasoning is that the simplified general information should enable the average investor to make better informed decisions about investing in that fund.

## EFFECTIVE DATE

The SEC expects that the practical result of the adoption of Rule 498 and revisions to prospectus disclosure requirements may be that funds begin using both documents at the same time. Because the profile's purpose is to provide investors with a new source of clear, concise information about funds, they believed that funds should have the option to use the profile as soon as possible and made rule 498 effective on June 1, 1998, with the amendments to Form N-1A becoming effective on the same date.

Although existing funds had until December 1, 1999, to comply with the Form N-1A amendments, a fund may have, at its option, prepared documents in accordance with the requirements of the amended Form at any time after the effective date of the amendments.


## NEED FOR SIMPLIFIED DISCLOSURE INFORMATION

In April 1999, there were 636 mutual fund companies in this country. At the end of 1998, 44% of the families held open-end funds with 77.3 million individuals owning shares in these funds. At that time, assets totaled $5.78 trillion, while in February 1999 commercial bank deposits were at $3.34 billion.

As more investors turn to funds for professional management of current and retirement savings, funds have introduced new investment options and shareholder services to appeal to investors. While benefiting from these developments, investors also faced an increasingly difficult task in choosing from the many different fund investments. The SEC, fund investors, and others realized it was in everyone's best interest to improve fund disclosure documents to help investors evaluate and compare them.

In the Commission's view, the growth of the fund industry and the diversity of fund investors warranted a new approach to fund disclosure to offer more choices in the format and the amount of information available about these investments. (Particularly, it would seem, since so many relatively "uninitiated" investors were testing the mutual fund market.)

The Profile summarizes key information about a fund, including its investment objectives, strategies, risks, performance, fees, investment adviser and portfolio manager, purchase and redemption procedures, distributions, tax information and the services available to the fund's investors.

It was designed to provide summary information about a fund that could assist an investor in deciding whether to invest in that particular fund immediately, or to request additional information about it before deciding whether or not to buy shares in it.

Rule 498 requires a fund to mail the prospectus and other information to the requesting investor within 3 business days of a request. An investor deciding to purchase fund shares based on the Profile receives the fund's prospectus with the purchase confirmation.

## PROFILE REQUIREMENTS UNDER RULE 498

1) **Standardized Fund Summaries.** The profile includes concise disclosure of 9 items of key information about a fund in a specific sequence.

2) **Improved Risk Disclosure.** A risk/return summary (also required at the beginning of a fund's *prospectus*) provides information about a fund's investment objectives, principal strategies, risks, performance, and fees.

3) **Graphic Disclosure of Variability of Returns.** The risk/return summary provides a bar chart of a fund's annual returns over a 10-year period that illustrates the variability of those returns and gives investors some idea of the risks of an investment in the fund. To help investors evaluate a fund's risks and returns relative to "the market," a table accompanying the bar chart compares the fund's average annual returns for 1-, 5-, and 10-year periods to that of a broad-based securities market index.

4) **Other Fund Information.** The profile includes information on the fund's investment adviser and portfolio manager, purchase and redemption procedures, tax considerations, and shareholder services.

5) **Plain English Disclosure.** The Commission's recently adopted plain English disclosure requirements, which are designed to give investors understandable disclosure documents, will apply to the profile. The plain English rule requires the use of plain English writing principles, including short sentences, everyday language, active voice, tabular presentation of complex material, no legal or business jargon, and no multiple negatives. (For a discussion of this rule, see Chapter 4.)

## PROFILES FOR TAX-DEFERRED ARRANGEMENTS

Rule 498 also permits a fund that serves as an investment option for a participant-directed defined contribution plan (or for certain other tax-deferred arrangements) to provide investors with a profile that includes disclosure that is tailored for the plan (or other arrangement).

Profiles tailored for such use can exclude information relating to the purchase and sale of fund shares, fund distributions, tax consequences, and fund services otherwise required in a profile.

## Pilot Profile Program

The Commission tested various options for improving fund disclosure documents in a pilot program conducted with participation by the Investment Company Institute (ICI) and several large fund groups, in which the funds used profile-like summaries with their prospectuses. The Pilot Profile summarized important information about specific funds to determine whether investors found these profiles helpful in making investment decisions. Focus groups conducted on the Commission's behalf responded positively to the profile concept, indicating that a disclosure document of this type would assist them in making investment decisions. Fund investors participating in a survey sponsored by the ICI also strongly supported the profile idea.

## Other Investment Companies Excluded from Profile Option

The Commission has decided that other types of investment companies, such as closed-end investment companies, unit investment trusts, and separate accounts that offer variable annuities do not come within the scope of Rule 498. It is available only to mutual funds.

Although the Agency recognizes that a short, summary disclosure document such as the profile could potentially benefit investors in other types of investment companies, it has concluded that it would be prudent to assess the use of profiles by mutual funds over a period of time before considering a rule to allow other types of investment companies to use similar summary documents. As the Commission gains experience with funds' use of the profile and analyzes the results of other pilot profile programs that are underway, it will undoubtedly consider expanding use of the concept to other types of investment companies if things work out as well as they anticipate.

## Multiple Funds Described in a Profile

The SEC decided that a profile that describes more than one fund can be consistent with the goal of a summary disclosure document that assists investors in evaluating and comparing funds. In fact they believe that describing more than one fund or class of a fund in a profile can be a useful means of providing investors with information about related investment alternatives offered by a fund group (e.g., a range of tax-exempt funds or different types of money market funds) or about the classes of a multiple class fund. However, profiles describing multiple funds must be organized in a clear, concise, summary manner in a format designed to communicate the information effectively. Thus, a profile that offers the securities of more than one fund or class does not need to repeat information that is the same for each one described in the document.

## COVER PAGE

Rule 498 requires the cover page of a fund's profile to include certain basic information about the fund and to disclose that the profile is a *summary disclosure document*. The cover page identifies it as a "profile" without using the term "prospectus." It includes a legend explaining the profile's purpose, and displays the fund's name. A fund also could describe its investment objectives or its type or category (e.g., that the fund is a growth fund or invests its assets in a particular country). The cover page must state the approximate date of the profile's first use.

### Required Legend

The new rule requires the following legend on the cover page, or at the beginning, of a profile:

This profile summarizes key information about a Fund that is included in the Fund's prospectus. The Fund's prospectus includes additional information about the Fund, including a more detailed description of the risks associated with investing in the Fund that you may want to consider before you invest. You may obtain the prospectus and other information about the Fund at no cost by calling _____.

A toll-free (or collect) telephone number that investors can use to obtain the prospectus and other information must be provided. The fund may also indicate, as applicable, that the prospectus and other information is available on the fund's Internet site or by E-mail request.

When additional information is requested, a 3-business day mailing requirement applies. Since many funds use intermediaries in distributing or servicing their shares, revised Rule 498 also permits the legend to state that additional information in such a case may be obtained from financial intermediaries. The 3-business day rule applies here also.

## RISK / RETURN SUMMARY

The first 4 items of the profile must contain information that would be substantially identical to the proposed risk/return summary at the beginning of every prospectus. The following discussion summarizes the main features of the risk/return summary required by Form N-1A and discusses specific disclosure required in the profile.

## Fund Investment Objectives/Goals

To assist investors in identifying funds that meet their general investment needs, the risk/return summary requires a fund to disclose its investment objectives or goals.

## Principal Investment Strategy

The risk/return summary requires a fund to summarize, based on the information provided in its prospectus, how the fund intends to achieve its investment objectives. The purpose of this disclosure is to provide a summary of the fund's principal investment strategies, including the specific types of securities in which the fund invests or will invest principally, and any policy of the fund to concentrate its investments in an industry or group of industries.

In addition, a fund (other than one that has not yet been required to deliver a semi-annual or annual report) must provide the following disclosure:

"Additional information about the Fund's investments is available in the Fund's annual and semi-annual reports to shareholders. In the Fund's annual report you will find a discussion of the market conditions and investment strategies that significantly affected the Fund's performance during the last fiscal year. You may obtain either or both of these reports at no cost by calling _____."

## Principal Risks of Investing in the Fund

*Summary Risk Disclosure.* The risk summary gives a fund the option to include disclosure in its profile about the types of investors for whom the fund is intended and the types of investment goals that may be consistent with an investment in the fund.

*Special Risk Disclosure Requirements.* A mutual fund profile is required to provide a special disclosure in the risk summary for money market funds to the effect that, "An investment in the Fund is not insured or guaranteed by the Federal Deposit Insurance Corporation or any other government agency. Although the Fund seeks to preserve the value of your investment at $1.00 per share, it is possible to lose money by investing in the Fund."

A fund advised by or sold though a bank would disclose in the risk summary of its profile: "An investment in the Fund is not a deposit of the bank and is not insured or guaranteed by the Federal Deposit Insurance Corporation or any other government agency."

***Risk/Return Bar Chart and Table.*** The risk/return summary requires a fund's profile to include a bar chart showing the fund's annual returns for each of the last 10 calendar years and a table comparing the fund's average annual returns for the last 1, 5, and 10 fiscal years to those of a broad-based securities market index.

Obviously, this provision requires a fund to have at least one calendar year of returns before including the bar chart. It requires a fund whose profile does not include a bar chart, because the fund does not have annual returns for a full calendar year, to modify the narrative explanation to refer only to information presented in the table. The provision also requires the bar chart of a fund in operation for fewer than 10 years to include annual returns for the life of the fund.

To show a fund's highest and lowest returns (or "range" of returns) for annual or other periods as an alternative, or in addition, to the bar chart, the Profile ruling requires that a fund disclose (in addition to the bar chart) its best and worst returns for a quarter during the 10-year (or other) period reflected in the bar chart. This information is aimed at disclosing the variability of a fund's returns and the risks by pointing out that a fund's shares may very well be subject to short-term price fluctuations.

***Presentation of Return Information.*** To help investors use the information in the bar chart and table, the profile risk/return summary requires a fund to provide a brief narrative explanation of just how the information illustrates the variability of the fund's returns.

***Bar Chart Return Information.*** The risk/return summary requires calendar-year periods for both the bar chart and table. Under Rule 498, the average annual return information in the table in a fund's profile risk/return summary must be as of the most recent calendar quarter and updated quarterly.

***Bar Chart Presentation.*** The bar chart may include return information for more than one fund. However, the presentation of the bar chart is subject to the general requirement that disclosure should be presented in a format designed to communicate information *clearly and effectively.*

The risk/return summary requires a fund offering more than one class of shares in a profile to include annual return information in its bar chart for only one class. The ruling permits a fund to choose the class to be reflected in the bar chart, subject to certain limitations: the chart must reflect the performance of a class that has returns for at least 10 years (e.g., a fund could not present a class in the bar chart with 2 years of returns when another class has returns for at least 10 years). In addition, if two or more classes offered in the profile have returns for less than 10 years, the bar chart must reflect returns for the class that has returns for the longest period.

## Fees and Expenses of the Fund

The risk/return summary requires a bar chart showing the fund's fees and expenses, including any sales loads charged in connection with an investment in the fund. The fee table must be included in both the profile and the prospectus. This emphasis underlines the SEC's belief that fees and expenses of a fund figure high in a typical investor's decision to invest in a fund. The fee table is designed to help them understand the costs of investing in a particular fund and to compare those costs with the costs of other funds.

### OTHER DISCLOSURE REQUIREMENTS

The profile of a fund must include not only the risk/return summary, but also disclosure about other key aspects of investing in the fund—the other items to be disclosed in sequence: Investment Adviser, Sub-Adviser(s) and Portfolio Manager(s) of the Fund.

The profile requirements are very precise in this respect. This section requires:

1) Identification of the fund's investment adviser.
2) Identification of the fund's sub-adviser(s) (if any):
   a) A fund need not identify a sub-adviser(s) whose sole responsibility for the fund is limited to day-to-day management of the fund's holdings of cash and cash equivalent instruments, unless the fund is a money market fund or other fund with a principal investment strategy of regularly holding cash and cash equivalent instruments.
   b) A fund having three or more sub-advisers, each of which manages a portion of the fund's portfolio, need not identify each such sub-adviser, except that the fund must identify any sub-adviser that is (or is reasonably expected to be) responsible for the management of a significant portion of the fund's net assets. For purposes of this paragraph, a significant portion of a fund's net assets generally will be deemed to be 30% or more of the fund's net assets.
   c) State the name and length of service of the person or persons employed by or associated with the fund's investment adviser (or the fund) who are primarily responsible for the day-to-day manage-

ment of the fund's portfolio and summarize each person's *business experience* for the last five years.

A fund with three or more such persons, each of whom is (or is reasonably expected to be) responsible for the management of a portion of the Fund's portfolio, need not identify each person, except that a fund must identify and summarize the business experience for the last five years of each person who is (or is reasonably expected to be) responsible for the management of a significant portion of the fund's net assets. For purposes of this paragraph, a significant portion of a fund's net assets generally will be deemed to be 30% or more of the fund's net assets.

## Purchase of Fund Shares

Under Rule 498, a fund must disclose the minimum initial or subsequent investment requirements, the initial sales load (or other loads), and, if applicable, the initial sales load breakpoints or waivers.

## Sale of Fund Shares

Rule 498 also requires a fund to state that its shares are redeemable; to identify the procedures for redeeming shares (e.g., on any business day by written request, telephone, or wire transfer); to identify any charges or sales loads that may be assessed upon redemption (including, if applicable, the existence of waivers of these charges).

## Fund Distributions and Tax Information

Rule 498 requires a mutual fund's profile to describe how frequently the fund intends to make distributions and what reinvestment options for distributions (if any) are available to its investors.

It also requires a fund to disclose whether its distributions to shareholders may be taxed as ordinary income or capital gains and that the rates shareholders pay on capital gains may be taxed at different rates depending upon the length of time that the fund holds its assets.

If a fund expects that its distributions, as a result of its investment objectives or strategies, primarily will consist of ordinary income or capital gains, it must provide disclosure to that effect. Funds subject to this requirement would include, for example, those often described as "tax-managed," "tax-sensitive," or "tax-advantaged," which have investment strategies to maximize long-term capital gains and minimize ordinary income.

If a fund has a *principal* investment objective or strategy to achieve tax-managed results of this type, the fund would be required to provide disclosure to that effect in the discussion of its investment objectives.

For a fund that describes itself as investing in securities generating tax-exempt income, it must provide, as applicable, a general statement to the effect that a portion of the fund's distributions may be subject to federal income tax.

## Other Services Provided by the Fund

A fund profile should provide a brief summary of services available to the fund's shareholders (e.g., any exchange privileges or automated information services), unless this information has already been provided in earlier sections of the profile. A fund should disclose only those services that generally are available to typical investors in the fund.

### APPLICATION TO PURCHASE SHARES

The profile may include an application that a prospective investor can use to purchase the fund's shares as long as the application explains with equal prominence that an investor has the option of purchasing shares of the fund after reviewing the information in the profile or after requesting and reviewing the fund's prospectus (and other information) before making a decision about investing in the fund.

### FILING REQUIREMENTS

A profile is to be filed with the Commission at least 30 days before the date that it is first sent or given to a prospective investor. The first profile filing must be accompanied by the submission of a profile in the format in which it will be distributed to investors. Subsequent filings will not require the additional formatted profile. An amended form of any profile must be filed with the Commission within 5 business days after it is used.

### MODIFIED PROFILES FOR CERTAIN FUNDS

Funds can tailor disclosure for profiles to be used for investments in defined contribution plans qualified under the Internal Revenue Code, and for funds offered through variable insurance contracts. The Commission believes that this revision will help to ensure that profiles contain information that investors will find meaningful and useful.

Rule 498 permits a profile for a fund offered as an investment option for a plan to include, or be accompanied by, an enrollment form for the plan. An application or enrollment form for a variable insurance contract may accompany the profile for the funds that serve as investment options; however, this is only if the form also is accompanied by a full prospectus for the contract.

The Rule also permits funds to modify the legend and other disclosure in profiles intended for use in connection with defined contribution plans, other tax-deferred arrangements described in the Rule, and variable insurance contracts.

# Chapter 6
## Mutual Funds

## KINDS OF DISTRIBUTIONS

There are several kinds of distributions that a shareholder can receive from a mutual fund. They include:

1) Ordinary dividends.
2) Capital gain distributions.
3) Exempt-interest dividends.
4) Return of capital (nontaxable) distribution.

### Tax-Exempt Mutual Fund

Distributions from a tax-exempt mutual fund—one that invests primarily in tax-exempt securities—can consist of ordinary dividends, capital gains distributions, undistributed capital gains, or return of capital like any other mutual fund. These contributions follow the same rules as a regular mutual fund. Distributions designated as exempt-interest dividends are not taxable.

A mutual fund may pay exempt-interest dividends to its shareholders if it meets certain requirements. These dividends are paid from tax-exempt interest earned by the fund. Since the exempt-interest dividends keep their tax-exempt character, the taxpayer does not have to include them in income, but may need to report them on his or her return. The mutual fund will send the taxpayer a statement within 60 days after the close of its tax year showing the amount of exempt-interest dividends. Although exempt-interest dividends are not taxable, they must be reported on the tax return if one is required to be filed. This is an information reporting requirement and does not convert tax-exempt interest to taxable interest.

## Return of Capital

A distribution that is not out of earnings and profits is a return of the investment, or capital, in the mutual fund. The return of capital distributions are not taxed as ordinary dividends and are sometimes called tax-free dividends or nontaxable distributions that may be fully or partly taxable as capital gains.

A return of capital distribution reduces the basis in the shares. The basis cannot be reduced below zero. If the basis is reduced to zero, the taxpayer must report the return of capital distribution on the tax return as a capital gain. The distribution is taxable if, when added to all returns of capital distribution received in past years, it is more than the basis in the shares. Whether it is a long-term or short-term capital gain depends on how long the shares had been held.

## Reinvestment of Distributions

Most mutual funds permit shareholders to automatically reinvest distributions, including dividends and capital gains, in more shares in the fund. Instead of receiving cash, distributions are used to purchase additional shares. The reinvested amounts must be reported to the IRS in the same way as if the reinvestment were received in cash. Reinvested ordinary dividends and capital gains distributions must be reported as income; reinvested exempt-interest dividends are not reported as income.

## FOREIGN TAX DEDUCTION OR CREDIT

Some mutual funds invest in foreign securities or other instruments. A mutual fund may choose to allow an investor to claim a deduction or credit for the taxes the fund paid to a foreign country or U.S. possession. The notice to the fund's investors will include their share of the foreign taxes paid to each foreign country or possession, and the part of the dividend derived from sources in each country or possession.

## BASIS

The basis in shares of a regulated investment company (mutual fund) is generally figured in the same way as the basis of other stock. The cost basis of purchased mutual fund shares often includes a sales fee, also known as a *load charge.* In certain cases, the entire amount of a load charge incurred after October 3, 1989, cannot be added to the cost basis, if the load charge gives the purchaser a reinvestment right.

## Commissions and Load Charges

The fees and charges paid to acquire or redeem shares of a mutual fund are not tax deductible. They are usually added to the cost of the shares and increase the basis. A fee paid to redeem the shares is usually a reduction in the redemption price (sales price) in the case of mutual funds.

## Keeping Track of the Basis

The investor in mutual funds should keep careful track of his or her basis because the basis is needed to figure any gain or loss on the shares when they are sold, exchanged, or redeemed. When mutual fund shares are bought or sold, the confirmation statements should be kept to show the price paid for the shares, and the price received for the shares when sold. If the shares are acquired by gift or inheritance, the investor needs information that is different from that in a confirmation statement for figuring the basis of those shares. The basis of shares of a mutual fund is important to know in figuring a gain or loss, with the basis dependent upon how the shares are acquired.

## Shares Acquired by Inheritance

If mutual funds shares are inherited shares, the basis is the fair market value (FMV) at the date of the decedent's death, or at the alternate valuation date, if chosen for estate tax purposes. In community property states, each spouse is considered to own half the estate. If one spouse dies and at least half of the community interest is includable in the decedent's gross estate, the FMV of the community property at the date of death becomes the basis of both halves of the property.

## Adjusted Basis

After mutual fund shares are acquired, adjustments may need to be made to the basis. The adjusted basis of stock is the original basis, increased or reduced. The basis is increased in a fund by 65% of any undistributed capital gain that is included in the taxpayer's income. This has the effect of increasing the basis by the difference between the amount of gain included in income and the credit claimed for the tax considered paid on that income. The mutual fund reports the amount of undistributed capital gain.

## Reduction of the Basis

The basis must be reduced in the fund by any return of capital distributions received from the fund. The basis is not reduced for distributions that are exempt-interest dividends.

## SALES, EXCHANGES, AND REDEMPTIONS

When mutual fund shares are sold, exchanged, or redeemed, the investor will usually have a taxable gain or deductible loss. This includes shares in a tax-exempt mutual fund. The amount of the gain or loss is the difference between the adjusted basis in the shares and the amount realized from the sale, exchange, or redemption.

Gains and losses are figured on the disposition of shares by comparing the amount realized with the adjusted basis of the owner's shares. If the amount realized is more than the adjusted basis of the shares, a gain results; if the amount realized is less than the adjusted basis of the shares, a loss results. The amount received from a disposition of mutual fund shares is the money and value of any property received for the shares disposed of, minus expenses of sale such as redemption fees, sales commissions, sales charges, or exit fees.

The exchange of one fund for another fund is a taxable exchange, regardless of whether shares in one fund are exchanged for shares in another fund that has the same distributor or underwriter without paying a sales charge. Any gain or loss on the investment in the original shares as a capital gain or loss must be reported in the year in which the exchange occurs. Service charges or fees paid in connection with an exchange can be added to the cost of the shares acquired. Mutual funds and brokers must report to the IRS the proceeds from sales, exchanges, or redemptions. The broker must give each customer a written statement with the information by January 31 of the year following the calendar year the transaction occurred. The broker must be given a correct taxpayer identification number (TIN); a social security number is acceptable as a TIN.

## Identifying the Shares Sold

When mutual fund shares are disposed of, the investor must determine which shares were sold and the basis of those shares. If the shares were acquired all on the same day and for the same price, figuring their basis is not difficult; however, for shares that are acquired at various times, in various quantities, and at various prices, determining the cost basis can be a difficult process. Two methods can be used to figure the basis, the cost basis, or the average basis.

Under the cost basis one of the following methods can be chosen:

1) Specific share identification.
2) First-in first-out (FIFO).

If the shares sold can be definitely identified, the adjusted basis of those particular shares can be used to figure a gain or loss. The shares can be adequately identified, even if bought in different lots at various prices and times, if:

1) The buyer specifies to the broker or other agent the particular shares to be sold or transferred at the time of the sale or transfer.
2) The buyer receives confirmation of the specification from his or her broker in writing within a reasonable time.

The confirmation by the mutual fund must state that the seller instructed the broker to sell particular shares. The owner of the shares has to be able to prove the basis of the specified shares at the time of sale or transfer.

If the shares were acquired at different times or at different prices, and the seller cannot identify which shares were sold, the basis of the shares acquired initially (first-in, first-out) is used as the basis of the shares sold. Therefore, the oldest shares still available arc considered sold first. An adequate record should be kept of each purchase and any dispositions of the shares, until all shares purchased at the same time have been disposed of completely.

## Average Basis

The average basis can be used to figure a gain or loss when all or part of the number of shares in a regulated investment company are sold. This choice can be made only if acquired at various times and prices, and the shares were left on deposit in an account handled by a custodian or agent who acquires or redeems those shares. The investor may be able to find the average basis of the shares from information provided by the fund. Once the average basis is used, it must continue to be used for all accounts in the same fund. However, a different method can be used for the shares in other funds.

To figure average basis, one of the following methods can be used:

1) Single-category method.
2) Double-category method.

***Single-category method.*** In the single-category method, the average cost is found of all shares owned at the time of each disposition, regardless of how long the shares were owned. Shares acquired with reinvested dividends or capital gains distributions must be included. Even if only one category is used to compute the basis, it is possible to have short-term or long-term gains or losses. To determine the holding period, the shares disposed of are considered to be those acquired first. The following steps are used to compute the basis of shares sold:

1) The cost of all shares owned is added.
2) The result of Step 1 is divided by the number of shares owned. This gives the *average basis* per share.
3) The result of Step 2 is multiplied by the number of shares sold. This gives the basis of the shares sold.

The basis of the shares determined under average basis is the basis of all the shares in the account at the time of each sale. If no shares were acquired or sold since the last sale, the basis of the remaining shares at the time of the next sale is the same as the basis of the shares sold in the last sale.

*Double-category method.*    In the double-category method, all shares in an account at the time of each disposition are divided into two categories: short-term and long-term. The adjusted basis of each share in a category is the total adjusted basis of all shares in that category at the time of disposition, divided by the total shares in the category.

The investor can specify to the custodian or agent handling the account from which category the shares are to be sold or transferred. The custodian or agent must confirm in writing the seller's specification. If the investor does not specify or receive confirmation, the shares sold must first be charged against the long-term category and then any remaining shares sold against the short-term category.

When a share has been held for more than one year, it must be transferred from the short-term category to the long-term category. When the change is made, the basis of a transferred share is its actual cost or adjusted basis; if some of the shares in the short-term category have been disposed of, its basis falls under the average basis method. The average basis of the undisposed shares would be figured at the time of the most recent disposition from this category.

## Holding Period

When mutual fund shares are disposed of, the holding period must be determined. The period starts by using the trade date—the *trade date* is the date on which the holder of the shares bought or sold the mutual fund shares. Most mutual funds will show the trade date on confirmation statements of the purchases and sales.

## INVESTMENT EXPENSES

The expenses of producing taxable investment income on a *nonpublicly* offered mutual fund during the year are generally deductible expenses; these include counseling and advice, legal and accounting fees, and investment newsletters. These are deductible as miscellaneous itemized deductions to the extent that they exceed 2% of adjusted gross income. Interest paid on money to buy or carry investment property is also deductible.

A nonpublicly offered mutual fund is one that:

**1)** Is not continuously offered pursuant to a public offering.

**2)** Is not regularly traded on an established securities market.

**3)** Is not held by at least 500 persons at all times during the tax year.

Generally, mutual funds are *publicly* offered funds. Expenses of publicly offered mutual funds are not treated as miscellaneous itemized deductions because these mutual funds report only the net amount of investment income after the investor's share of the investment expenses has been deducted. Expenses on the shares of nonpublicly offered mutual funds can be claimed as a miscellaneous itemized deduction subject to the 2% limit.

Expenses cannot be deducted for the collection or production of exempt-interest dividends. Expenses must be allocated if they were for both taxable and tax-exempt income. One accepted method for allocating expenses is to divide them in the same proportion that the tax-exempt income from the mutual fund is to the total income from the fund.

The amount that can be deducted as investment interest expense must be limited in two different ways. First, the interest cannot be deducted for the expenses borrowed to buy or carry shares in a mutual fund that distributes only tax-exempt dividends. Second, investment interest is limited by the amount of investment income. Deductions for interest expense are limited to the amount of net investment income. Net investment is figured by subtracting investment expenses other than interest from investment income. Investment income includes gross income derived from property held for investment, such as interest, dividends, annuities, and royalties. It does not include net capital gains derived from disposing of investment property, or capital gains distributions from mutual fund shares. Investment interest that cannot be deducted because of the 2% limit can be carried forward to the next tax year, provided that net investment income exceeds investment interest in the later year.

# Chapter 7

## Business Use of a Home

New rules that went into effect in 1999 make it easier to claim a deduction for the business use of a home. Under the new rules, a taxpayer may qualify to claim the deduction, even though never having qualified before. The following information explains the new rules.

### PRINCIPAL PLACE OF BUSINESS: NEW FOR 1999

Under the new rules for deducting expenses for the business use of a home, it is easier for a home office to qualify as the principal place of business. Under the old rules, a taxpayer had to consider the relative importance of the activities carried out at each business location when determining if a home was the principal place of business. The place where the taxpayer conducted the most important activities was the place where meetings were held with clients, customers, or patients, or the location where goods or services were delivered. Performing administrative or management duties in the home office was considered less important.

In 1998, an outside salesperson's home office did not qualify as a principal place of business. The place where he or she met with customers to explain available products and take orders was considered more important than the home office where administrative duties were conducted. Beginning in 1999, however, a home office would qualify as a principal place of business for deducting expenses for the use of it:

**1)** If the home office is used exclusively for administration or management activities of a trade or business.

**2)** If the taxpayer has no other fixed location for conducting substantial administrative or management activities relating to a trade or business.

There are many activities that are administrative or managerial in nature. Some of these activities are:

**1)** Billing customers, clients, or patients.

**2)** Keeping books and records.

**3)** Ordering supplies.

**4)** Setting up appointments.

**5)** Forwarding orders or writing reports.

The following administrative or management activities performed at other locations will *not* disqualify a home office as a principal place of business:

**1)** When others conduct a taxpayer's administrative or management activities at locations other than the home.

**2)** The conduct of administrative or management activities at places that are not fixed locations of a business, such as in a car or a hotel room.

**3)** The taxpayer occasionally conducts minimal administrative or management activities at a fixed location outside of the home.

**4)** The taxpayer conducts substantial *non*administrative or *non*management business at a fixed location outside the home.

**5)** Suitable space to conduct administrative or management activities is available outside the home office, but a home office is used for those activities instead.

## OTHER CRITERIA FOR DETERMINING PLACE OF BUSINESS

If the new 1999 rules do not appear to cover the taxpayer's particular situation, the older rules may give an indication of other aspects when considering deductions for business use of the home—or the IRS may add further rules for the upcoming tax season.

It is permissible to have more than one business location, including a home, for a single trade or business. To qualify to deduct the expenses for the business use of a home, the home must be a principal place of business of that trade or business. To determine the principal place of business, all of the facts and circumstances must be considered. If, after considering the business locations, one cannot be identified as a principal place of business, then home office expenses cannot be deducted. The two primary factors to consider are:

1) The relative importance of the activities performed at each location.
2) The time spent at each location.

To determine whether a home is the principal place of business, the taxpayer must consider the relative importance of the activities carried out at each business location. The relative importance of the activities performed at each business location is determined by the basic characteristics of the business. If the business requires that meetings or conferences be held with clients or patients, or that goods or services be delivered to a customer, then the place where contacts are made must be given great weight in determining where the most important activities are performed.

If the relative importance of the activities does not clearly establish the principal place of business, such as when to deliver goods or services at both the office, in the home, and elsewhere, then the time spent at each location is important. Comparison should be made of the time spent on business at the home office with the time spent at other locations.

## SEPARATE STRUCTURES

Expenses can be deducted for a separate free-standing structure, such as a studio, garage, or barn, if the structure is used exclusively and regularly for the business. The structure does not have to be the principal place of business, or a place where patients, clients or customers are met.

## FIGURING THE DEDUCTION

Once it has been determined that the "home office" does qualify for a deduction, the next step is determining how much the taxpayer can deduct. Certain expenses related to the business use of a home can be deducted, but deductions are limited by the following:

1) Percentage of the home used for business, i.e., the business percentage.
2) Deduction limit.

To find the *business percentage*, the taxpayer must compare the size of the part of the home used for business to the entire house. The resulting percentage is used to separate the business part of the expenses from the expenses for operating the entire home. Any reasonable method to determine the business percentage can be used. Two commonly used methods are:

1) Dividing the square foot area of the "business space" by the total area of the home.

2) Dividing the number of rooms used for business by the total number of rooms in the home. This method can be used if the rooms in the home are all about the same size.

## DEDUCTION LIMIT

If gross income from the business use of a home equals or exceeds the total business expenses (including depreciation), all of the business expenses can be deducted. If the gross income from that use is less than the total business expenses, the deduction for certain expenses for the business use is limited. The deduction of otherwise nondeductible expenses, such as insurance, utilities, and depreciation (with depreciation taken last), allocable to business is limited to the gross income from the business use of the home minus the sum of the following:

1) The business part of expenses that could be deducted even if the home was not used for business (such as mortgage interest, real estate taxes, and casualty and theft losses).

2) The business expenses that relate to the business activity in the home (for example, salaries or supplies), but not to the use of the home itself.

A self-employed individual may not include in (2) above the deduction for half of the self-employment tax.

If deductions are greater than the current year's limit, it is possible to carry over the excess to the next year. Any carryover is subject to the gross income limit from the business use of the home for the next tax year. The amount carried over will be allowable only up to the taxpayer's gross income in the next tax year from the business in which the deduction arose whether the individual lives in the home during that year or not.

## ASSORTED USE TESTS

To qualify under the *regular use test*, a specific area of the home must be used for business on a continuing basis. The regular-use test is not met if the business use of the area is only occasional, even if that area is not used for any other purpose.

To qualify under the *trade or business use* test requires that part of a home be used in connection with a trade or business. If part of the home is used for some other profit-seeking activity that is not a trade or business, a deduction cannot be taken for a business use.

A taxpayer who is an employee must qualify under the *convenience-of-the-employer* test. If an employer provides suitable work space for administrative management activities, this fact must be considered in determining whether this test is met. Even if expenses qualify for a deduction for the business use of a home, the deduction may be limited. If the employee's gross income from the business use of a home is less than the employee's total business expenses, the deduction for some of the expenses—utilities, insurance, depreciation, for example—is limited.

## Exclusive Use

To qualify under the *exclusive use* test, a specific area of a home must be used only for a trade or business. The area used for business can be a room or other separately identifiable space. The space does not need to be marked off by a permanent partition. If the home area in question is used both for business and personal purposes, it does not meet the requirements of the exclusive use test rule.

The exclusive use test does not have to be met if space is used for the *storage of inventory or product samples*, or for a *day-care facility*. When part of a home is used for the storage of inventory or product samples, the following 5 tests must all be met:

1) The inventory or product samples are kept for use in a trade or business.
2) The trade or business is a wholesale or retail selling of products.
3) The home is the only fixed location of a trade or business.
4) The storage space must be used on a regular basis.
5) The space is an identifiably separate space suitable for storage.

## Part-Year Use

Expenses for the business use of a home *may not* be incurred during any part of the year it was not being used for business purposes. Only those expenses for the portion of the year in which it was actually used for business may be used in figuring the allowable deduction.

## DAY-CARE FACILITY

If space in the home is used on a regular basis for providing day care, it may be possible to deduct the business expenses for that part of the home even though the same space is used for nonbusiness purposes. To qualify for this exception to the exclusive use rule, the following requirements must be met:

1) The space must be used in the trade or business of providing day care for children, persons 65 or older, or persons who are physically or mentally unable to care for themselves.

2) The taxpayer must have applied for, been granted or be exempt from having a license certification registration, or approval as a day-care center or as a family or group day-care home under state law. An individual does not meet this requirement if an application was rejected or license or other authorization was revoked.

If a part of the home is regularly used for day care, it is necessary to figure the percentage of that part which is used for day care, as explained above under *business percentage*. All the allocable expenses subject to the deduction limit, as explained earlier, may be deducted for that part used exclusively for day care. If the use of part of the home as a day-care facility is regular, but not exclusive, it is necessary to figure what part of available time it is actually used for business.

A room that is available for use throughout each business day and that is regularly used in the business is considered to be used for day care throughout each business day. It is not necessary to keep records to show the specific hours the area was used for business. The area may be used occasionally for personal reasons; however, a room used only occasionally for business does not qualify for the deduction.

To find that part of the available time the home is actually used for business, the total business-use time is compared to the total time that part of the home can be used for all purposes. The comparison may be based upon the hours of business use in a week with the number of hours in a week (168), or the hours of business use for the tax year with the number of hours in the tax year (8,760 in 1998).

### Meal Allowance

If food is provided for a day-care business, the expense is not included as a cost of using the home for business. It is a separate deduction on the taxpayer's Schedule C (Form 1040). The cost of food consumed by the taxpayer or his or her family may not be deducted. However, 100% of the cost of food consumed by the day-care recipients and generally only 50% of the cost of food consumed by employees can be deducted. However, 100% of the cost of food consumed by employees can be deducted if its value can be excluded from their wages as a de minimis fringe benefit. For tax years beginning after 1997, the value of meals provided to employees on business premises is generally de minimis if more than half of these employees are provided the meals for the taxpayer's convenience.

If cost of food for the day-care business is deducted, a separate record (with receipts) must be maintained of the family's food costs. Reimbursements received from a sponsor under the Child and Adult Food Care Program of the Department of Agriculture are taxable only to the extent they exceed expenses for food for eligible children. If reimbursements are more than expenses for food, the difference is shown as income in Part I of Schedule C. If food expenses are greater than the reimbursements, the difference is shown as an expense in Part V of Schedule C.

## INCREASE IN SECTION 179 DEDUCTION FOR 1998 AND 1999

On certain property bought for use in a business, the taxpayer may be able to elect to deduct (rather than depreciate) all or a part of its cost as a Section 179 deduction. For 1998 the total the taxpayer can elect to deduct was increased to $18,500. In 1999 the total increases to $19,000.

## BUSINESS FURNITURE AND EQUIPMENT

Depreciation and Section 179 deductions may be used for furniture and equipment that an employee uses in his or her home for business or work. These deductions are available whether or not the individual qualifies to deduct expenses for the business use of a home. Following are explanations of the different rules for:

1) Listed property.
2) Property bought for business use.
3) Personal property converted to business use.

### Listed Property

Special rules apply to certain types of property, called listed property, used in the home. Listed property includes any property of a type generally used for entertainment, recreation, and amusement (including photographic, phonographic, communication, and video recording equipment). But "listed property" also includes computers and related equipment.

Listed property bought and placed in service in 1998 must be used more than 50% for business (including work as an employee) to be claimed as a Section 179 deduction or an accelerated depreciation deduction. If the business use of listed property is 50% or less, a Section 179 deduction cannot be taken and the property must be depreciated using the Alternate Depreciation System (ADS) (straight-line method). Listed property meets the more-than-50%-use test for any tax year if its qualified business use is more than 50% of its total use. Allocation among its various uses must be made for the use of any item of listed property used for more than one purpose during the tax year. The *percentage of investment use may not be used* as part of the percentage of qualified business use to meet the more-than-50%-use test. However, the taxpayer should use the combined total of business and investment use to figure the depreciation deduction for the property.

If an employee uses his or her own listed property (or listed rented property) for work as an employee, the property is business-use property only if both of the following requirements are met.

1)  The use is for the convenience of the employer.
2)  The use is required as a condition of employment.

"As a condition of employment" means that the use of the property is *necessary* for proper performance of work. Whether the use of the property is required for this purpose depends on all the facts and circumstances. The employer does not have to tell the employee specifically to have a computer for use in the home, nor is a statement by the employer to that effect sufficient.

If, in a year after placing an item of listed property in service, the taxpayer fails to meet the more-than-50%-use test for that item of property, he or she may be required to do both of the following.

1)  Figure depreciation, beginning with the year the property is no longer used more than 50% for business, using the straight-line method.
2)  Figure any excess depreciation and Section 179 deduction on the property and add it to:
    a)  Gross income.
    b)  The adjusted basis of the property.

It is not possible to take any depreciation of the Section 179 deduction for the use of listed property unless business/investment use can be proved with adequate records or sufficient evidence to support the individual's own statements. To meet the adequate records requirement, the taxpayer must maintain an account book, diary, log, statement of expense, trip sheet, or similar record or other documentary evidence that is sufficient to establish business/investment use.

## Property Bought for Business Use

The taxpayer who has bought certain property to use in his or her business can do any one of the following (subject to the limits discussed below).

1) Elect a Section 179 deduction for the full cost of the property.
2) Take part of the cost as a Section 179 deduction.
3) Depreciate the full cost of the property.

## Section 179 Deduction

A Section 179 deduction can generally be claimed on depreciable tangible personal property bought for use in the active conduct of business. The taxpayer can choose how much (subject to the limit) of the cost to deduct under Section 179 and how much to depreciate. The Section 179 deduction can be spread over several items of property in any way selected as long as the total does not exceed the maximum allowable. However, the taxpayer cannot take a Section 179 deduction for the basis of the business part of the home.

## Section 179 Deduction Limits

The Section 179 deduction cannot be more than the business cost of the qualifying property. In addition, the following limits apply when figuring a Section 179 deduction.

1) Maximum dollar limit.
2) Investment limit.
3) Taxable income limit.

The total cost of Section 179 property the taxpayer can elect to deduct for 1998 cannot be more than $18,500 ($19,000 for 1999). This *maximum dollar limit* is reduced if the individual goes over the investment limit in any tax year.

If the cost of the qualifying Section 179 property is over the *investment limit*—$200,000 in 1998—the taxpayer must reduce the maximum dollar limit for each dollar over $200,000.

The total cost that can be deducted each tax year is subject to the total *taxable income limit*. This is figured on the income from the active conduct of all trade or business activities, including wages, during the tax year. The taxable income for this purpose is figured in the usual way, but without regard to all of the following.

1) The Section 179 deduction.
2) The self-employment tax deduction.
3) Any net operating loss carryback or carryforward.

## DEPRECIATION

Part II of Form 4562 is used to claim a deduction for depreciation on property placed in service in 1998. It does not include any costs deducted in Part I (Section 179 deduction).

Most business property used in a home office is either 5-year or 7-year property under MACRS.

- 5-year property includes computers and peripheral equipment, typewriters, calculators, adding machines, and copiers.
- 7-year property includes office furniture and equipment such as desks, files, and safes.

Under MACRS, the half-year convention is generally used, which allows deduction of a half-year of depreciation in the first year the property is used in the business. If more than 40% of the depreciable property was placed in service during the last 3 months of the tax year, the mid-quarter convention must be used instead of the half-year convention.

## PERSONAL PROPERTY CONVERTED TO BUSINESS USE

If property is used in the home office that was used previously for personal purposes, a Section 179 deduction cannot be taken for the property, but it can be depreciated. The method of depreciation depends upon when the property was first used for personal purposes.

# Chapter 8
## Miscellaneous Deductions

This chapter covers which expenses the taxpayer can claim as miscellaneous itemized deductions. The taxpayer must reduce the total of most miscellaneous itemized deductions by 2% of the adjusted gross income (AGI). The following topics will be covered:

1) Deductions subject to the 2% limit.
2) Deductions not subject to the 2% limit.
3) Expenses that cannot be deducted.
4) How to report permissible deductions.

Records *must* be kept to verify deductions. Receipts, canceled checks, financial account statements, and other documentary evidence must be available for the IRS in case of an audit of the taxpayer's return and deductions claimed.

## DEDUCTIONS SUBJECT TO 2% LIMIT

The 2% of AGI is figured by subtracting 2% of the AGI from the total amount of the claimed expenses after any other deductions are applied. For example, the 50% limit on business-related meals and entertainment is applied before the 2% of adjusted gross income is subtracted.

## Unreimbursed Employee Expenses

The only unreimbursed employee expenses that can be deducted are:

**1)** Paid or incurred during the tax year.
**2)** For carrying on a trade or business of being an employee.
**3)** Ordinary and necessary business expenses.

An expense is *ordinary* if it is common and accepted in the taxpayer's trade or business. An expense is *necessary* if it is appropriate and helpful to a trade or business. The following unreimbursed expenses are usually deductible:

- Business bad debt of an employee.
- Business liability insurance premiums.
- Damages paid to a former employer for breach of an employment contract.
- Depreciation on a computer or cellular telephone the employee is required to use in his or her work.
- Dues to chamber of commerce if membership helps an employee on the job.
- Dues to professional societies.
- Education that is employment related.
- Home office or part of home used regularly and exclusively in work.
- Job search expenses in the taxpayer's present occupation.
- Laboratory breakage fees.
- Licenses and regulatory fees.
- Malpractice insurance premiums.
- Medical examination required by employer.
- Occupational taxes.
- Passport for business trip.
- Repayment of income aid payment.
- Research expenses of a college professor.
- Subscriptions to professional journals and trade magazines related to the taxpayer's work.
- Tools and supplies used in work.
- Travel, transportation, entertainment, and gift expenses related to the employee's work.

- Union dues and expenses.
- Work clothes and uniforms if required and not suitable for everyday use.

## Other Expenses

Certain other expenses can be deducted as miscellaneous itemized deductions subject to the 2% of adjusted gross income limit. These expenses are:

1) To produce or collect income that must be included in gross income.
2) To manage, conserve, or maintain property held for producing income.
3) To determine, contest, pay, or claim a refund of any tax.

Other expenses an employee pays can be deducted for the purposes in (1) and (2) *only* if they are reasonably and closely related to these purposes. These other expenses include:

- Appraisal fees for a casualty loss or charitable contribution.
- Casualty and theft losses from property used in performing services as an employee.
- Clerical help and office rent in handling investments.
- Depreciation on home computers used for investments.
- Excess deductions, including administrative expenses, allowed a beneficiary on termination of an estate or trust.
- Fees to collect interest and dividends.
- Hobby expenses, but not more than hobby income.
- Indirect miscellaneous deductions of pass-through entities.
- Investment fees and expenses.
- Legal fees related to producing or collecting taxable income, doing or keeping a job, or getting tax advice.
- Losses on deposits in an insolvent or bankrupt financial institution.
- Repayments of income.
- Repayments of Social Security benefits.
- Safe deposit box rental.
- Service charges on dividend investment plans.
- Tax advice and preparation fees, including fees for electronic filing.
- Trustee's fees for an IRA, if separately billed and paid.

The following expenses *cannot be deducted*:

- Burial or funeral expenses, including the cost of a cemetery lot.
- Campaign expenses.
- Capital expenses.
- Check-writing fees.
- Certain club dues.
- Commuting expenses.
- Expenses of attending stockholders' meeting.
- Expenses of earning or collecting tax-exempt income.
- Expenses to improve professional reputation.
- Fees and licenses, such as car licenses and marriage licenses.
- Fines and penalties, such as parking tickets.
- Hobby losses.
- Home repairs, insurance, and rent.
- Illegal bribes and kickbacks.
- Investment-related seminars.
- Life insurance premiums.
- Lobbying expenses.
- Losses from the sales of a home, furniture, personal car, etc.
- Lost or misplaced cash or property.
- Lunches with co-workers.
- Meals while working late.
- Personal disability insurance premiums.
- Personal legal expenses.
- Personal, living, or family expenses.
- Political contributions.
- Professional accreditation fees.
- Relief fund contributions.
- Residential telephone line.
- Travel expenses for another individual.
- Voluntary unemployment benefit fund contributions.
- Wristwatches.

## Depreciation on Home Computers

Depreciation on a home computer can be deducted if it is used to produce income such as managing investments that produce taxable income. If a person works as an employee and uses a computer for work, a deduction may be permissible.

## Legal Expenses

Legal expenses can usually be deducted when incurred in attempting to produce or collect taxable income or if paid in connection with the determination, collection, or refund of any tax. Legal expenses can also be deducted that are:

1)  Related to either doing or keeping a job.
2)  For tax advice related to a divorce if the bill specifies how much is for tax advice and is determined in a reasonable way.
3)  To collect taxable alimony.

Expenses can be deducted for resolving tax issues relating to profit or loss from business rentals or royalties. Expenses can be deducted for resolving nonbusiness tax issues.

## Business Bad Debt

A business bad debt is a loss from a debt created or acquired in a trade or business. Any other worthless debt is a business bad debt only if there is a very close relationship between the debt and the trade or business when the debt becomes worthless. A debt has a very close relationship to a trade or business of being an employee if the main motive for incurring the debt is a business reason.

## Business Liability Insurance

Insurance premiums can be deducted if paid for protection against personal liability for wrongful acts on the job by an employee if the damages are attributable to the pay the employee received from the employer.

## Damages for Breach of Employment Contract

If an employee breaks an employment contract, the damages can be deducted by the employee who paid his or her former employer for the damages. The damages must be attributable to the pay the employee received from that employer.

## Depreciation: Computers and Cellular Telephones

If a computer or cellular telephone was purchased by an employee and used in connection with the employee's work, the use generally must be:

**1)** For the convenience of the employer.

**2)** Required as a condition of employment.

*For the convenience of the employer* means that the computer or cellular telephone is for a substantial business reason of the employee's employer. All the facts in making this determination must be considered, including the use of a computer or cellular phone during regular working hours to carry on the employer's business.

*Required as a condition of employment* means that the employee cannot properly perform his or her duties without it. Whether or not the employee can properly perform required duties without the computer or cellular telephone depends on all the facts and circumstances. It is not necessary for the employer to explicitly require an employee to use a computer or cellular telephone; but neither is it enough that the employer merely states that employee use of these items is a condition of the employee's employment.

## Which Depreciation Method Can Be Used

If an employee uses more than 50% of a home computer or cellular telephone in the employee's work, an accelerated depreciation deduction can be taken. If the home computer or cellular telephone system is not used predominantly in the employee's work, the depreciation of these items must be the straight-line method.

## Dues to Chamber of Commerce and Professional Societies

Dues may be deductible that are paid to professional organizations and to chambers of commerce and similar organizations, if membership helps an employee to carry out the duties of a job. Dues cannot be deducted when paid to an organization if one of its main purposes is to conduct entertainment activities for members or their guests, or to provide members or their guests with access to entertainment facilities.

## Education That Is Employment Related

Education expenses can be deducted even if the education may lead to a degree, if the education meets one of the following two requirements:

1) The education maintains or improves skills required in the present work.
2) The education:
   a) Is required by the employer, or the law, to keep the employee's salary, status, or job.
   b) Serves a business purpose of the employer.

If an employee's education meets either of these two requirements, the employee can deduct expenses for tuition, books, supplies, laboratory fees, and similar items, and certain transportation costs. An employee cannot deduct as a miscellaneous deduction any qualified education expenses to the extent they were taken into account in determining the amount excludable as an education IRA.

Education expenses cannot be deducted even though one or both of the requirements are met, if the education:

1) Is needed to meet the minimum educational requirements to qualify in the work or business of an employee.
2) Will lead to qualify an employee in a new trade or business.

## DEDUCTIONS NOT SUBJECT TO THE 2% LIMIT

The expenses listed below can be deducted as miscellaneous itemized deductions. They are *not* subject to the 2% limit.

- Amortizable premium on taxable bonds.
- Casualty and theft losses from income-producing property.
- Federal estate tax on income in respect of a decedent.
- Gambling losses up to the amounts of gambling winnings.
- Impairment-related work expenses of persons with disabilities.
- Repayments of more than $3,000 under a claim of right.
- Unrecovered investment in a person

## GAMBLING LOSSES UP TO THE AMOUNT OF GAMBLING WINNINGS

The full amount of both gambling winnings and gambling losses must be reported. Gambling losses that exceed gambling winnings cannot be deducted. Gambling winnings cannot be reduced by gambling losses and the difference reported. The full amount of winnings must be reported as income and losses claimed up to the amount of winnings are reported as itemized deductions. The taxpayer's records must show winnings separately from losses. Only gambling losses incurred during the year can be deducted.

An accurate diary or similar record must be kept of losses and winnings. The diary should contain at least the following information:

1) The date and type of specific wager or wagering activity.
2) The name and address or location of the gambling establishment.
3) The names of other persons present with the taxpayer at the gambling establishment.
4) The amount won or lost.

In addition to a diary, taxpayers should also have other documentation, such as wagering tickets, canceled checks, credit records, bank withdrawals, and statement of actual winnings on payment slips provided by the gambling establishment.

For specific wagering transactions, the following items can be used to support winnings and losses:

- *Keno.* Copies of the keno tickets purchased that were validated by the gambling establishment, copies of casino credit records, and copies of casino check cashing records.
- *Slot Machines.* A record of the machine number and all winnings by date and time the machine was played.
- *Table Games.* Twenty-one (blackjack), craps, poker, baccarat, roulette, wheel of fortune, etc. The number of the table at which the taxpayer was playing. Casino credit card data indicating whether the credit was issued at the tables or at the cashier's cage.
- *Bingo.* A record of the number of games played, cost of tickets purchased and amounts collected on winning tickets. Supplemental records include any receipts from the casino, parlor, etc.
- *Racing.* Horses, harness, dog, etc. A record of the races, amounts of wagers, amounts collected on winning tickets, and amounts lost on losing tickets. Supplemental records include unredeemed tickets and payment records from the race track.
- *Lotteries.* A record of ticket purchases, dates, winnings, and losses. Supplemental records include unredeemed tickets, payments slips, and winnings statements. These record keeping suggestions are intended as general guidelines to help a taxpayer establish winnings and losses. They are not all-inclusive; tax liability depends on particular facts and circumstances.

## Impairment-Related Work Expenses

If a taxpayer has a physical or mental disability that limits being employed, or substantially limits one or more of major life activities, such as performing manual tasks, walking, speaking, breathing, learning, and working, the impairment-related work expenses can be deducted.

Impairment-related work expenses are ordinary and necessary business expenses for attendant care services at the place of work, and other expenses in connection with the place of work that are necessary for a person to be able to work.

# Chapter 9

## Change in Accounting Methods and Consideration of Accounting Periods

To simplify the procedures to obtain IRS consent for taxpayers to change methods of accounting for federal income tax purposes, the IRS has modified and/or eliminated a number of the complicated rules governing changes in these accounting methods. The purpose of the new procedures is to provide incentives to encourage prompt, voluntary compliance with proper tax accounting principles. Under this approach, a taxpayer usually receives more favorable terms and conditions by filing a request for a change in method before the IRS contacts the taxpayer for an examination. A taxpayer who is contacted for an examination and required by the IRS to change his or her method of accounting generally receives less favorable terms and conditions and may also be subject to penalties.

### SIGNIFICANT CHANGES

Probably the single most important change for the taxpayer is that Form 3115 requesting a change in method may now be filed any time during the year. Other new rules reduce or eliminate many of the complex provisions of the previous procedure including:

1) The Category A and Category B, and Designated A and Designated B have been eliminated.

2) The 90-day window at the *beginning* of an examination has been eliminated.

3) The 30-day window for taxpayers under *continuous examination* has been increased to 90 days.

4) The number of consecutive months the taxpayer is required to be under examination has been reduced from 18 to 12.

5) The definition of "under examination" has been clarified.

6) The consent requirement for taxpayers before an appeals officer or a federal court has been replaced with a notification procedure.

7) The various adjustment periods have been replaced with a single 4-year adjustment period for both positive and negative adjustments.

8) Several of the terms and conditions relating to the adjustment have been eliminated.

## CHANGE IN METHOD OF ACCOUNTING DEFINED

A change in method of accounting includes a change in the overall plan of accounting for gross income or deductions, or a change in the treatment of any material item. A *material item* is any item that involves the proper time for the inclusion of the item in income or the taking of the item as a deduction.

In determining whether a taxpayer's accounting practice for an item involves timing, the relevant question is whether the practice permanently changes the amount of the taxpayer's lifetime income. If the practice does not permanently affect the taxpayer's lifetime income, but does or could change the taxable year in which income is reported, it involves timing and is, therefore, a method of accounting.

*Consistency:* Although a method of accounting may exist under this definition without a pattern of consistent treatment of an item, a method of accounting is not adopted in most instances without consistent treatment. The treatment of a material item in the same way in determining the gross income or deductions in two or more consecutively filed tax returns, without regard to any change in status of the method as permissible or not permissible, represents consistent treatment of that item. If a taxpayer treats an item properly in the first return that reflects the item, however, it is not necessary for the taxpayer to treat the item consistently in two or more consecutive tax returns to have adopted a method of accounting. If a taxpayer has adopted a method of accounting under the rules, the taxpayer cannot change the method by amending prior income tax returns.

*Classification:* A change in the classification of an item can constitute a change in the method of accounting if the change has the effect of shifting income from one period to another. A change in method of accounting does not include correction of mathematical or posting errors, or errors in the computation of a tax liability.

# FILING FORM 3115

Except as otherwise provided, a taxpayer must secure the consent of the Commissioner before changing a method of accounting for federal income tax purposes. In order to obtain the Commissioner's consent for a method change, a taxpayer must file a Form 3115, *Application for Change in Accounting Method* during the taxable year in which the taxpayer wants to make the proposed change.

The Commissioner can prescribe administrative procedures setting forth the limitations, terms, and conditions deemed necessary to permit a taxpayer to obtain consent to change a method of accounting. The terms and conditions the Commissioner can prescribe include the year of change, whether the change is to be made with an adjustment or on a cutoff basis, and the adjustment period.

Unless specifically authorized by the Commissioner, a taxpayer cannot request, or otherwise make, a retroactive change in method, regardless of whether the change is from a permissible or an impermissible method.

## METHOD CHANGE WITH ADJUSTMENT

Adjustments necessary to prevent amounts from being duplicated or omitted must be taken into account when the taxpayer's taxable income is computed under a method of accounting different from the method used to compute taxable income of the preceding tax year. When a change in method is applied, income for the taxable year preceding the year of change must be determined under the method of accounting that was then employed. Income for the year of change and the following taxable years must be determined under the new method as if the new method had always been used.

Required adjustments can be taken into account in determining taxable income in the manner and subject to the conditions agreed to by the Commissioner and the taxpayer. In the absence of an agreement, the adjustment is taken into account completely in the year of change, which limits the amount of tax where the adjustment is substantial. However, under the Commissioner's authority to prescribe terms and conditions for changes in method, specific adjustment periods are permitted that are intended to achieve an appropriate balance between mitigating distortions of income that result from accounting method changes and providing appropriate incentives for voluntary compliance.

## METHOD CHANGE USING A CUTOFF METHOD

Certain changes can be made in a method and without an adjustment, using a cutoff method. Under a cutoff method, only the items arising on or after the beginning of the year of change are accounted for under the new method. Certain changes, such as changes in the last-in first-out (LIFO) inventory method, *must* be made using the cutoff method. Any items arising before the year of change or other operative date continue to be accounted for under the taxpayer's former method of accounting. Because no items are duplicated or omitted from income when a cutoff method is used to make a change, no adjustment is necessary.

## Initial Method

A taxpayer can generally choose any permitted accounting method when filing the first tax return. IRS approval is not needed for the choice of the method. The method chosen must be used consistently from year to year and clearly show the taxpayer's income. A change in an accounting method includes a change not only in an overall system of accounting, but also in the treatment of any material item. Although an accounting method can exist without treating an item the same all the time, an accounting method is not established for an item, in most cases, unless the item is treated the same every time.

## IRS Approval

After a taxpayer's first return has been filed, the taxpayer must get IRS approval to change the accounting method. If the current method clearly shows the income, the IRS will consider the need for consistency when evaluating the reason for changing the method used. The following changes require IRS approval:

1) A change from the cash method to an accrual method or vice versa unless this is an automatic change to an accrual method.
2) A change in the method or basis used to value inventory.
3) A change in the method of figuring depreciation, except certain permitted changes to the straight-line method for property placed in service before 1981.

   Approval is not required in the following instances:

1) Correction of a math or posting error.
2) Correction of an error in computing tax liability.
3) An adjustment of any item of income or deduction that does not involve the proper time for including it in income or deducting it.
4) An adjustment in the useful life of a depreciable asset.

## Reflections of Income

The important point to remember is that methods of accounting should clearly reflect income on a continuing basis, and that the IRS exercises its discretion and in a manner that generally minimizes distortion of income across taxable years on an annual basis. Therefore, if a taxpayer asks to change from a method of accounting that clearly reflects income, the IRS, in determining whether to consent to the taxpayer's request, will weigh the need for consistency against the taxpayer's reason for desiring to change the method of accounting.

## Need for Adjustment

The adjustment period is the applicable period for taking into account an adjustment, whether positive (an increase in income) or negative (a decrease in income), required for the change in method of accounting. Adjustments necessary to prevent amounts from being duplicated or omitted are taken into account when the taxpayer's taxable income is computed under a method of accounting different from the method used to compute taxable income for the preceding taxable year. When there is a change in method of accounting, income for the year preceding the year of change must be determined under the method of accounting that was then employed, and income for the year of change and the following years must be determined under the new method of accounting.

## 90-Day and 120-Day Window Periods

A taxpayer under examination cannot file a Form 3115 to request a change in accounting methods except as provided in the 90-day window and 120-day window periods, and the consent of the district director. A taxpayer filing a Form 3115 beyond the time periods provided by the 90-day and 120-day windows will not be granted an extension of time to file except in unusual and compelling circumstances.

A taxpayer can file a Form 3115 during the first 90 days of any taxable year if the taxpayer has been under examination for at least 12 consecutive months as of the first day of the taxable year. The 90-day window is not available if the method of accounting the taxpayer is requesting to change is an issue under consideration at the time the Form 3115 is filed, or is an issue the examining agent has placed in suspense at the time.

A taxpayer requesting a change under the 90-day window must provide a copy of the Form 3115 to the examining agent at the same time the original form is filed with the IRS. The form must contain the name and telephone number of the examining agent, and the taxpayer must attach to the form a separate statement signed by the taxpayer certifying that, to the best of his or her knowledge, the same method of accounting is not an issue under consideration or an issue placed in suspense by the examining agent.

A taxpayer can file a Form 3115 to request a change in accounting method during the 120-day period following the date an examination ends regardless of whether a subsequent examination has commenced. The 120-day window is not available if the method of accounting the taxpayer is requesting to change is an issue under consideration at the time the form is filed or is an issue the examining agent has placed in suspense at the time of the filing.

A taxpayer requesting a change under the 120-day window rule must provide a copy of the Form 3115 to the examining agent for any examination that is in process at the same time the original form is filed with the IRS. The form must contain the name and telephone number of the examining agent, and must have a separate signed statement attached certifying that, to the best of the taxpayer's knowledge, the same method of accounting is not an issue under consideration or an issue placed in suspense by the examining agent.

## UNDER EXAMINATION

A taxpayer is "under examination" if the taxpayer has been contacted in any manner by a representative of the IRS for the purpose of scheduling any type of examination of any of its federal income tax returns. If a consolidated return is being examined, each member of the consolidated group will be considered under examination for purposes of the accounting method change requirements.

However, according to the 1997 ruling, on the date a new subsidiary becomes affiliated with a consolidated group, a 90-day window period can be provided within which the parent of the group may request a method change on behalf of the new member, unless the subsidiary itself is already under examination. Previously, if a consolidated group was being examined, each member of the consolidated group was considered under examination regardless of the tax year under examination.

An examination of a taxpayer, or consolidated group of which the taxpayer is a member, is considered to end at the earliest of the date:

1) The taxpayer or consolidated group of which the taxpayer is a member receives a "no-change" letter.
2) The taxpayer or consolidated group of which the taxpayer is a member pays the deficiency—or proposed deficiency.
3) The taxpayer or consolidated group requests consideration by an appeals officer.

**4)**  The taxpayer requests consideration by a federal court.

**5)**  The date on which a deficiency, jeopardy, termination, bankruptcy, or receivership assessment is made.

A taxpayer under examination cannot ask to change an impermissible method of accounting if under examination for the year in which the taxpayer adopted the method, and it was an impermissible method of accounting in the year of adoption. A taxpayer under examination cannot ask to change a method to which it changed without permission if under examination for the year in which the unauthorized change was made. Under any other circumstance, a taxpayer under examination can change an accounting method only if the taxpayer requests the change under the applicable procedures, terms, and conditions set forth in the regulation.

## APPLICATION PROCEDURES

The IRS can decline to process any Form 3115 filed in situations in which it would not be in the best interest of sound tax administration to permit the requested change. In this regard, the IRS will consider whether the change in method of accounting would clearly and directly interfere with compliance efforts of the IRS to administer the income tax laws.

A change in the method of accounting filed must be made pursuant to the terms and conditions provided in the regulations. The rule notwithstanding, the IRS can determine, based on the unique facts of a particular case, terms and conditions more appropriate for a change different from the changes provided in the regulations.

In processing an application for a change in an accounting method, the IRS will consider all the facts and circumstances, including whether:

**1)**  The method of accounting requested is consistent with the Tax Code regulations, revenue rulings, revenue procedures, and decisions of the United States Supreme Court.

**2)**  The use of the method requested will clearly reflect income.

**3)**  The present method of accounting clearly reflects income.

**4)**  The request meets the need for consistency in the accounting area.

**5)**  The taxpayer's reasons for the change are valid.

**6)**  The tax effect of the adjustment is appropriate.

**7)**  The taxpayer's books and records and financial statements will conform to the proposed method of accounting.

**8)**  The taxpayer previously requested a change in the method of accounting for the same item but did not make the change.

If the taxpayer has changed the method of accounting for the same item within the four taxable years preceding the year of requesting a change for that item, an explanation must be furnished stating why the taxpayer is again requesting a change in the method for the same item. The IRS will consider the explanation in determining whether the subsequent request for change in method will be granted.

## Consolidated Groups

Separate methods of accounting can be used by each member of a consolidated group. In considering whether to grant accounting method changes to group members, the IRS will consider the effects of the changes on the income of the group. A parent requesting a change in method on behalf of the consolidated group must submit any information necessary to permit the IRS to evaluate the effect of the requested change on the income of the consolidated group. A Form 3115 must be submitted for each member of the group for which a change in accounting method is requested. A parent can request an identical accounting method change on a single Form 3115 for more than one member of a consolidated group.

## Separate Trades or Businesses

When a taxpayer has two or more separate and distinct trades or businesses, a different method of accounting may be used for each trade or business, provided the method of accounting used for each trade or business clearly reflects the overall income of the taxpayer as well as that of each particular trade or business. No trade or business is separate and distinct unless a complete and separate set of books and records is kept for that trade or business. If the reason for maintaining different methods of accounting creates or shifts profits or losses between the trades or businesses of the taxpayer so that income is not clearly reflected, the trades or businesses of the taxpayer are not separate and distinct.

## Resolving Timing Issues: Appeals and Counsel Discretion

An appeals officer or counsel for the government may resolve a timing issue when it is in the interest of the government to do so. To reflect the hazards of litigation, they are authorized to resolve a timing issue by changing the taxpayer's method of accounting using compromise terms and conditions or they may use a nonaccounting method change basis using either an alternative-timing or a time-value-of-money resolution.

## Requirement to Apply the Law to the Facts

An appeals officer or counsel for the government resolving a timing issue must treat the issue as a change in method of accounting. The law must be applied without taking into account the hazards of litigation when determining the new method of accounting. An appeals officer or government official can change a taxpayer's method of accounting by agreeing to terms and conditions that differ from those applicable to an "examination-initiated" accounting method change.

The appeals officer may compromise on several points:

1) The year of change (by agreeing to a later year of change).
2) The amount of the adjustment (a reduced adjustment).
3) The adjustment period (a longer adjustment period).

If an appeals officer agrees to compromise the *amount* of an adjustment, the agreement must be in writing.

A change in a taxpayer's method of accounting ordinarily will *not defer the year of change* to later than the most recent taxable year under examination on the date of the agreement finalizing the change, and in no event will the year of change be deferred to later than the taxable year that includes the date of the agreement finalizing the change.

## Alternative Timing

An appeals officer can resolve a timing issue by not changing the taxpayer's method of accounting, and by the IRS and the taxpayer agreeing to alternative timing for all or some of the items arising during/prior to and during, the taxable years before appeals or a federal court. The resolution of a timing issue on an alternative-timing basis for certain items will not affect the taxpayer's method of accounting for any items not covered by the resolution.

## Time-Value-of-Money

An appeals officer or government counsel may resolve a timing issue by not changing the taxpayer's method of accounting, and by the IRS and the taxpayer agreeing that the taxpayer will pay the government a specified amount that approximates the time-value-of-money benefit the taxpayer derived from using its method of accounting for the taxable years before appeals or a federal court. This approach is instead of the method of accounting determined by the appeals officer to be the proper method of accounting. The "specified amount" is reduced by an appropriate factor to reflect the expense of litigation. The specified amount is not interest and cannot be deducted or capitalized under any provision of the law. An appeals officer may use any reasonable manner to compute the specified amount.

## Taxpayer's Advantage

As outlined above, these IRS requirements, which are part of the "new" IRS image, cover timing problems that have been resolved by the IRS on a nonaccounting-method change basis. They provide terms and conditions for IRS-initiated changes that are intended to encourage taxpayers to *voluntarily request a change from an impermissible method of accounting* rather than being contacted by an agent for examination. Under this approach, a taxpayer who is contacted for *examination* and required to change methods of accounting by the IRS generally receives less favorable terms and conditions than if the taxpayer had filed a request to change before being contacted for examination.

The new regulations may be consistent with the policy of encouraging prompt voluntary compliance with proper tax accounting principles, but they appear to have some limitations. It is now easier for the taxpayer to change an accounting method, but the IRS ordinarily will not initiate an accounting method change if the change will place the taxpayer in a more favorable position than if the taxpayer had been contacted for examination. An examining agent will not initiate a change from an impermissible method that results in a negative adjustment. If the IRS declines to initiate such an accounting method change, the district director will consent to the taxpayer requesting a voluntary change.

## Resolving Timing Issues: Discretion of Examining Agent

An examining agent proposing an adjustment on a timing issue will treat the issue as a change in method of accounting. In changing the taxpayer's method of accounting, the agent will properly apply the law to the facts without taking into account the hazards of litigation when determining the new method of accounting. An examining agent changing a taxpayer's method of accounting will impose an adjustment.

The change can be made using a cutoff method only in rare and unusual circumstances when the examining agent determines that the taxpayer's books and records do not contain sufficient information to compute the adjustment and the adjustment is not susceptible to reasonable estimation. An examining agent changing a taxpayer's method of accounting will effect the change in the earliest taxable year under examination (or, if later, the first taxable year the method is considered impermissible) with a one-year adjustment period.

## Method Changes Initiated by the IRS

If a taxpayer does not regularly employ a method of accounting that clearly reflects his or her income, the computation of taxable income must be made in a manner that, in the opinion of the Commissioner, does clearly reflect income. The Commissioner has broad discretion in determining whether a taxpayer's method of accounting clearly reflects income, and the Commissioner's determination must be upheld unless it is clearly unlawful.

The Commissioner has broad discretion in selecting a method of accounting that properly reflects the income of a taxpayer once it has been determined that the taxpayer's method of accounting does not clearly reflect income. The selection can be challenged only upon showing an abuse of discretion by the Commissioner.

The Commissioner has the discretion to change a method of accounting even though the IRS had previously changed the taxpayer to that method if it is determined that the method of accounting does not clearly reflect the taxpayer's income. The discretionary power does not extend to requiring a taxpayer to change from a method of accounting that clearly reflects income to a method that, in the Commissioner's view, more clearly reflects income.

The accounting method of a taxpayer that is under examination, before an appeals office, or before a federal court, can be changed except as otherwise provided in published guidance. The service is generally precluded from changing a taxpayer's method of accounting for an item for prior taxable years if the taxpayer timely files a request to change the method of accounting for the item.

### Retroactive Method Change

Although the Commissioner is authorized to consent to a retroactive accounting method change, the taxpayer does not have a right to a retroactive change, regardless of whether the change is from a permissible or impermissible method.

Except under unusual circumstances, if a taxpayer who changes the method of accounting is subsequently required to change or modify that method of accounting, the required change or modification will not be applied retroactively provided that:

1)  The taxpayer complied with all the applicable provisions of the consent agreement.
2)  There has been no misstatement nor omission of material facts.
3)  There has been no change in the material facts on which the consent was based.

**4)** There has been no change in the applicable law.

**5)** The taxpayer to whom consent was granted acted in good faith in relying on the consent, and applying the change or modification retroactively would be to the taxpayer's detriment.

## New Method Established

An IRS-initiated change that is final establishes a new method of accounting. As a result, a taxpayer is required to use the new method of accounting for the year of change and for all subsequent taxable years unless the taxpayer obtains the consent of the commissioner to change from the new method or the IRS changes the taxpayer from the new method on subsequent examination. As indicated above, the IRS is not precluded from changing a taxpayer from the new method of accounting if the IRS determined that the new method does not clearly reflect the taxpayer's income. A taxpayer who executes a closing agreement finalizing an IRS initiated accounting method change will not be required to change or modify the new method for any taxable year for which a federal income tax return has been filed as of the date of the closing agreement, provided that:

**1)** The taxpayer has complied with all the applicable provisions of the closing agreement.

**2)** There has been no taxpayer fraud, malfeasance, or misrepresentation of a material fact.

**3)** There has been no change in the material facts on which the closing agreement was based.

**4)** There has been no change in the applicable law on which the closing agreement was based.

## Required Change or Modification of New Method

The IRS may require a taxpayer to change or modify the new method in the earliest open taxable year if the taxpayer fails to comply with the applicable provisions of the closing agreement, or upon a showing of taxpayer's fraud, malfeasance, or misrepresentation of a material fact. The taxpayer can be required to change or modify the new method in the earliest open taxable year in which the material facts have changed, and can also be required to change or modify the new method in the earliest open taxable year in which the applicable law has changed. For this purpose, a change in the applicable law includes:

**1)** A decision of the U.S. Supreme Court.

**2)** The enactment of legislation.

**3)** The issuance of temporary or final regulations.

**4)** The issuance of a revenue ruling, revenue procedure, notice, or other guidance published in the Internal Revenue Bulletin.

Except in rare and unusual circumstances, a retroactive change in applicable law is deemed to occur when one of the events described in the preceding sentence occurs and not when the change in law is effective.

## ACCOUNTING PERIODS

Taxable income must be figured on the basis of a tax year. A *tax year* is an annual accounting period for keeping records and reporting income and expenses. The tax years usable are:

**1)** A calendar year.

**2)** A fiscal year.

The tax year is adopted in the first year that an income tax return is filed. The tax year must be adopted by the due date, not including extensions, for filing a return for that year. The due date for individual and partnership returns is the 15th day of the 4th month after the end of the tax year. "Individuals" include sole proprietorships, partners, and S corporation shareholders. The due date for filing returns for corporations and S corporations is the 15th day of the 3rd month after the end of the tax year. If the 15th day of the month falls on a Saturday, Sunday, or legal holiday, the due date is the next business day.

### Calendar Year

If a calendar year is chosen, the taxpayer must maintain books and records and report income and expenses from January 1 through December 31 of each year. If the first tax return uses the calendar year and the taxpayer later begins business as a sole proprietor, becomes a partner in a partnership, or becomes a shareholder in an S corporation, the calendar year must continue to be used unless the IRS approves a change. Anyone can adopt the calendar year. However, if any of the following apply, the calendar year must be used:

**1)** The taxpayer does not keep adequate records.

**2)** The taxpayer has no annual accounting period.

**3)** The taxpayer's tax year does not qualify as a fiscal year.

## Fiscal Year

A fiscal year is 12 consecutive months ending on the last day of any month except December. A 52–53-week tax year is a fiscal year that varies from 52 to 53 weeks. If a fiscal year is adopted, books and records must be maintained, and income and expenses reported using the same tax year.

A 52–53-week tax year may be elected if books and records are kept, and income and expenses are reported on that basis. If this election is chosen, the tax year will be 52 or 53 weeks long, and will always end on the same day of the week. The tax year can end only on the same day of the week that:

**1)**   Last occurs in a particular month.

**2)**   Occurs nearest to the last day of a particular calendar month.

To make the choice, a statement with the following information is attached to the tax return for the 52–53-week tax year:

**1)**   The month in which the new 52–53-week tax year ends.

**2)**   The day of the week on which the tax year always ends.

**3)**   The date the tax year ends. It can be either of the following dates on which the chosen day:

    **a)**   Last occurs in the month in (1).

    **b)**   Occurs nearest to the last day of the month in (1).

When depreciation or amortization is figured, a 52–53-week tax year is considered a year of 12 calendar months unless another practice is consistently used. To determine an effective date, or apply provisions of any law, expressed in terms of tax years beginning, including, or ending on the first or last day of a specified calendar month, a 52–53-week tax year is considered to:

**1)**   Begin on the first day of the calendar month beginning nearest to the first day of the 52–53-week tax year.

**2)**   End on the last day of the calendar month ending nearest to the last day of the 52–53-week tax year.

If the month in which a 52–53-week tax year ends is changed, a return must be filed for the short tax year if it covers more than 6 but less than 359 days. If the short period created by the change is 359 days or more, it should be treated as a full tax year. If the short period created is 6 days or less, it is not a separate tax year. It is to be treated as part of the following year.

A corporation figures tax for a short year under the general rules described for individuals. There is no adjustment for personal exemptions.

## Improper Tax Year

A calendar year is a tax year of 12 months that ends on December 31, and a fiscal year is a tax year of 12 months that ends on the last day of any month except December, including a 52–53-week tax year. If business operations start on a day other than the last day of a calendar month and adopt a tax year of exactly 12 months from the date operations began, the taxpayer has adopted an *improper* tax year. The requirements for a calendar or fiscal tax year, including a 52–53-week tax year, have not been met. To change to a proper tax year, one of the following requirements must be met:

1) An amended tax return should be based on a calendar year.
2) IRS approval should be sought to change to a tax year, other than a calendar year.

## Business Purpose Tax Year

A business purpose tax year is an accounting period that has a substantial business purpose for its existence.

In considering whether there is a business purpose for a tax year, significant weight is given to tax factors. A prime consideration is whether the change would create a substantial distortion of income. The following are examples of distortions of income:

1) Deferring substantial income or shifting substantial deductions from one year to another to reduce tax liability.
2) Causing a similar deferral or shifting for any other person, such as a partner or shareholder.
3) Creating a short period in which there is a substantial net operating loss.

The following nontax factors, based on convenience for the taxpayer, are generally not sufficient to establish a business purpose for a particular year:

1) Using a particular year for regulatory or financial accounting purposes.
2) Using a particular pattern, such as typically hiring staff during certain times of the year.
3) Using a particular year for administration purposes, such as:

    **a)** Admission or retirement of partners or shareholders.

    **b)** Promotion of staff.

    **c)** Compensation or retirement arrangements with staff, partners, or shareholders.

**4)** Using a price list, model year, or other item that changes on an annual basis.

**5)** Deferring income to partners or shareholders.

## Natural Business Year

One nontax factor that may be sufficient to establish a business purpose for a tax year is an annual cycle of business, called a "natural business year." A natural business year exists when business has a peak and a nonpeak period. The natural business year is considered to end at or soon after the end of the peak period. A business whose income is steady from month-to-month all year would not have a natural business year as such. A natural business year is considered a substantial business purpose for an entity changing its accounting period. The IRS will ordinarily approve this change unless it results in a substantial deferral of income or another tax advantage.

The IRS provides a procedure for a partnership, an S corporation, or a personal service corporation to retain or automatically change to a natural business year as determined by the 25% test. It also allows an S corporation to adopt, retain, or change to a fiscal year that satisfies the "ownership tax year test." The 25% test uses the method of accounting used for the tax returns for each year involved. To figure the 25% test:

**1)** The gross sales and services receipts for the most recent 12-month period that includes the last month of the requested fiscal year are totaled for the 12-month period that ends before the filing of the request. Gross sales and services receipts for the last 2 months of that 12-month period are then totaled.

**2)** The percentage of the receipts for the 2-month period is then determined by dividing the total of the 2-month period by the total for the 12-month period. The percentage should be carried to two decimal places.

**3)** The percentage following steps 1 and 2 should then be figured for the two 12-month periods just preceding the 12-month period used in 1.

If the percentage determined for each of the three years equals or exceeds 25%, the requested fiscal year is the *natural business year.* If the partnership, S corporation, or personal service corporation qualifies for more than one natural business year, the fiscal year producing the higher average of the three percentages is the natural business year. If the partnership, S corporation, or personal service corporation does not have at least 47 months of gross receipts—which may include a predecessor organization's gross receipts—it cannot use this automatic procedure to obtain permission to use a fiscal year.

If the requested tax year is a 52–53-week tax year, the calendar month ending nearest the last day of the 52–53-week tax year is treated as the last month of the requested tax year for purposes of computing the 25% test.

An S corporation or corporation electing to be an S corporation qualifies for automatic approval if it meets the ownership tax year test. The test is met if the corporation is adopting, retaining, or changing to a tax year and shareholders holding more than 50% of the issued and outstanding shares of stock on the first day of the requested tax year have, or are all changing to, the same tax year.

## Change in Tax Year

A tax year change must be approved by the IRS. A current Form 1128 must be filed by the 15th day of the end calendar month after the close of the short tax year to get IRS approval. The *short tax year* begins on the first day after the end of the present tax year and ends on the day before the first day of the new tax year. If the short tax year required to effect a change in tax years is a year in which the taxpayer has a net operating loss (NOL), the NOL must be deducted ratably over a 6-year period from the first tax year after the short period.

A husband and wife who have different tax years cannot file a joint return. There is an exception to this rule if their tax years began on the same date and ended on different dates because of the death of either or both. If a husband and wife want to use the same tax year so they can file a joint return, the method of changing a tax year depends on whether they are newly married. A newly married husband and wife with different tax years who wish to file a joint return can change the tax year of one spouse without first getting IRS approval.

The correct user fee must be included, if any. The IRS charges a user fee for certain requests to change an accounting period or method, certain tax rulings, and determination letters. The fee is reduced in certain situations and for certain requests, such as a request for substantially identical rulings for related entities.

## Year of Change

While this heading and the one above are similar, the connotation is somewhat different. The year of change is the taxable year for which a change in the method of accounting is effective, that is, the first taxable year the new method is used even if no affected items are taken into account for that year. The year of change is also the first taxable year for taking an adjustment and complying with all the terms and conditions accompanying the change.

## Partnership

A partnership must conform its tax year to its partners' tax years unless the partnership can establish a business purpose for a different period. The rules for the required tax year for partnerships are:

1) If one or more partners having the same tax year own a majority interest—more than 5%—in partnership profits and capital, the partnership must use the tax year of those partners.

2) If there is no majority interest tax year, the partnership must use the tax year of its principal partners. A principal partner is one who has a 5% or more interest in the profits or capital of the partnership.

3) If there is no majority interest tax year and the principal partners do not have the same tax year, the partnership generally must use a tax year that results in the least aggregate deferral of income to the partners.

If a partnership changes to a required tax year because of these rules, the change is considered to be initiated by the partnership with IRS approval. No formal application for change in the tax year is needed. Any partnership that changes to a required tax year must notify the IRS by writing at the top of the first page of its tax return for its first required tax year: *Filed Under Section 806 of the Tax Reform Act of 1986.*

The tax year that results in the least aggregate deferral of income is determined by:

1) Figuring the number of months of deferral for each partner using one partner's tax year. The months of deferral are found by counting the months from the end of that tax year forward to the end of each other partner's tax year.

2) Each partner's months of deferral figured in step (1) are multiplied by that partner's share of interest in the partnership profits for the year used in step (1).

**3)** The amounts in step (2) are added to get the aggregate (total) deferral for the tax year used in step (1).

**4)** Steps (1) through (3) are repeated for each partner's tax year that is different from the other partners' years.

The partners' tax year that results in the lowest aggregate—total—number is the tax year that must be used by the partnership. If more than one year qualifies as the tax year that has the least aggregate deferral of income, the partnership can choose any year that qualifies. If one of the tax years that qualifies is the partnership's existing tax year, the partnership must retain that tax year.

## S Corporations

If a business meets the requirements of a small business corporation, it can elect to be an S corporation. All S corporations, regardless of when they became an S corporation, must use a *permitted tax year.* A permitted tax year is the calendar year or any other tax year for which the corporation establishes a business purpose.

## Personal Service Corporation

A personal service corporation must use a calendar year unless it can establish a business purpose for a different period or it makes a Section 444 election (discussed below). For this purpose, a corporation is a personal service corporation if all of the following conditions are met:

**1)** The corporation is a C corporation.

**2)** The corporation's principal activity during the testing period is the performance of personal services.

**3)** Employee-owners of the corporation perform a substantial part of the services during the testing period.

**4)** Employee-owners own more than 10% of the corporation's stock on the last day of the testing period.

The principal activity of a corporation is considered to be the performance of personal services if, during the testing period, the corporation's compensation costs for personal service activities is more than 50% of its total compensation costs.

Generally, the *testing period for a tax year is the prior tax year.* The testing period for the first tax year of a new corporation starts with the first day of the tax year and ends on the earlier of the following dates:

1) The last day of its tax year.
2) The last day of the calendar year in which the tax year begins.

The *performance of personal services* involves any activity in the fields of health, veterinary services, law, engineering, architecture, accounting, actuarial science, performing arts, or certain consulting services.

An employee-owner of a corporation is a person who:

1) Is an employee of the corporation on any day of the testing period.
2) Owns any outstanding stock of the corporation on any day of the testing period.

A further clarification of the definition of an independent contractor by the 1997 Act states, "A person who owns any outstanding stock of the corporation and who performs personal services for or on behalf of the corporation is treated as an *employee* of the corporation. This rule applies even if the legal form of the person's relationship to the corporation is such that the person would be considered an independent contractor for other purposes."

## Section 444 Election

A partnership, S corporation, or personal service corporation can elect under Section 444 of the Internal Revenue Code to use a tax year different from its required tax year. Certain restrictions apply to the election. In addition, a partnership or S corporation may have to make a payment for the deferral period. The Section 444 election does not apply to any partnership, S corporation, or personal service corporation that establishes a business purpose for a different period.

A partnership, S corporation, or personal service corporation can make a Section 444 election if it meets all the following requirements:

1) It is not a member of a tiered structure.
2) It has not previously had a Section 444 election in effect.
3) It elects a year that meets the deferral period requirement.

The determination of the *deferral period* depends on whether the partnership, corporation, or personal service corporation is retaining its current tax year or adopting or changing its tax year with a Section 444 election.

A partnership, S corporation, or personal service corporation can make a Section 444 election to *retain* its tax year only if the deferral period of the new tax year is three months or less. The deferral period is the number of months between the beginning of the retained year and the close of the first required tax year.

If the partnership, S corporation, or personal service corporation is *changing* to a tax year other than its required year, the deferral period is the number of months from the end of the new tax year to the end of the required tax year. The IRS will allow a Section 444 election only if the deferral period of the new tax year is less than the shorter of:

**1)** Three months.

**2)** The deferral period of the tax year being changed. This is the tax year for which the partnership, S corporation, or personal service corporation wishes to make the Section 444 election.

If the tax year is the same as the required tax year, the deferral period is zero.

A Section 444 election is made by filing a form with the IRS by the earlier of:

**1)** The due date of the income tax return resulting from the 444 election.

**2)** The 15th day of the 6th month of the tax year for which the election will be effective. For this purpose, the month in which the tax year begins is counted, even if it begins after the first day of that month. The Section 444 election stays in effect until it is terminated. If the election is terminated, another Section 444 election cannot be made for any tax year. The election ends when any of the three corporations does any of the following:

**1)** Changes its tax year to a required tax year.

**2)** Liquidates.

**3)** Willfully fails to comply with the required payments or distributions.

**4)** Becomes a member of a tiered structure.

The election also ends if:

**1)** An S corporation's election is terminated. However, if the S corporation immediately becomes a personal service corporation, it can continue the Section 444 election of the S corporation.

**2)** A personal service corporation ceases to be a personal service corporation. If the personal service corporation elects to be an S corporation, it can continue the election of the personal service corporation.

## Corporations

A new corporation establishes its tax year when it files its first return. A newly reactivated corporation that has been inactive for a number of years is treated as a new taxpayer for the purpose of adopting a tax year. A corporation other than an S corporation, a personal service corporation, or a domestic international sales corporation (C-DISC) can change its tax year without getting IRS approval if all the following conditions are met:

1) It must not have changed its tax year within the 10 calendar years ending with the calendar year in which the short tax year resulting from the change begins.

2) Its short tax year must not be a tax year in which it has a net operating loss.

3) Its taxable income for the whole tax year, if figured on an annual basis, is 80% or more of its taxable income for the tax year before the short tax year.

4) If a corporation is one of the following for either the short tax year or the tax year before the short tax year, it must have the same status for both the short tax year and the prior tax year.

   a) Personal holding company.

   b) Foreign personal holding company.

   c) Exempt organization.

   d) Foreign corporation not engaged in a trade or business within the United States.

5) It must not apply to become an S corporation for the tax year that would immediately follow the short tax year required to effect the change.

The corporation must file a statement with the IRS office where it files its tax return. The statement must be filed by the due date for the short tax year required by the change. It must indicate the corporation is changing its annual accounting period, and show that all the preceding conditions have been met. If the corporation does not meet all the conditions because of later adjustments in establishing tax liability, the statement will be considered a timely application to change the corporation's annual accounting period to the tax year indicated in the statement.

The IRS will waive conditions (1) and (5) above, as well as conditions (2) and (3)(c) outlining automatic approval criteria for a corporation that:

1) Meets all the other conditions.

**2)** Elected to be an S corporation for the tax year beginning January 1, 1997.
**3)** It must:
   **a)** Write "Filed" at the top of the forms required.
   **b)** Write "Attention, Entity Control" on the envelope.
   **c)** Mail the forms to the IRS where the corporation files its return.

Corporations can automatically change their tax year if it cannot meet the five conditions and has not changed its annual accounting period within 6 calendar years or in any of the calendar years of existence, and if the corporation is *not any of the following*:

**1)** A member of a partnership.
**2)** A beneficiary of a trust or an estate.
**3)** An S corporation.
**4)** An interest-charging DISC or a foreign sales corporation (FSC).
**5)** A personal service corporation.
**6)** A controlled foreign corporation.
**7)** A cooperative association.
**8)** Certain tax-exempt organizations.

## CHANGES DURING THE TAX YEAR

A corporation, other than an S corporation, a personal service corporation, or a domestic international sales corporation (IC-DISC) can change its tax year without getting IRS approval if all the following conditions are met:

**1)** It must not have changed its tax year within the 10 calendar years in which the short tax year resulting from the change begins.
**2)** Its short tax year must not be a tax year in which it has a net operating loss (NOL).
**3)** Its taxable income for the short tax year, when figured on an annual basis, annualized, is 80% or more of its taxable income for the tax year before the short tax year.
**4)** If a corporation is one of the following for either the short tax year or the tax year before the short tax year, it must have the same status for both the short tax and the prior tax year.
**5)** It must not apply to become an S corporation for the tax year that would immediately follow the short tax year required to effect the change.

The corporation must file a statement with the IRS office where it files its tax return. The statement must be filed by the due date, including extensions, for the short tax year required by the change. It must indicate the corporation is changing its annual accounting period, and that all the preceding conditions have been met.

Certain corporations can *automatically* change their tax year by meeting all the following criteria:

1) It cannot meet the conditions listed earlier.
2) It has not changed its annual accounting period within 6 calendar years of existence, or in any of the calendar years of existence, if less than 6 years.

# Chapter 10

## More "Taxpayer Rights" and Some IRS Changes

### NEW IMAGE FOR THE IRS

This year, along with their tax bills, taxpayers received new and revised publications delineating their rights and obligations in handling various and sundry tax problems. Some of the points made are reminiscent of those previously publicized in the Taxpayer Bill of Rights 1, 2, and 3. (The last may be better known as the *IRS Restructuring and Reform Act of 1998*, but more on that below.) These two publications emphasize some of the measures adopted in the Congressional Bills, but are also based on IRS regulations and other legislation. They are not a Taxpayer Bill of Rights 4. Regardless, it does appear that the Service is attempting to serve the public and make tax paying as painless as possible.

At some point, between the time that Congress passed the 1998 bill and the IRS started sending out information publications for the 1998 tax season, it had picked up a subtitle and become known as the *Taxpayer Bill of Rights 3*.

In fact, the IRS states, "The *IRS Restructuring Reform Act of 1998* contains the Taxpayer Bill of Rights 3. It preserves the balance between safeguarding the rights of the individual taxpayers and enabling the Internal Revenue Service to administer the tax laws efficiently, fairly, and with the least amount of burden to the taxpayer."

Under this bill, taxpayer rights have been expanded in several areas:

1) The burden of proof will shift to the IRS in certain court proceedings.

2) In certain cases, taxpayers may be awarded damages and fees, and get liens released.

3) Penalties will be eased when the IRS exceeds specified time limits between when a return is filed and when the taxpayer is notified of a tax liability.

4) Interest will be eliminated in certain cases involving federally-declared disaster areas.

5) There are new rules for collection actions by levy.

6) Innocent spouse relief provisions have been strengthened.

7) In certain situations, taxpayer-requested installment agreements must be accepted. Taxpayers will get annual status reports of their installment agreements.

Included are requirements that IRS employees are now required to be more polite and responsive. For example, any IRS correspondence not computer generated must include the name and telephone number of an employee whom a taxpayer can contact. The new law also establishes a nine-member board to oversee the general administration of the agency. And to assure that key decision making will not remain in the self-protecting hands of IRS career employees, six of the board's members will be "outsiders." Many of these provisions are contained in the material that follows.

## DECLARATION OF TAXPAYER RIGHTS

The first part of this discussion explains some of a taxpayer's most important rights. The second part explains the examination, appeal, collection, and refund procedures.

I. *Protection of a Taxpayer's Rights.* IRS employees will explain and protect a taxpayer's rights throughout his or her contact with the IRS.

II. *Privacy and Confidentiality.* The IRS will not disclose to anyone the information given to the IRS, except as authorized by law.

III. *Professional and Courteous Service.* If a taxpayer believes an IRS employee has not treated him or her in a professional, fair, and courteous manner, the employee's supervisor should be told. If the supervisor's response is not satisfactory, the taxpayer should write to the IRS District Director or Service Center Director.

IV. *Representation.* A taxpayer can either represent himself or herself or, with proper written authorization, have someone else as a representative. The taxpayer's representative must be a person allowed to practice before the IRS, such as an attorney, certified public accountant, or enrolled agent.

If a taxpayer is in an interview and asks to consult such a person, then the IRS must stop and reschedule the interview in most cases. Someone may accompany the taxpayer to an interview, and make recordings of any meetings with the IRS examining agent, appeal or collection personnel, provided the taxpayer tells the IRS in writing 10 days before the meeting.

**V.** *Payment of Only the Correct Amount of Tax.* Taxpayers are responsible for paying the correct amount of tax due under the law—no more, no less. If a responsible taxpayer cannot pay all of his or her tax when it is due, it may be possible to make monthly installment payments. Arrangements for payments are made with the IRS.

**VI.** *Help with Unresolved Tax Problems.* The National Taxpayer Advocate's Problem Resolution Program can help a taxpayer who has tried unsuccessfully to resolve a problem with the IRS. A local Taxpayer Advocate can offer special help for a significant hardship as a result of a tax problem. The taxpayer may call toll-free or write to the Taxpayer Advocate at the IRS office that last contacted him or her.

**VII.** *Appeals and Judicial Review.* If a taxpayer disagrees with the IRS about the amount of a tax liability or certain collection actions, it is the taxpayer's right to ask the Appeals Office to review the case. The taxpayer also has the right to ask a court to review the case.

**VIII.** *Relief from Certain Penalties and Interest.* The IRS will waive penalties when allowed by law if a taxpayer can show he or she has acted reasonably and in good faith or relied on the incorrect advice of an IRS employee. The IRS will waive interest that is the result of certain errors or delays caused by an IRS employee.

## EXAMINATIONS, APPEALS, COLLECTIONS, AND REFUNDS

*Examinations (Audits).* The IRS accepts most taxpayers' returns as filed. If the IRS inquires about a return or selects it for examination, it does not suggest the taxpayer is dishonest. The inquiry or examination may or may not result in more tax. A case can be closed without change, or the taxpayer may receive a refund.

The process of selecting a return for examination usually begins in one of two ways:

**1)** Computer programs are used to identify returns that may have incorrect amounts. These programs may be based on:

   **a)** Information returns, such as Forms 1099 and W-2.

   **b)** Studies of past examinations.

    **c)** Certain issues identified by compliance projects.

**2)** Information is used from outside sources that indicate that a return has incorrect amounts. These sources include:

    **a)** Newspapers.

    **b)** Public records.

    **c)** Individuals.

If it is determined that the information is accurate and reliable, this information may be used to select a particular tax return for examination.

*Examinations by Mail.* The IRS processes many examinations and inquiries by mail. They will send a letter to a taxpayer with either a request for more information or a reason the IRS believes a change in a return may be needed. The taxpayer can respond by mail or can request a personal interview with an examiner. If the taxpayer mails the requested information or provides an explanation, the IRS may or may not agree with the taxpayer's explanation, and will explain the reasons for any changes. The IRS urges taxpayers not to hesitate to write about anything they do not understand.

*By Interview.* If the IRS notifies a taxpayer that they will conduct an examination through a personal interview, or the taxpayer requests such an interview, the taxpayer has the right to ask that the examination take place at a reasonable time and place that is convenient for both the taxpayer and the IRS. If an examiner proposes any changes to a return, the examination will make clear the reasons for the changes. If the taxpayer does not agree with these changes, he or she can meet with the examiner's supervisor.

*Repeat Examinations.* If the IRS examined a return for the same items in either of the two previous years and proposed no change to the taxpayer's tax liability, he or she should contact the IRS as soon as possible so that the IRS can determine if the current examination should be discontinued.

*Appeals.* If a taxpayer does not agree with an examiner's proposed changes, he or she can appeal them to the Appeals Office of the IRS. Most differences can be settled without expensive and time-consuming court trials. If the taxpayer does not want to use the Appeals Office or disagrees with its finding, the case can be taken to the U.S. Tax Court, U.S. Court of Federal Claims, or the U.S. District Court where the taxpayer lives. If a case is taken to court, the IRS will have the burden of proving certain facts. These would include whether the taxpayer:

1) Kept audit records to show the tax liability.
2) Cooperated fully with the IRS.
3) Met certain other conditions.

If the court agrees with the taxpayer on most issues in a case, and finds that the IRS position was largely unjustified, the taxpayer may be able to recover some of the administrative and litigation costs. However, the taxpayer cannot recover these costs unless he or she tried to resolve a case administratively, including going through the appeals system, and giving the IRS the information necessary to resolve the case.

***Innocent Spouse Relief.*** Generally, both spouses are responsible, jointly and individually, for paying the full amount of any tax, interest, or penalties due on their joint return. However, one spouse may not have to pay the tax, interest, and penalties related to the other spouse or former spouse.

New tax law changes make it easier to qualify for innocent spouse relief and add two other ways to get relief through "separation of liability" and "equitable relief." Thus, there are now three types of relief available:

1) Innocent spouse relief which applies to all joint filers.
2) Separation of liability, which applies to joint filers who are divorced, widowed, legally separated, or have not lived together for the past 12 months.
3) Equitable relief, which applies to all joint filers and married couples filing separate returns in community property states.

Innocent spouse relief and separation of liability apply only to items incorrectly reported on the return. If a spouse does not qualify for innocent spouse relief or separation of liability, the IRS may grant equitable relief.

***Refunds.*** A taxpayer can file a claim for a refund if he or she thinks too much tax was levied The claim must generally be filed within 3 years from the date the original return was filed, or 2 years from the date the tax was paid, whichever is later. The law generally provides for interest on a refund if it is not paid within 45 days of the date the return was filed or the refund was claimed.

## THE IRS COLLECTION PROCESS

There are steps the IRS can take to collect overdue taxes. The information in this discussion applies to all taxpayers—for individuals who owe income taxes and employers who owe employment tax. Special rules that apply only to employers are given at the end of this discussion.

By law, taxpayers have the right to be treated professionally, fairly, promptly, and courteously by IRS employees. Some of those rights are to:

1)  Disagree with claims on the tax bill.
2)  Meet with an IRS manager if the taxpayer disagrees with the IRS employee who handles the tax case.
3)  Appeal most IRS collection actions.
4)  Transfer a case to a different IRS office.
5)  Be represented by someone when dealing with IRS matters.
6)  Receive a receipt for any payment he or she makes.

*Disagreement with an IRS Decision.* If a taxpayer disagrees with a decision of an IRS employee at any time during the collection process, the taxpayer can ask the employee's manager to review the case. The employee will then refer the taxpayer to a manager who will either speak with the taxpayer then or return a call by the next work day.

If the taxpayer disagrees with a manager's decision, the taxpayer has the right to file an appeal which enables him or her to appeal most collection actions taken by the IRS, including filing a lien, placing a levy on the taxpayer's wages or bank account, or seizing a taxpayer's property.

*Someone to Represent a Taxpayer.* When dealing with the IRS, a taxpayer can choose to represent himself or herself, or can have an attorney, a certified public accountant, an enrolled agent, or any person enrolled to practice before the IRS as a representative.

*Problem Resolution Program.* This program ensures that taxpayers' problems are handled promptly and properly. If repeated attempts have been made to sort out a tax problem with the IRS, but have been unsuccessful, then the taxpayer can first ask any IRS employee or manager for help. If the problem continues, the taxpayer may ask for an appointment with the Taxpayer Advocate in the local IRS office. The Taxpayer Advocate determines whether the taxpayer qualifies for the Problem Resolution Program.

*IRS Sharing Information.* By law the IRS can share a taxpayer's information with city and state tax agencies and, in some cases, with the Department of Justice, other federal agencies, and with people the taxpayer authorizes to receive that information. Such information can also be shared with certain foreign governments under tax treaty provisions.

The IRS can contact other sources, such as neighbors, banks, employers or employees, to investigate a case. However, after January 18, 1999, the new law provides that before contacting other persons, the IRS must notify the individual that, in examining or collecting tax liability, they may contact third parties. In addition, the new law requires the Service to provide a list of persons who were questioned. This information is to be provided periodically and upon request.

The notification provision does not apply in the following circumstances:

1) Pending criminal investigations.
2) When providing notice would jeopardize collection of any tax liability.
3) Where providing notice may result in reprisal against any person.
4) When the taxpayer authorized the contact.

If a taxpayer is involved in a bankruptcy proceeding, the proceeding may not eliminate the tax debt, but it may temporarily stop IRS enforcement action from collecting a debt related to the bankruptcy.

***If a Taxpayer Owes Child Support.*** If a taxpayer is entitled to a federal or state tax refund while still owing unpaid taxes or child support, the IRS can apply the refund toward the debt and send the taxpayer the remaining balance, if there is any.

***When a Taxpayer Can't Pay.*** When a tax return is filed, the IRS checks to see if the mathematics is accurate and if the taxpayer has paid the correct amount. If the taxpayer has not paid all that is owed, the IRS will send a bill called a *Notice of Tax Due and Demand for Payment*. The bill will include the taxes, plus penalties and interest, and the IRS encourages a taxpayer to pay the tax bill by check or money order as quickly as possible.

If the taxpayer has received a bill for unpaid taxes, the entire amount should be paid, or the IRS should be notified why the taxpayer cannot pay. If the taxpayer does not pay the taxes owed and makes no effort to pay them, the IRS can ask the taxpayer to take action to pay by selling or mortgaging any assets, or getting a loan. If the taxpayer still makes no effort to pay the taxes owed or to work out a payment plan, the IRS can also take more serious action, such as seizing the taxpayer's bank, levying his or her wages, or taking other income or assets.

***If a Taxpayer Believes the Bill Is Wrong.*** If a taxpayer believes a bill is wrong, the IRS should be contacted as soon as possible by:

1) Calling the number on the bill.
2) Writing to the IRS office that sent the bill.
3) Visiting the local IRS office.

To help IRS consideration of the problem, the taxpayer should send a copy of the bill along with copies (not originals) of any records, tax returns, and canceled checks that will help the IRS understand why the taxpayer believes the bill to be wrong. When writing to the IRS, the taxpayer should state clearly why he or she believes the bill is wrong. If the IRS finds the taxpayer is correct, the account will be adjusted, and, if necessary, the taxpayer will be sent a corrected bill.

If the total amount owed cannot be paid immediately, as much as possible should be paid. By paying that portion, the amount of interest and penalty will be reduced. The taxpayer should call, write, or visit the nearest IRS office to explain the situation. The IRS will ask for a completed form, *Collection Information Statement,* to help them consider the amount the taxpayer can pay based upon the taxpayer's monthly income and expenses. The IRS will then help to figure out a payment plan that fits the situation. The IRS will work with the taxpayer to consider several different ways to pay what is owed:

1) The taxpayer may be able to make monthly payments through an installment agreement.
2) The taxpayer may be able to apply for an offer in compromise.
3) The taxpayer may qualify for a temporary delay, or the case may be considered a significant hardship.

**An Installment Agreement.** Installment agreements allow the full payment of taxes in smaller, equal monthly payments. The amount of each installment payment is based on the amount of tax owed and the taxpayer's ability to pay that amount within the time available to the IRS to collect the tax debt.

Previously, the IRS did not have to agree to accept the payment of taxes in installments. However, as of July 22, 1998, they must enter into an installment agreement for the payment of income tax if the taxpayer meets all of the following conditions on the date he or she offers to enter into the agreement:

1) The total income tax owed is not more than $10,000.
2) In the last 5 years, the taxpayer (and spouse if the liability relates to a joint return) has:
   a) Filed all required income tax returns.

    **b)** Paid all taxes shown on the returns filed.

    **c)** Not entered into an installment agreement to pay any income tax.

**3)** The taxpayer shows (and the IRS agrees) that the individual cannot pay the income tax in full when due.

**4)** The taxpayer agrees to pay the tax in full in 3 years or less.

**5)** The taxpayer agrees to comply with the tax laws while the agreement is in effect.

An installment agreement is a reasonable payment option for some taxpayers, but they should be aware that an installment agreement is more costly than paying all the tax owed and may be more costly than borrowing funds to pay the full amount. Why? Because the IRS charges interest and *penalties* on the tax owed and also charges interest on the unpaid penalties and interest that have been charged to the taxpayer's account. This means that while the taxpayer is making payments on his or her tax debt through an installment agreement, the IRS continues to charge interest and penalties on the unpaid portion of that debt.

The interest rate on a bank loan or on a cash advance on a credit card may be lower than the combination of penalties and interest the IRS charges. There is also another cost associated with an installment agreement. To set up the payment program, the IRS charges a $43 user fee. If a taxpayer owes $10,000 or less in tax, the taxpayer can call the number on the tax bill to set up a plan. The IRS will inform the taxpayer what has to be done to begin immediately.

If more than $10,000 is owed, the IRS may still be able to set up an installment agreement with the taxpayer based on the completed form, *Collection Information Statement.* Even though a taxpayer agrees to an installment plan, the IRS can still file a *Notice of Federal Tax Lien* to secure the government's interest until the taxpayer makes the final payment.

However, the IRS cannot levy against the taxpayer's property:

**1)** While a request for an installment agreement is being considered.

**2)** While an agreement is in effect.

**3)** For 30 days after the request for an agreement has been rejected.

**4)** For any period while an appeal of the rejection is being evaluated by the IRS.

If an installment agreement is arranged, the taxpayer can pay with personal or business checks, money orders, certified funds, or payroll deductions the employer takes from the taxpayer's salary and regularly sends to the IRS, or by electronic transfers from the employee's bank account or other means.

An installment agreement is based on the taxpayer's financial situation. If a change in the financial situation makes it necessary to change the terms of the installment agreement, the IRS will inform the taxpayer by letter 30 days before changing the established plan. The payments on an installment agreement must be paid on time; if a payment cannot be made, the IRS should be informed immediately. The IRS can end an agreement if the taxpayer does not furnish updated financial information when the IRS requests it, or if the taxpayer fails to meet the terms of the agreement.

An agreement could end if the taxpayer misses a payment, or does not file or pay all required tax returns. In that case, the IRS can take enforced collection action. In some cases, the IRS will accept an offer in compromise. On the other hand, if taxes are not paid when they are due, the taxpayer may be subject to a failure-to-pay penalty of 5% of the unpaid taxes for each month they are not paid. But if a return was filed on time, the penalty will be reduced to 2.5% for any month beginning after 1999 in which the taxpayer has an installment agreement in effect.

***Offer in Compromise.***   In some cases, the IRS may accept an Offer in Compromise to settle an unpaid tax account, including any interest and penalties. With such an arrangement, they can accept less than the amount owed when it is doubtful that they would be able to collect all of the taxpayer's debt any time in the near future.

***Temporary Delay.***   If the IRS determines that the taxpayer cannot pay *any* of a tax debt, they may temporarily delay collection until the taxpayer's financial condition improves. If the IRS does delay collection, the debt will increase because penalties and interest are charged until the full amount is paid. During a temporary delay, the IRS will review the individual's ability to pay, and may file a *Notice of Federal Tax Lien* to protect the government's interest in the taxpayer's assets.

***A Significant Hardship.***   The IRS can consider whether a significant hardship exists for a taxpayer to pay a tax liability. It would be judged a significant hardship if the taxpayer cannot afford to maintain even the necessities to live day to day (adequate food, clothing, shelter, transportation, and medical treatment). Other cases that can be considered as significant hardship by law:

1)   An immediate threat of adverse action.
2)   Delay of more than 30 days in resolving taxpayer account problems.
3)   Incurring significant costs (including fees for professional representation) if relief is not granted.
4)   Irreparable injury to, or long-term adverse impact on, the taxpayer if relief is not granted.

A taxpayer may apply for emergency relief if facing a significant hardship. He or she should call the toll-free IRS Taxpayer Assistant number or visit the district's Taxpayer Advocate. A qualifying taxpayer will be assisted in filling out the form, *Application for Taxpayer Assistance Order*.

## EMPLOYMENT TAXES FOR EMPLOYERS

To encourage prompt payment of withheld income and employment taxes, including Social Security taxes, railroad retirement taxes, or collected excise taxes, Congress passed a law that provides for the trust fund recovery penalty. (These taxes are called *trust fund taxes* because the employer actually holds the employee's money in trust until making a federal tax deposit in that amount.)

If the IRS plans to assess an employer for the trust fund recovery penalty, they will send a letter stating that the employer is the *responsible* person. An employer has 60 days after receiving the letter to appeal the IRS proposal. If the employer does not respond to the letter, the IRS will assess the penalty and send a *Notice and Demand for Payment*. The IRS can apply this penalty even if the employer has gone out of business.

***Responsible Person.*** A responsible person is a person or group of people having the duty to perform and the power to direct the collecting, accounting, and paying of trust fund taxes. This person may be:

1) An officer or an employee of a corporation.
2) A member or employee of a partnership.
3) A corporate director or shareholder.
4) A member of a board of trustees of a nonprofit organization.
5) Another person with authority and control over funds to direct their disbursement.

***Assessing the Trust Fund Recovery Penalty.*** The IRS may assess the penalty against anyone who:

1) Is responsible for collecting or paying withheld income and employment taxes, or for paying collected excise taxes.
2) Willfully fails to collect or pay them.

For *willfulness* to exist, the responsible person must:

1) Have known about the unpaid taxes.
2) Have used the funds to keep the business going or allowed available funds to be paid to other creditors.

*Employment Taxes.* Employment taxes include the amount the employer should *withhold* from employees for both income and Social Security tax, plus the amount of Social Security tax paid on behalf of each employee.

If the employer fails to pay employment taxes on time, or if required to but did not include payment with the return, the IRS will charge interest and penalties on any unpaid balance. They may charge penalties of up to 15% of the amount not deposited, depending on how many days late the payment is.

If withheld trust fund taxes are not paid, the IRS may take additional collection action. They may require the employer to:

1) File and pay the employee's taxes monthly rather than quarterly, or
2) Open a special bank account for the withheld amounts, under penalty of prosecution.

## AWARD OF ADMINISTRATIVE COSTS

A new law expands the rules for awarding reasonable administrative costs and certain fees incurred after January 18, 1999.

*Qualified Offer Rule.* The taxpayer can receive reasonable costs and fees as a prevailing party in a civil action or proceeding when all of the following occur:

1) The taxpayer makes a qualified offer to the IRS to settle the case.
2) The IRS rejects that offer.
3) The tax liability (not including interest) later determined by the Court is not more than the the qualified offer.

The Court can consider the IRS not to be the prevailing party in a civil action or proceeding based on the fact that the IRS has lost in other courts of appeal on substantially similar issues.

*Qualified Offer.* This is a written offer made by the taxpayer during the qualified offer period. It must specify both of the following:

1) The amount of the taxpayer's liability (not including interest).
2) That it is a qualified offer when made.

It must remain open until the earliest of the following dates:

1) The date the offer is rejected.

**2)** The date the trial begins.

**3)** 90 days from the date of the offer.

The qualified offer period is the period beginning with the date that the 30-day letter is mailed by the IRS to the taxpayer and ending on the date that is 30 days before the date the case is first set for trial.

Administrative costs can be awarded for costs incurred after the earliest of the following dates:

**1)** The date of the notice of deficiency.

**2)** The date the first letter of proposed deficiency is sent that allows an opportunity to request administrative review in the IRS Office of Appeals.

**3)** The date the taxpayer receives the IRS Office of Appeals' decision

***Attorney Fees.*** The basic rate of an award for attorney fees has been raised from $110 to $125 per hour and it can be higher in certain circumstances. Those circumstances now include the difficulty level of the issues in the case and the availability of tax expertise locally. The basic rate is subject to adjustment each year.

Attorney fees now include the fees paid for the services of anyone who is authorized to practice before the Tax Court or before the IRS. In addition, attorney fees can be awarded in civil actions taken for unauthorized inspection or disclosure of the taxpayer's tax return or return information.

Fees can be awarded in excess of the actual amount charged if all of the following apply:

**1)** The fees are charged at less than the $125 basic rate.

**2)** The taxpayer is represented for no fee, or for a nominal fee, as a pro bono service.

**3)** The award is paid to the taxpayer's representative or to the representative's employer.

## EXPLANATION OF CLAIM FOR REFUND DISALLOWANCE

Beginning January 19, 1999, the IRS must explain the specific reasons that a claim for refund is disallowed or partially disallowed. This puts into law an existing practice of the IRS. Claims for refund can be disallowed based on a preliminary review or on examination by a revenue agent. This means that the taxpayer must receive one of the following:

**1)** A form explaining that the claim is disallowed for one of the following reasons:

   **a)** The claim was filed late.

   **b)** It was based solely on the unconstitutionality of the revenue acts.

   **c)** It was waived as part of a settlement.

   **d)** It covered a tax year or issues that were part of a closing agreement or an offer in compromise.

   **e)** It was related to a return closed by a final court order.

**2)** A revenue agent's report explaining the reasons that the claim is disallowed.

## TAX COURT PROCEEDINGS

*Burden of Proof.* Generally, for court proceedings resulting from examinations started after July 22, 1998, the IRS will have the burden of proving any factual issue if the taxpayer has introduced credible evidence relating to the issue. However, the taxpayer must also have done all of the following:

**1)** Complied with all substantiation requirements of the Internal Revenue Code.

**2)** Maintained all records required by the Internal Revenue Code.

**3)** Cooperated with all reasonable requests by the IRS for information regarding the preparation and related tax treatment of any item reported on a tax return.

**4)** Had a net worth of $7 million or less at the time the tax liability is contested in any court proceeding if the tax return is for a corporation, partnership, or trust.

*Use of Statistical Information.* The IRS has the burden of proof in court proceedings that are based on any reconstruction of an individual's income solely through the use of statistical information on unrelated taxpayers.

*Penalties.* The IRS has the burden of proof in court proceedings with respect to the liability of any individual taxpayer for any penalty, addition to tax, or additional amount imposed by the tax laws.

*Refund or Credit of Overpayments Before Final Decision.* Beginning July 22, 1998, any court with proper jurisdiction, including the Tax Court, can order the IRS to refund any part of a tax deficiency that the IRS collects from the taxpayer during a period when the IRS is not permitted to assess, levy, or engage in any court proceeding to collect that tax deficiency.

In addition, the court can order a refund of any part of a tax deficiency that is not at issue in a taxpayer's appeal to the court. The court can order these refunds before its decision on the case is final. Generally, the IRS is not permitted to take action on a tax deficiency during the following periods.

1)   The 90-day (or 150-day if outside of the United States) period that the taxpayer has to petition a notice of deficiency to the Tax Court.

2)   The period that the case is under appeal.

Under prior law, no authority existed for ordering the IRS to refund any amount collected during an Impermissible period, or to refund any amount that was not at issue in an appeal, before the final decision of the Tax Court.

***Small Case Procedures.***   For proceedings beginning after July 22, 1998, small tax case procedures are available for disputes that involve $50,000 or less. Under prior law, small tax case procedures were limited to disputes involving $10,000 or less. Small tax case procedures can be used, at the taxpayer's request and with the Tax Court's concurrence, for income, estate, gift, certain employment, and certain excise taxes. The proceedings are conducted as informally as possible. Neither briefs nor oral arguments are required. Most taxpayers represent themselves, although they may be represented by anyone admitted to practice before the Tax Court.

## DEPRECIATION DOLLAR CAP FOR LUXURY AUTOS

As with other inflation-adjusted figures for 1999, the IRS has announced lower *depreciation dollar caps* for "luxury" passenger automobiles placed in service during 1999 and generally lower adjusted inclusion amounts for autos first leased in 1999. Effective for autos first placed in service in 1999, the annual dollar maximum depreciation limitations for gasoline powered vehicles are:

| | |
|---|---|
| 1st year | $3,060, |
| 2nd year | $5,000, |
| 3rd year | $2,950, |
| later years | $1,775. |

The IRS also publishes separate tables to reflect the higher limits applicable to electric vehicles. The automobile lease inclusion amounts for the year is $15,500, down $300 from 1998. The lease add-backs and luxury auto caps apply uniformly throughout the entire year, starting retroactively to January 1, 1999.

## Estimated Tax Safe Harbor

For 1999, the *estimated tax safe harbor* for higher income taxpayers (other than farmers and fishermen) has been modified. If the 1998 adjusted gross income shown on that return is more than $150,000 or, if married filing separately for 1999, more than $75,000, the taxpayer will need to pay the lower of 90% of the expected tax for 1999, or 105% (up from 100%) of tax on the 1998 return (covering 12 months). Otherwise, the filer could be subject to an estimated tax penalty.

## Self-Employed Health Deduction Increased

For 1999, the self-employed health insurance deduction is increased from 45% to 60% of medical insurance expenses for the taxpayer and his or her family.

## Standard Deduction for 1999

If no deductions are itemized, the 1999 standard deduction can be taken.
Filing Status Standard Deduction:

- Married filing jointly or qualifying widow(er)     $7,200
- Head of Household                                  $6,350
- Single                                             $4,300
- Married filing separately                          $3,600

If the taxpayer can be claimed as a dependent on another person's 1999 return, his or her standard deduction is the greater of $700, or the taxpayer's earned income plus $250 up to the standard deduction amount.
An additional amount is added to the standard deduction if:

**1)**  65 or Older or Blind                $860
**2)**  65 or Older and Blind               $1,700
**3)**  Both spouses 65 or older and blind  $3,400

## Child Credit

The child credit goes up $100 in 1999 to $500 for each dependent under age 17 at the end of 1999. Income tax might be reduced as a result, for taxpayers with large families.

## DEPRECIATION

For property placed in service after December 31, if the taxpayer chooses to use the 150% declining balance rate under the General Depreciation System (GDS), the same recovery periods should be used that would have been used if the 200% declining balance rate had been chosen.

## DEPRECIATION AND ALTERNATIVE MINIMUM TAX (AMT)

For property placed in service after 1998, the same recovery period is to be used to figure depreciation for regular tax purposes to calculate any AMT adjustment.

## IRS POSTPONES 1999 STANDARD MILEAGE RATE

Late in 1998, the IRS announced that it was lowering the automobile standard mileage rate for 1999 to 31 cents per mile—the first decrease ever in the standard mileage rate—effective January 1, 1999. Early in 1999 the IRS announced that it was delaying the effective date of the change until April 1, 1999. The IRS postponed the change because of numerous complaints that taxpayers needed more time to apply the new rate to mileage calculations. The IRS had explained that it was lowering the rate because reduced oil prices and other automobile expenses caused a corresponding decline in automobile operating costs. The standard mileage rate for use of a car to obtain medical care or in connection with a job-connected move remains 10 cents per mile; the mileage rate for charitable use of a car remains at the 1998 figure of 14 cents per mile. The 1999 fixed and variable rate method that employers may use to reimburse employees for the business use of their personal cars remains at its 1998 level of $27,100.

## PER DIEM RATES

The IRS announced that the per diem rates for business travel away from home have gone up across the board for 1999. The per diem rate is increased from $180 to $185 for travel to any high-cost locality, and from $113 to $115 to any other locality within the continental United States. The federal meals and incidental expense rates under the optional high-low method likewise have increased to $42 from $40 for high-cost localities, and to $34 from $32 in other localities.

# Chapter 11
## Higher Education Incentives

There are many new tax benefits for those saving for or paying higher education costs for themselves and members of their families or who are repaying student loans. Most of these benefits first became available in 1998 as a result of measures included in The Taxpayer Relief Act of 1997. The new benefits include tax credits, individual retirement account options, and a deduction for student loan interest.

## IMPORTANT CONSIDERATIONS

Consideration was given in formulation of these incentives to providing coverage for assorted levels of higher education, to covering different types of costs in different plans, and to designating staggered income limits for different plans. Thus, as a result of the last element, the assortment of benefits provides step-ups to various limits rather than a blank wall which could effectively penalize the taxpayer for earning a few extra dollars. With such a varied assortment, there should be something for everyone. On the other hand, it may well take a knowledgeable accountant/adviser/tax preparer to guide the taxpayer, if he or she expects to take full advantage of the several provisions.

It would be premature to attempt to evaluate any "benefit" that may have resulted from the expanded list of tax incentives intended to raise the educational level in the U.S., but there can be no question that Congress and the Administration are trying their best to foster a better educated citizenry.

The discussion of tax benefits for persons who are saving for or paying higher education costs for themselves and members of their families includes the following:

1) Two education credits—the Hope credit and the lifetime learning credit.
2) Education individual retirement accounts (education IRAs).
3) Withdrawals from traditional or Roth IRAs.
4) Interest paid on certain student loans.
5) The cancellation of certain student loans.
6) Qualified state tuition programs.
7) Interest earned on certain savings bonds.
8) Employer-provided educational assistance benefits.

Two of the available tax credits that have received the most publicity (along with the education IRA) are the Hope credit and the lifetime learning credit. They have many features in common, but they also differ in a number of respects. Therefore, it is important, particularly if both appear to cover a particular individual, to figure which provides the most benefit.

## Applicable to Both Hope and Lifetime Learning Credits

The amount of each credit is determined by:

1) The amount paid for qualified tuition and related expenses for students.
2) The amount of the individual's modified adjusted gross income.

These education credits are subtracted from the individual's tax but they are nonrefundable. This means if the credits are more than the tax, the excess is not refunded. (Married taxpayers filing separate returns cannot claim the higher education credits.)

### Qualified Expenses

The tax credits are based on qualified tuition and related expenses the taxpayer pays for himself or herself, a spouse, or a dependent claimed on the tax return. In general, qualified tuition and related expenses are tuition and fees required for enrollment or attendance at an eligible educational institution. Fees for course-related books, supplies and equipment, and student activity fees are included in qualified tuition and related expenses *only if the fees must be paid to the institution* as a condition of enrollment or attendance.

Qualified tuition and related expenses *do not include* the cost of insurance, medical expenses (including student health fees), room and board, transportation or similar personal, living or family expenses, even if the fee must be paid to the institution as a condition of enrollment or attendance.

## Prepaid Expenses

When qualified tuition and related expenses for an academic period that begins in the first three months of the following year are prepaid, the taxpayer can use the prepaid amount in figuring the credit.

## The Dependent

A dependent is a person for whom a dependency exemption is claimed. This generally includes an unmarried child who is under age 19 or who is a full-time student under age 24 if the taxpayer supplies more than half the child's support for the year.

## Eligible Educational Institution

An eligible educational institution is any accredited college, university, vocational school, or other accredited postsecondary educational institution eligible to participate in a student aid program administered by the Department of Education. It includes virtually all accredited, public, nonprofit, and proprietary (privately owned profit making) postsecondary institutions. The school should be able to inform the taxpayer if it is an "eligible educational institution."

## Academic Period

An academic period includes a semester, trimester, quarter, or any other period designated by the educational institution as a period of instructional time. For purposes of the education credits an academic period begins on the first day of classes and does not include periods of student orientation, counseling, or vacation.

## Special Situations

1) If a deduction for higher education expenses is claimed on a tax return, a credit cannot be claimed for those same expenses.

**2)** If higher education expenses are paid with certain tax-free funds, a credit cannot be claimed for those amounts. Tax-free funds could include:

  **a)** Scholarships.

  **b)** Pell grants.

  **c)** Employer-provided educational assistance.

  **d)** Veterans' educational assistance.

  **e)** Any other nontaxable payments (other than gifts, bequests, or inheritances) received for educational expenses.

**3)** A credit can be claimed for expenses paid with the student's earnings, loans, gifts, inheritances, and personal savings.

**4)** If a student receives a tax-free withdrawal from an education IRA in a particular tax year, none of that student's expenses can be used as the basis of a higher education credit for that tax year. However, the student can waive the tax-free treatment.

**5)** If, in a later tax year, the taxpayer receives a refund of an expense used to figure a higher education credit, all or part of the credit may have to be refunded.

## HOPE CREDIT

For expenses paid after December 31, 1997, for academic periods beginning after that date, the taxpayer may be able to claim a Hope credit of up to $1,500 for the qualified tuition and related expenses paid for *each* eligible student. This credit may be claimed for only two taxable years for each eligible student.

### Eligible Student for Hope Credit

A Hope credit may be claimed only for an eligible student who meets all of the following requirements:

**1)** Has not completed the first two years of postsecondary education (generally, the freshman or sophomore years of college).

**2)** Is enrolled in a program that leads to a degree, certificate, or other recognized educational credential.

**3)** Is taking at least one-half of the normal full-time work load for his or her course of study for at least one academic period beginning during the calendar year.

**4)** Is free of any felony conviction for possessing or distributing a controlled substance.

## Amount of Credit

The amount of the Hope credit is 100% of the first $1,000 plus 50% of the next $1,000 paid for each eligible student's qualified tuition and related expenses. The maximum amount of Hope credit that could be claimed in 1998 was $1,500 times the number of eligible students. In other words, the taxpayer can claim the full $1,500 for each eligible student for whom at least $2,000 was paid for qualified expenses.

However, the credit could be reduced based on the individual's modified adjusted gross income.

## LIFETIME LEARNING CREDIT

For expenses paid after June 30, 1998, for academic periods beginning after that date, the taxpayer may be able to claim a lifetime learning credit of up to $1,000 for the total qualified tuition and related expenses paid during the tax year for all students who were enrolled in eligible educational institutions. Unlike the Hope credit:

1)   The lifetime learning credit is not based on the student's work load. It is allowed for one or more courses.
2)   The lifetime learning credit is not limited to students in the first two years of postsecondary education.
3)   Expenses for graduate-level degree work are eligible.
4)   There is no limit on the number of years for which the lifetime learning credit can be claimed for each student.
5)   The amount that can be claimed as a lifetime learning credit does not vary (increase) based on the number of students for whom qualified expenses are paid.

## Amount of Credit

The amount of the lifetime learning credit is 20% of the first $5,000 paid for qualified tuition and related expenses for all students in the family. The maximum amount of lifetime learning credit that could be claimed for 1998 was $1,000 (20% times $5,000). However, that amount could be reduced based on an individual's modified adjusted gross income.

## POINTS TO CONSIDER IN CHOOSING WHICH CREDIT TO CLAIM

The following points should be considered when deciding which credit to claim:

**1)** For each student, the taxpayer can elect for any tax year only one of the credits or a tax-free withdrawal from an education IRA. For example, if he or she elects to take the Hope credit for a child on a tax return, the taxpayer cannot, for that same child, also claim the lifetime learning credit or take a tax-free withdrawal from an education IRA for the same year.

**2)** It is permissible to take the Hope credit for the first two years of a child's postsecondary education and claim the lifetime learning credit for that same child in later tax years.

**3)** If qualified expenses are paid for more than one student in the same year, it is possible to choose to take credits on a per-student, per-year basis. This means that the Hope credit could be claimed for one child and the lifetime learning credit for another child in the same tax year.

**4)** It should be fairly obvious that in any one tax year, only one person can claim a higher education credit for a student's expenses. If the taxpayer is paying higher education costs for a dependent child, one or the other, but not both, can claim a credit for a particular year.

**5)** If the taxpayer claims an exemption for a child on his or her tax return, the taxpayer should treat any expenses paid by the child as if the taxpayer had paid them. These expenses should be included when figuring the amount of the Hope or lifetime learning credit.

## INCOME PHASEOUT

Education credits are phased out (gradually reduced) if the individual's modified adjusted gross income is between $40,000 and $50,000 ($80,000 and $100,000 in the case of a joint return). No higher education credits can be claimed if modified adjusted gross income is over $50,000 ($100,000 in the case of a joint return).

For most taxpayers, modified adjusted gross income will be their adjusted gross income (AGI) as figured on their federal income tax return. However, each individual must make adjustments to AGI if they excluded income earned abroad or from certain U.S. territories or possessions or took a foreign housing deduction. When this applies, the individual should increase the AGI by the following amounts excluded or deducted from income:

**1)** Foreign earned income of U.S. citizens or residents living abroad.

**2)** Housing costs of U.S. citizens or residents living abroad.

**3)** Income from sources within Puerto Rico, Guam, American Samoa, or the Northern Mariana Islands.

The phaseout (reduction) works on a sliding scale. The higher the modified adjusted gross income, the more the credits are reduced.

## Claiming the Credits

Education credits are claimed by completing Form 8863 and attaching it to the income tax return. An eligible educational institution (the college or university) that receives payment of qualified tuition and related expenses should issue Form 1098-T, Tuition Payments Statement, to each student. The information on Form 1098-T will help to determine whether an education tax credit can be claimed for any particular year.

## EDUCATION INDIVIDUAL RETIREMENT ACCOUNT

The education IRA or ED IRA is another new savings device to be used in paying the qualified higher education expenses of a designated beneficiary under the age of 18. Those expenses include tuition, fees, books, supplies and equipment, as well as room and board if the designated beneficiary is at least a half-time student at an eligible educational institution.

Contributions to these IRAs are nondeductible, and earnings on the amount held in them will be nontaxable until distributed. Annual contributions by any individual, including the child, are limited to $500 per beneficiary. There is no limit on the *number* of education IRAs established for the same child; however, total contributions for a tax year may not exceed the $500 limit. Any individual may contribute to a child's education IRA if the individual's modified AGI is less than $110,000 or $160,000 for joint filers.

## Excess Withdrawals

Distributions from an education IRA are excludable from income to the extent the amount *does not exceed* the qualified higher education expenses of the eligible student during the year of distribution. If the distribution is in excess of the qualified higher education expenses, only a portion of the distribution may be excluded. In addition, distributions not used for higher education are subject to a 10% penalty. The Act requires any balance remaining in an education IRA at the time a beneficiary becomes 30 years of age to be distributed and taxed as income to the beneficiary (and subject to the 10% penalty). However, the balance may be rolled over tax free to another education IRA benefiting another under-age-30 family member.

## Requirements

But what *is* this education IRA? And how does one go about setting one up? It is a trust or custodial account designated as an education IRA and created for the express purpose of paying the qualified higher education expenses of the beneficiary. The document creating and governing the trust must be in writing and abide by the following requirements:

1) It must be created or organized in the U.S.
2) The trustee must be a bank, credit union, or other entity approved by the IRS.
3) The trust must provide that the trustee can accept only cash contributions made before the beneficiary reaches age 18 that would not exceed $500 in the tax year (not including rollover contributions).
4) Money in the account may not be invested in life insurance contracts.
5) Money in the account may not be combined with other property except in a common trust fund or common investment fund.
6) The balance in the account generally must be withdrawn within 30 days after the earlier of the following events.
   a) The beneficiary reaches age 30.
   b) The beneficiary's death.

## Qualified Expenses

These are expenses required for the enrollment or attendance of the designated beneficiary at an eligible educational institution. Included are the following items:

1) Tuition and fees.
2) Books, supplies, and equipment.
3) Amounts contributed to a qualified state tuition program. (See below.)
4) Room and board if the designated beneficiary is at least a half-time student at an eligible educational institution. (A student is enrolled "at least half time" if he or she is enrolled for at least half the full-time academic work load for the course of study the student is pursuing as determined under the standards of the school where the student is enrolled.) The expense for room and board is limited to one of the following two amounts.
   a) The school's posted room and board charge for students living on campus.
   b) $2,500 each year for students living off campus and not at home.

## Excess Contributions

A 6% excise tax applies each year to excess contributions made to an education IRA. They include the following amounts:

1) Contributions that are more than the contribution limit.

2) Contributions to the account if any amount is also contributed to a qualified state tuition program on behalf of the same child in the same tax year. The excise tax will not apply, however, if funds were withdrawn from the education IRA to be contributed to the qualified state tuition program.

3) Excess contributions for the preceding year reduced by the total of:

    a) Withdrawals (other than rollovers) made during the year, and

    b) The contribution limit for the current year minus the amount contributed for the current year.

However, the excise tax does not apply if the excess contributions (and any earnings on them) are withdrawn before the due date of the beneficiary's tax return (including extensions). If the beneficiary does not have to file a return, the tax does not apply if the excess contributions (and the earnings) are withdrawn by April 15 of the year following the year the contributions are made. The withdrawn earnings must be included in the beneficiary's income for the year in which the excess contribution is made.

The excise tax also does not apply to any rollover contribution.

## Rollovers and Other Transfers

Assets can be rolled over from one education IRA to another, the designated beneficiary can be changed, or the beneficiary's interest can be transferred to a spouse or former spouse because of divorce.

***Rollovers.*** Any amount withdrawn from an education IRA and rolled over to another education IRA for the benefit of the same beneficiary or certain members of the beneficiary's family is not taxable. A rollover to an education IRA of a family member is not taxable only if that family member is under age 30. An amount is rolled over if it is paid to another education IRA within 60 days after the date of the withdrawal. Only one rollover for an education IRA is permitted during a twelve-month period ending on the date of the payment or withdrawal.

The beneficiary's spouse and the following individuals (and their spouses) are members of the beneficiary's family:

- The beneficiary's child, grandchild, or stepchild.
- A brother, sister, half-brother, half-sister, stepbrother, or stepsister of the beneficiary.
- The father, mother, grandfather, grandmother, stepfather, or stepmother of the beneficiary.

- A brother or sister of the beneficiary's father or mother.
- A son or daughter of the beneficiary's brother or sister.
- The beneficiary's son-in-law, daughter-in-law, father-in-law, mother-in-law, brother-in-law, or sister-in-law.

## WITHDRAWALS FROM TRADITIONAL OR ROTH IRAS

Withdrawals may be made from a traditional or Roth IRA for qualified higher education expenses. (A traditional IRA is an IRA that is not a Roth IRA, SIMPLE IRA, or education IRA.) Income tax must be paid on at least part of the amount withdrawn, but the 10% additional tax on early withdrawals will not apply.

### Tax Liability of Withdrawals

Part (or all) of any withdrawal may not be subject to the 10% additional tax on early withdrawals. The part *not* subject to the tax is generally the amount that is not more than the qualified higher education expenses at an eligible educational institution. The education must be for the taxpayer, spouse, children, or grandchildren of the taxpayer or spouse.

When determining the amount of the withdrawal that is not subject to the 10% additional tax, the qualified higher education expenses paid with any of the following may be included:

1) An individual's earnings.
2) A loan.
3) A gift.
4) An inheritance given either to the student or the individual making the withdrawal.
5) Personal savings (including savings from a qualified state tuition program).

Expenses paid with any of the following funds may not be included:

1) Tax-free withdrawals from an education IRA.
2) Tax-free scholarships, such as a Pell grant.
3) Tax-free employer-provided educational assistance.
4) Any tax-free payment (other than a gift, bequest, or devise) due to enrollment at an eligible educational institution.

## Qualified Expenses

Qualified higher education expenses are tuition, fees, books, supplies, and equipment required for the enrollment or attendance of a student at an eligible educational institution. In addition, if the individual is at least a half-time student, room and board are qualified higher education expenses.

## QUALIFIED EDUCATION STUDENT LOAN DEDUCTIONS

An above-the-line maximum deduction for up to $2,500 of interest paid by taxpayers on qualified education loans is provided in the 1997 legislation. The $2,500 limit is phased in (i.e., $1,500 in 1999, $2,000 in 2000, and $2,500 in 2001).

Interest deductions are allowed only for the first 60 months that interest payments are required. The deduction is phased out for taxpayers with modified AGI between $40,000 and $55,000, or $60,000 and $75,000 for joint filers.

This deduction is an adjustment to income; therefore, it can be claimed even though the taxpayer does not itemize deductions. Married taxpayers must file jointly to take the deduction. Furthermore, the credit may not be claimed on the tax return of anyone who is claimed as a dependent by another person.

## Qualifying Loan

This is a loan taken out solely to pay qualified higher education expenses. The expenses must have been:

1) For the taxpayer, spouse, or a person who was a dependent when the indebtedness was incurred.
2) Paid or incurred within a reasonable time before or after the loan was taken out.
3) For education furnished during a period when the recipient of the education was an eligible student.

## Qualified Expenses

These expenses are the costs of attending an eligible educational institution, including graduate school. Generally, these costs include tuition, fees, room and board, books, equipment, and other necessary expenses, such as transportation. But these costs must be reduced by the following items:

1) Nontaxable employer-provided educational assistance benefits.
2) Nontaxable withdrawals from an education IRA.
3) U.S. savings bond interest that is nontaxable because qualified higher education expenses have been paid.
4) Qualified scholarships that are nontaxable.
5) Veterans' educational assistance benefits.
6) Any other nontaxable payments (other than gifts, bequests, or inheritances) received for educational expenses.

In addition to the definition of "eligible educational institution" given earlier, for purposes of the student loan interest deduction, the term also includes an institution conducting an internship or residency program leading to a degree or certificate from an institution of higher education, a hospital, or a health care facility that offers postgraduate training.

## Eligible Student

An eligible student is one who:

1) Is enrolled in a degree, certificate, or other program (including a program of study abroad that is approved for credit by the institution at which the student is enrolled) leading to a recognized educational credential at an eligible educational institution, and
2) Is carrying at least one-half the normal full-time workload for the course of study the student is pursuing.

## Related Person Loan

Interest cannot be deducted on a loan obtained from a related person. Related persons include brothers and sisters, half-brothers and half-sisters, spouse, ancestors (parents, grandparents, etc.), and lineal descendants (children, grandchildren, etc.). Related persons also include certain corporations, partnerships, trusts, and exempt organizations.

## Refinanced Loan

If a qualified student loan is refinanced, the new loan can also be a qualified student loan, but refinancing a loan does not extend the 60-month period described earlier. The 60-month period is based on the original loan.

## CANCELLATION OF DEBT ON STUDENT LOANS

Certain student loans contain a provision that all or part of the debt incurred to attend the qualified educational institution will be canceled if the recipient works for a certain period of time in certain professions for any of a broad class of employers. If the conditions were met and the loan was canceled, the canceled debt does not have to be included in income. The loan must be made by one of the following:

1) A governmental unit—federal, state, or local, or an instrumentality, agency, or subdivision thereof.

2) A tax-exempt public benefit corporation that has assumed control of a state, county, or municipal hospital, and whose employees are considered public employees under state law.

3) An educational institution if the loan is made:

   a) Under an agreement with an entity described in one of the categories above that provided the funds to the educational institution to make the loan.

   b) Under a program of the educational institution as part of its program designed to encourage students to serve in occupations or areas with unmet needs, and the services provided are for or under the direction of a governmental unit or a qualifying Section 501 (c)(3) tax-exempt organization. These include any corporation, community chest, fund or foundation organized and operated exclusively for one or more of the following purposes:

   • charitable

   • religious

   • educational

   • scientific

   • literary

   • testing for public safety

   • fostering national or international amateur sports competition (but only if none of its activities involve providing athletic facilities or equipment)

   • prevention of cruelty to children or animals.

A loan will also qualify if it was made by an educational institution, or a tax-exempt organization to refinance a student loan that meets these requirements. This is true if the new loan is made:

1) To assist the student in attending the educational institution, and

**2)** Under a program of the new lender that meets the conditions of (3)(b) above.

## STATE TUITION PROGRAM

Certain states and agencies maintain programs that allow people to purchase credits or certificates or make contributions to an account to pay for future education. Contributions to a qualified state tuition program are not deductible, and withdrawals are taxable only to the extent they are more than the amount contributed to the program. (See "Excess Withdrawals" under "Education IRA.") A qualified state tuition program is one that is established and maintained by a state or agency and that:

**1)** Allows a person to:
   **a)** Buy tuition credits or certificates for a designated beneficiary who would then be entitled to a waiver or payment of qualified higher educational expenses, or
   **b)** Make contributions to an account that is set up to meet the qualified higher educational expenses of a designated beneficiary of the account.
**2)** Requires all purchases or contributions to be made only in cash,
**3)** Prohibits the contributor and the beneficiary from directing the amount invested,
**4)** Allows a rollover or a change of beneficiary to be made only between members of the same family (defined earlier in "Rollovers" under "Education IRA"), and
**5)** Imposes a penalty on any refund of earnings that does not meet at least one of the following conditions:
   **a)** The amount is used for qualified higher educational expenses of the beneficiary.
   **b)** The refund is made because of the death or disability of the beneficiary.
   **c)** The refund is made because the beneficiary received (and the refund is not more than) a scholarship, a veterans' educational assistance allowance, or another nontaxable payment (other than a gift, bequest, or inheritance) for educational expenses.

For more information on a specific state tuition program, the taxpayer should contact the state or agency that established and maintains it.

## The Education Savings Bond Program

This program makes it possible to exclude from income all or part of the interest received on the redemption of qualified U.S. savings bonds during the year if the taxpayer pays qualified higher educational expenses during that same year. If married, the taxpayer can exclude the interest from income only if a joint return is filed with the spouse.

A qualified U.S. savings bond is a Series EE U.S. savings bond issued *after* 1989, or a Series I bond. The bond must be issued either in the sole owner's name or in the owner and his or her spouse's names as co-owners. The taxpayer must be at least 24 years old before the bond's issue date. The date a bond is issued can be earlier than the date the bond is purchased, because bonds are issued as of the first day of the month in which they are purchased. Any individual, including a child, can be designated a beneficiary of the bond payable on death.

### Excludable Amounts

If the total proceeds (interest and principal) from the qualified U.S. savings bonds redeemed during the year are not more than the qualified higher educational expenses for the year, all of the interest can be excluded. If the proceeds are more than the expenses, part of the interest can be excluded.

The interest exclusion is phased out if the modified adjusted gross income is:

1) $52,250 to $67,250 for taxpayers filing singly or as head of household.
2) $78,350 to $108,350 for married taxpayers filing jointly.

(The individual does not qualify for the interest exclusion if the modified adjusted gross income is equal to or more than the upper limit.)

Modified adjusted gross income for purposes of this exclusion is AGI figured on the individual's federal income tax return and modified by adding back any of the following amounts that may have been deducted or excluded from income:

1) Foreign-earned income of U.S. citizens or residents living abroad.
2) Foreign housing costs exclusion or deduction.
3) Income from sources within Puerto Rico, American Samoa, Guam, or the Northern Mariana Islands.
4) U.S. savings bond interest that is nontaxable because qualified higher education expenses were paid.
5) Adoption benefits received under an employer's adoption benefits assistance program.
6) Student loan interest.

If an interest exclusion is claimed, a written record must be kept of the Series EE U.S. savings bonds issued after 1989 that are redeemed. The written record must include the serial number, issue date, face value, and redemption proceeds of each bond. Any bills, receipts, canceled checks or other documentation must be kept that show qualified higher educational expenses were paid during the year.

## Qualified Expenses

Qualified higher education expenses include the following items paid for the taxpayer, his or her spouse, or a dependent for whom they claim an exemption.

1) Tuition and fees required to enroll at or attend an eligible educational institution (defined earlier). Qualified expenses do not include expenses for room and board or for courses involving sports, games, or hobbies that are not part of a degree program.
2) Contributions to a qualified state tuition program.
3) Contributions to an education IRA.

## Reduced Expenses

Educational expenses are reduced by the amount of any of the following benefits the student received:

1) Tax-free scholarships.
2) Tax-free withdrawals from an education IRA.
3) Any nontaxable payments (other than gifts, bequests, or inheritances) received for educational expenses or for attending an eligible educational institution. Such benefits include:
   a) Veterans' educational assistance benefits.
   b) Benefits under a qualified state tuition program.
   c) Tax-free employer-provided educational assistance.
4) Any expenses used in figuring the Hope and lifetime learning credits.

### EMPLOYER-PROVIDED EDUCATIONAL ASSISTANCE

Educational assistance benefits received from an employer under an educational assistance program are tax-free, up to $5,250 each year. This means the employer should not include the benefits with wages, tips, and other compensation.

An employee must reduce deductible educational expenses by the amount of any tax-free educational assistance benefits received for those expenses.

To qualify as an educational assistance program, the plan must be written and meet certain other requirements. The employer can inform an employee whether or not there is a qualified program in effect.

## Assistance Coverage

Tax-free educational assistance benefits include payments by the employer for tuition, fees and similar expenses, books, supplies, and equipment. The payments must be for undergraduate-level courses that begin before June 1, 2000. The payments do not have to be for work-related courses.

Educational assistance benefits do not include payments for the following items.

1)  Meals, lodging, transportation, or tools or supplies (other than text-books) that the student can keep after completing the course of instruction.

2)  Education involving sports, games, or hobbies unless the education has a reasonable relationship to the business of the employer, or is required as part of a degree program.

3)  Graduate-level courses that began after June 30, 1996, and are normally taken under a program leading to a law, business, medical, or other advanced academic or professional degree.

## Benefit Over $5,250

If the employer provides more than $5,250 of educational assistance benefits during the year, the amount over $5,250 is generally taxable. The employer should include the taxable amount in wages.

However, if the payments also qualify as a working condition fringe benefit, the employer can exclude all of the payments from wages. A working condition fringe benefit is a benefit which, had the employee paid for it, could be deducted as an employee business expense.

## Expenses Paid with Benefits

If the taxpayer received tax-free benefits under an employer's qualified educational assistance program, he or she cannot take a deduction for qualified educational expenses.

# Chapter 12

## Growing Niche for Accountants: Expert Witness

With the plethora of high profile legal cases which have inundated the news in the last few years, we've all become trial experts. After being briefed on a variety of cases, we're aware of all the legal terms—and ramifications.

But of a less spectacular nature has been the steady increase of experts in more dignified, straightforward, less publicized cases; in fact, to the lay person, these are often downright boring. However, to the accountant who has found his niche as an "expert witness," they are not only fascinating, but can be quite remunerative. (After all, it was accounting that finally put Al Capone behind bars.) Many accountants are discovering they can increase business, gain public awareness, and enjoy using their special knowledge and experience as expert witnesses. Their financial knowledge and ability to follow a paper trail of figures gives them importance as investigators as well as witnesses in complicated court cases involving financial dealings. There can also be pitfalls along the way.

The need for the accountant as an "expert witness" has increased proportionately with the growing complexity of business affairs. For a number of years, the courts had permitted a rather liberal use of experts in trials; however, the days of relative immunity from prosecution of the expert witness seem to have ended as litigation threatened to become a national pastime. Obviously, the more lawsuits, the more losers. And the loser has to take it out on someone. (That loser may be the opposing party—or it could be the accountant's client.) Why not go after that expert who caused all the trouble? And his firm, too!

## Engagement Letter

Therein lies the raison d'être of a well thought-out, carefully constructed engagement agreement containing buffers against both parties. This agreement needs, at the minimum, to spell out carefully:

1) What the accountant has agreed to do.
2) What information the client *must* make available to the expert witness to enable him or her to investigate the evidence and reach an opinion.
3) Lines of effective communication with both the client(s) and the attorney(s).
4) What the client can expect if the accountant is *required* to reveal on the stand any and all information on which his opinion is based.
5) That the attorney *must* keep the accountant informed in a timely fashion of any and all legal requirements such as filing times, submission of written documents, when any graphic presentations are due, and the like.

The corollary of this is, of course, that the accountant needs to guarantee to do or not do several things of concern to the client and/or attorney. If the accountant feels that he may not "fit the bill" as an expert witness in a case, he must not accept the engagement. The accountant must:

1) Possess the necessary qualifications and background.
2) Be cognizant of the accounting profession's technical and ethical standards applicable to litigation services, specifically those applying to expert witnesses.
3) Schedule adequate time and opportunity to investigate the case thoroughly.
4) Be prepared to furnish testimony in a forceful, confident manner.
5) Be prepared to defend a position "properly taken" in a polite, matter-of-fact manner in cross-examination.
6) Keep foremost in mind that the objective is to aid the client and attorney in winning the case, but *not* at the cost of the accountant's integrity.
7) Remember that the expert witness is *not* a client advocate, but an advocate of the accountant's own opinion and point of view.
8) Be positive that there can be no taint of conflict of interest that could be detrimental to the case.
9) Steer away from any engagement where there could be a possibility of divulging privileged information.

**10)**   Withdraw as expeditiously as possible if there are any doubts about the litigation in question.

**11)**   Adhere to the strategy of the lawyer, but here again, *not* at the expense of the accountant's integrity.

## PREP TIME

Preparing for the first trial may be the most difficult part of joining the growing number of accountants entering the expert witness niche. This is the time when the accountant, if he's been lucky or hasn't served on a jury, really becomes familiar with the down-to-earth (non-Night Court or Rumpole) aspect of the judicial system.

There's nothing like familiarity in developing confidence and ease of presentation; therefore, preparation should include:

**1)**   Becoming familiar with the general rules governing real-life courtroom procedure in the locale where the testimony will be given.

**2)**   A visit to a court, preferably one where there is a trial being held involving an accountant expert witness. In metropolitan areas, this should be relatively easy.

**3)**   When apprised of the specific court assignment of the case, the accountant should visit the particular judge's courtroom to observe his attitude and demeanor.

**4)**   Role playing. This activity is recommended for all sorts of therapy, where it may or may not work, but it definitely works in a situation like this. (The attorneys had to play out their role for moot court in law school. Why not the accountant turning expert witness?) Partners, staff and/or family members make great critics—as well as actors in this courtroom drama. Even a full-length mirror can ask questions and talk back.

## DEFINITION OF AN EXPERT WITNESS

The courts uniformly agree that the accountant possesses the qualifications of an expert witness on any subject matter falling within the scope of his experience, training, and education.

There are perhaps as many definitions of an "expert witness" as there are statutes, judges, and writers concerned with testimony. The following definition of an expert witness is designed to cover all aspect of "expert" definitions (without any whereases or wherefores): *A witness is an expert witness and is qualified to give expert testimony if the judge finds that to perceive, know, or understand the matter concerning which the witness is to testify requires special knowledge, skill, experience, training, and/or education, and that the witness has the requisite special knowledge, skill, experience, training, and/or education deemed necessary and appropriate.*

If the opposing party offers any objection to the use of an expert's testimony, the accountant's special knowledge, skill, experience, training, or education must be shown before the witness may testify as an expert. Regardless, this information should be made known to the court. A witness's special knowledge, skill, training, or education may be shown by his own testimony, but it will probably "set" better with the jury if the lawyer elicits the pertinent information from the witness relating to his or her education, experience, and specialized knowledge.

Since the basic requirement of an expert witness is that the witness possess the ability to interpret, analyze, and evaluate the significant facts on a question concerning which just a judge or a judge and jury need assistance to resolve, it is imperative that they be aware of the accountant's background. This expertise must be demonstrated in a positive but unassuming manner to be effective. No one likes a braggart.

The courts have uniformly accepted the accountant as an expert. In the majority of cases, the primary and most significant criteria in guidance of a trial court's determination of qualifications of an expert witness are based on occupational experience. Equally significant is the judicial recognition of the special knowledge acquired by an accountant relating to a particular industry, trade, occupation, or profession to qualify her as an expert on particular business and trade practices and on other factors relating to costs and gross profit margins.

In actual practice, it is rare that the trial court will refuse to permit the witness to testify as an expert because he is insufficiently qualified. Rather, any weakness or deficiency will show up in the quality and impact of the testimony rather than its admissibility.

Therefore, it is imperative that an accountant be very cautious about accepting an assignment that may be beyond his or her area of expertise.

## FUNCTION OF THE EXPERT WITNESS

The function of the expert witness is to form an opinion or inference on matters when individuals in the normal course of affairs would probably not be able to do so. Therefore, an expert witness is needed in any case where by reason of his special knowledge, the expert is able to form a valid opinion on the facts while the man on the street would—or should—not.

Courts vary in their conception of when the expert is needed. Some courts maintain that expert testimony is admissible only when the subject matter is beyond the common experience of the ordinary juror who would then be unable to reach an informed opinion or draw a valid inference from the facts. In effect, they apply a "strict" test of necessity. More often, the determination is made on the basis of whether this testimony would be of "assistance" to the judge or jury.

## Basis of Investigation

In his investigation preparatory to giving testimony, an expert may rely upon various sources. He may:

1) Rely on known facts if such facts are material to the inquiry.
2) Obtain information gained from a demonstrably reliable source.
   This could include previous audit reports, certified financial statements, books and records of the business—even though they were not kept by the expert witness—or demonstrable customs and practices within the business or industry of the client for whom the expert is testifying.
3) If the expert has firsthand knowledge of the situation, inferences or opinions may be stated directly. However, care should be taken to be absolutely sure that the practitioner states fully the facts relied upon, the reliable source, and the permissibility of the basis upon which an opinion was founded. Otherwise, the testimony will do more harm than good. If a judge and/or jury become aware of even one instance in which the accountant has slipped up, his expertise will henceforth be open to question.

In addition, the expert witness must have a thorough knowledge of the substantive issue in the case. The investigation and subsequent conclusion may be incomplete and unrelated to the issue if he either has not been informed properly of the particulars in a case, or has not done his homework thoroughly. It is also necessary that he know the issues of the case so that he can anticipate and respond promptly and forcefully to cross-examination and avoid answers that are incomplete, confusing, and irrelevant. In other words, the expert must be made privy to all relevant facts in the case as well as to the direction of the lawyer's attack or counterattack.

The "need to know" policy should not be carried so far that the accountant appears "in the dark" or at best ill-informed. Therefore, it is important for the accountant to ascertain whether the attorney is willing to work closely with the "expert witness." If the accountant finds it impossible to work in good faith with a particular attorney or law firm, he should withdraw from the case, if possible, or at least refuse to work with that individual or firm in the future. Failure to be aware of or to consider all of the facts not only diminishes the value of the expert's testimony to the case but quite often leaves the expert vulnerable to attack on cross-examination. Not only can the accountant become surprised and confused by the additional facts, but the image as an expert will be damaged in the minds of the judge and jury. The individual's credibility and reputation could be severely damaged.

## Exhibits

It is almost mandatory that the expert witness prepare, or have prepared, some type of exhibit for several obvious reasons, not the least of which is the fact that very few individuals can make any sense of numbers from just *hearing* them. Oversize charts, graphs, schedules, diagrams—whatever aids the court in visualizing the accountant's findings—can be useful in focusing their attention. Visual aids not only help the expert witness explain his conclusions but they can have a greater impact on the judge and jury. *If* these graphics can be presented in an interesting, imaginative way, they might also tend to lessen the tedium of often very dry facts and figures.

This "demonstrative evidence" (in the parlance of the court) must not appear to be a way of "lecturing" to the judge and jury. At the same time, these are not people preparing for the CPA exam. The visual materials must present readily understood, clearly identifiable steps the accountant took in arriving at opinions and conclusions—not just a jumble of numbers.

It may be appropriate to provide copies of the material to the judge and the members of the jury so that they can use both eyes and ears to follow the testimony of the expert. Even then, it is probably better to have too little information on a graph or schedule than too much.

## Understandable Testimony

Expert testimony is valuable only when it is understood by the judge and jury. The expert must be able to explain and defend her opinion in language reasonably understood by the layman. Everyone complains about "legalese." What about "accountantese"? It should always be kept in mind that the very reason the expert is testifying is that the subject matter is beyond the common knowledge and experience of the average juror.

A common error committed by the accounting expert is to use technical language in testimony without offering an explanation of its meaning.

Terms like *earnings per share, stockholder's equity,* and *retained earnings* may have a nice ring to them. However, if the testimony must necessarily involve technical accounting terms and concepts of this caliber, they must be defined and explained in a clear and simple manner.

## CROSS-EXAMINATION

An accountant testifying as an expert may be cross-examined to the same extent as any other witness.

Therefore, the expert should assume that his opinion will be rigorously challenged on cross-examination. The fact that the subject matter is being litigated indicates conflicting theories or facts upon which an opinion may be based. In order to preserve the value and effectiveness of testimony given as an expert, the witness should anticipate what may be brought up in cross-examination. Thorough preparation, awareness of other aspects of a case, anticipation of where the "attack" may come will all aid in the individual's holding up well in this phase of a court appearance. Now is the time when the opposing counsel will attempt to discredit the expert witness concerning qualifications, knowledge of the subject matter, the validity of the source of relevant information, and the basis for arriving at the stated opinion and conclusions.

It is important for the accountant to remember that this is the lawyer's job. Since the purpose of cross-examination is to diminish or destroy the expert's conclusions, the lawyer may be argumentative, supercilious, and aggressive in an attempt to catch the witness off balance—to make the expert react too quickly and speak before thinking. Instead, this is the time when remaining courteous, unemotional, and firmly convinced of the correctness of previous statements pays off.

One of the techniques used in cross-examination is to show a contradiction or omission of facts upon which the expert founded an opinion. For this reason, it is essential that the expert make a thorough investigation, have knowledge of all relevant theories and material facts, and be prepared to support that opinion rationally on cross-examination. If the expert has adequately prepared, she can reasonably anticipate any weak or questionable aspects of the testimony and be ready to cope with them quickly and spontaneously on cross-examination.

## REBUTTAL

Rebuttal testimony provides the opposing party with an opportunity to introduce evidence that refutes the prior evidence of the other side in the case. The opposing side may decide to offer in rebuttal its own expert to directly refute the testimony of the original expert. Rebuttal testimony may not go beyond the scope of the original evidence. In other words, a party may not introduce new evidence but is limited to a direct rebuttal of prior evidence. However, there is still plenty of opportunity for accounting expert witness No. 2 to question the validity of the original expert's assumptions, opinions, and conclusions concerning alternative ways of looking at a situation.

If the original expert has considered and discussed the cause for litigation from every possible angle, the impact of a rebuttal expert witness who attempts to base opinion on opposing theories and facts has basically been forestalled, because that ground has already been covered, and discarded.

## LEGAL MATTERS

What are these weighty matters which the expert witness is going to investigate, form opinions concerning, testify to, be cross-examined about or offer rebuttal to? As might be expected, there may even be a "mini-niche" within this niche where the accountant could decide to specialize. Among the more likely spots are:

1) Tax cases-civil, criminal, fraud—both state and federal. It is difficult to imagine a tax case that does not involve accounting problems. Attorneys for both the government and the taxpayer can be expected to have a general knowledge of accounting principles, but they have other responsibilities in the case. Enter the practitioner investigator and witness to refute the charge of "willful attempt to evade taxes," or just an assertion of deficiency in tax payments.

2) Divorce cases. In states with community property laws, this can become extremely involved in tracing and determining which funds are community property, separate property, proceeds from separate property, commingled funds, and separate funds of various descriptions.

3) Probate proceedings. Wills, state inheritance taxes, and federal estate taxes in states with community property laws also often need testimony from investigative accountants. In fact, the distinction between separate and community property is often crucial in figuring the amount of state inheritance and federal estate taxes owed.

4) Partnership dissolution and/or valuation of partnership interest. The accountant is frequently employed as an expert to prepare a partnership accounting of a dissolved partnership. Following is a sampling of the items that will come to the attention of the accountant in preparing her report for submission to the court:

a) Contractual agreements among the partners expressly providing for a partnership accounting for capital or profits.

b) Capital contributions reflected in the partnership agreement, additional loans, and restrictions or limitations on the right of a partner to withdraw the profits or capital.

c) Present fair market value (FMV) of property previously contributed by a partner.

d) Allocation of profits and losses for the current year in accordance with the partnership agreement.

5) Corporate suits brought by shareholders; corporate fraud cases. These involve not only large corporations, but also very small ones that have been inundated in the flood of litigation in the U.S.

The accountant must, obviously, have an understanding of the pertinent substantive law before being competent to undertake an investigation of the facts and testify as an expert witness—giving an opinion and conclusions concerning a legal as well as a financial matter.

It becomes fairly obvious that the neophyte expert witness needs to do some investigating to determine just what laws apply to the niche he has chosen to delve into. The particular state laws are undoubtedly the place to begin the investigation since each will be somewhat different—some more than others.

## Federal Rule Changes Proposed

The Judicial Conference Advisory Committee on Evidence Rules has proposed dramatic amendments to Rules 701, 702 and 703. Rule 702 is particularly applicable to the accountant expert witness. The proposed amendment to the current rule is underlined below:

Rule 702: If scientific, technical, or other specialized knowledge will assist the trier of fact to understand the evidence or to determine a fact in issue, a witness qualified as an expert by knowledge, skill, experience training or education may testify thereto in the form of an opinion or otherwise, provided that (1) the testimony is sufficiently based on reliable facts or data, (2) the testimony is the product of reliable principles and methods, and (3) the witness has applied the principles and methods reliably to the facts of the case.

A decision on the changes to the rules is expected to be enacted and become effective in 2000. Basically what this means for the accountant expert witness is that he or she will have to be very sure of the basis of the testimony. The data and methodology leading up to the facts and opinions must be properly applied and "according to GAAP" or other equally recognized accounting literature and regulations. In other words, the testimony must be grounded in thorough, proper analytic procedure and authentication.

# Chapter 13

## Practice Before the IRS

This chapter discusses who can represent a taxpayer before the IRS and what forms or documents are used to authorize a person to represent a taxpayer. Usually, attorneys, certified public accountants (CPAs), enrolled agents, and enrolled actuaries can represent taxpayers before the IRS. Under special circumstances, others, including unenrolled return preparers, can represent taxpayers before the IRS.

### WHAT IS PRACTICE BEFORE THE IRS?

A person is practicing before the IRS if he or she does the following:

1) Communicates with the IRS for a taxpayer regarding the taxpayer's rights, privileges, or liabilities under laws and regulations administered by the IRS.
2) Represents a taxpayer at conferences, hearings, or meetings with the IRS.
3) Prepares and files necessary documents with the IRS for a taxpayer.

Just preparing a tax return, furnishing information at the request of the IRS, or appearing as a witness for the taxpayer is not practice before the IRS. These services can be performed by anyone.

## WHO CAN PRACTICE BEFORE THE IRS?

Any attorney who is not currently under suspension or disbarment from practice before the IRS, and who is a member in good standing of the bar of the highest court of any state, possessions, territory, commonwealth, or of the District of Columbia, can practice before the IRS. However, the attorney must file a written declaration with the IRS that he or she is currently qualified as an attorney and is authorized to represent the taxpayer.

Any CPA who is not currently under suspension or disbarment from practice before the IRS, and who is duly qualified to practice as a CPA in any state, possession, territory, commonwealth, or in the District of Columbia can practice before the IRS. However, the CPA must file a written declaration with the IRS that he or she is currently qualified as a CPA and is authorized to represent the taxpayer.

Any *enrolled agent* can practice before the IRS. Any individual who is enrolled as an *actuary* by the Joint Board for the Enrollment of Actuaries can practice before the IRS. However, the enrolled actuary must file a written declaration with the IRS that he or she is currently qualified as an enrolled actuary and is authorized to represent the taxpayer. The practice of enrolled actuaries is limited to certain Internal Revenue Code sections that relate to their area of expertise, principally those sections governing employee retirement plans.

Any individual other than an attorney, CPA, enrolled agent, or enrolled actuary who prepares a return and signs it as the return preparer is an *unenrolled return preparer.* An unenrolled return preparer can represent the taxpayer only concerning the return prepared. Also, an unenrolled return preparer is permitted to represent taxpayers only before the Examination Division of the IRS, and is not permitted to represent anyone before the Appeals, Collection, or any other division of the IRS.

The Director, after giving notice and an opportunity for a conference, can deny eligibility for limited practice before the IRS to any unenrolled preparer or other unenrolled individual who has engaged in disreputable conduct.

Because of their special relationship with a taxpayer, the following unenrolled individuals can represent the specified taxpayers before the IRS, provided they present satisfactory identification and, in most cases, proof of authority to represent:

1)  An individual can represent himself before the IRS.
2)  An individual family member can represent members of his immediate family.
3)  A bona fide officer of a corporation, including subsidiaries, or affiliated corporations, associations, organized group, or, in the course of

his official duties, an officer of a governmental unit, agency, or authority can represent it before the IRS.

4) A partner can represent the partnership before the IRS.

5) A trustee, receiver, guardian, administrator, or executor can represent the trust, receivership, guardianship, or estate.

6) A regular full-time employee can represent the employer. An employer can be, but is not limited to, an individual, partnership, corporation, including subsidiaries, affiliated corporations, association, trust, receivership, guardianship, estate, organized group, governmental unit, agency, or authority.

The Director of Practice can authorize an individual who is not otherwise eligible to practice before the IRS to represent another for a particular matter. This authorization is known as the *Commissioner's Special Authorization.* The prospective representative must request this authorization in writing from the Director of Practice. It is granted only when extremely compelling circumstances exist. If granted, the Director of Practice will issue a letter that details the particular tax matter for which the authorization is granted.

The *Commissioner's Special Authorization Letter* should not be confused with a letter from an IRS service center advising an individual that he has been assigned a *Centralized Authorization File (CAF)* number—an identifying number that the IRS assigns representatives. The issuance of a CAF number does not indicate that a person is either recognized or authorized to practice before the IRS. It merely confirms that a centralized file for authorizations has been established for the representative under that number.

## WHO CANNOT PRACTICE?

The following individuals are ineligible to practice before the IRS:

1) Individuals convicted of any criminal offense under the revenue laws of the U.S.

2) Individuals convicted of any offense involving dishonesty or breach of trust.

3) Individuals under disbarment or suspension from practicing as attorneys, CPAs, public accountants, or actuaries in any state, possession, territory, commonwealth, or in the District of Columbia, any federal court, or any body or board of any federal agency.

4) Individuals whose applications for enrollment to practice before the IRS have been denied.

5) Individuals who are disbarred or suspended from practice before the IRS.

6) Individuals who refuse or have refused to comply with the regulations governing practice before the IRS.

7) Individuals whose conduct or practices are disreputable.

8) Officers or employees of the U.S. Government or of the District of Columbia.

9) Officers or employees of state governments with authority to act on tax matters, if that employment may disclose facts or information on federal tax matters.

10) Any member of Congress or Resident Commissioner, serving, in connection with any matter to which he or she directly or indirectly receives, agrees to receive, or seeks any compensation.

11) Corporations, associations, partnerships, and other entities that are not individuals are ineligible to practice before the IRS.

## How an Individual Becomes Enrolled

The Director of Practice can grant enrollment to practice before the IRS to an applicant who demonstrates special competence in tax matters by passing a written examination administered by the IRS. Enrollment can also be granted to an applicant who qualifies because of past employment with the IRS. An applicant must not have engaged in any conduct that would justify suspension or disbarment by the IRS.

Applicants can apply for enrollment by filing Form 23, *Application for Enrollment to Practice Before the Internal Revenue Service,* with the Director of Practice. The application must include a check or money order in the amount of the fee shown on Form 23.

An enrollment card will be issued to each individual whose application is approved. The individual is enrolled until the expiration date shown on the enrollment card. To continue practicing beyond the expiration date, the individual must request renewal of the enrollment.

## What Are the Rules of Practice?

An attorney, CPA, enrolled agent, or enrolled actuary authorized to practice before the IRS—referred to as a *Practitioner*—has the duty to perform certain acts and is restricted from performing other acts. In addition, a practitioner cannot engage in disreputable conduct. Any practitioner who does not comply with the rules of practice or engages in disreputable conduct is subject to disciplinary action. Also, unenrolled preparers must comply with most of these rules of practice and conduct to exercise the privilege of limited practice before the IRS.

## Duties

Practitioners must promptly submit records or information requested by officers or employees of the IRS. When the Director of Practice requests information concerning possible violations of the regulations by other parties, the practitioner must provide it and be prepared to testify in disbarment or suspension proceedings. A practitioner can be excepted from these rules if he or she believes in good faith and on reasonable grounds that the information requested is privileged, or that the request is of doubtful legality. A practitioner who knows that the client has not complied with the revenue laws, or has made an error in or omission from any return, document, affidavit, or other required paper, has the responsibility to advise the client promptly of the noncompliance, error, or omission.

## Due Diligence

A practitioner must exercise due diligence:

1) In preparing or assisting in the preparation of, approving, and filing returns, documents, affidavits, and other papers relating to Internal Revenue Service matters.
2) In determining the correctness of oral or written representations made by him or her to the Department of the Treasury.
3) In determining the correctness of oral or written representations made to him or her to clients with reference to any matter administered by the Internal Revenue Service.

## Restrictions

Practitioners are restricted from engaging in certain practices. The following are some of those restricted practices. A practitioner must not:

1) Unreasonably delay the prompt disposition of any matter before the IRS.

2) Accept assistance from disbarred or suspended persons and former IRS employees.

3) Employ or accept assistance from any person who is under disbarment or suspension from practice before the IRS.

4) Accept employment as associate, correspondent, or subagent from, or share fees with, any such person.

5) Accept assistance from any former government employee where provisions of these regulations or any federal law would be violated.

If a practitioner who is a notary public is employed as counsel, attorney, or agent in a matter before the IRS, or has a material interest in the matter, that person must not engage in any notary activities relative to the matter.

A partner of an officer or employee of the executive branch of the U.S. Government, of an independent agency of the U.S., or of the District of Columbia, cannot represent anyone in a matter before the IRS in which the officer or employee has, or had, a personal or substantial interest as a government employee.

# Chapter 14

## Tip Income

What's the big deal? An estimated $9 billion a year in unreported, untaxed tip income, that's what. Reporting all tip income has always been required by law. When the significant extent to which taxpayers were ignoring the law became evident, the IRS stepped up the emphasis on the requirements for both employee and employer to report tip income.

### TIP RATE DETERMINATION/EDUCATION PROGRAM

The Tip Rate Determination/Education Program (TRD/EP) was first promoted in the gaming industry (casino industry) in Las Vegas, Nevada, and has spread to the food and beverage industry. Other industries whose employees receive tips include beauty parlors, barber shops, taxi companies, and pizza delivery establishments.

The Tip Rate Determination/Education Program created in 1993 is a national program used in all states. The employer has the option to enter into one of two arrangements under this program: the Tip Rate Determination Agreement (TRDA) or the Tip Reporting Alternative Commitment (TRAC) created in June 1995.

With the introduction of the new programs, four options became available for tip reporting:

1) Tip Rate Determination Agreement (TRDA).
2) Tip Reporting Alternative Commitment (TRAC).

**3)** The status quo—the old basic method following the requirements listed below without any "formal" agreement.

**4)** Examination of Tip Income Reporting.

Under the Tip Rate Determination/Education Program (TRD/EP), the employer may enter into either the TRDA or TRAC arrangement. The IRS will assist applicants in understanding and meeting the requirements for participation. Many similarities exist between the two new alternatives, but there are some differences. Following is a descriptive list of the requirements for each, particularly in reference to the food and beverage industry:

## TRDA

**1)** Requires the IRS to work with the establishment to arrive at a tip rate for the various restaurant occupations.

**2)** Requires the employee to enter into a Tipped Employee Participation Agreement (TEPA) with the employer.

**3)** Requires the employer to get 75% of the employees to sign TEPAs and report at or above the determined rate.

**4)** Provides that if employees fail to report at or above the determined rate, the employer will provide the names of those employees, their social security numbers, job classification, sales, hours worked, and amount of tips reported.

**5)** Has no specific education requirement relating to legal responsibility to report tips under the agreement.

**6)** Participation assures the employer that prior periods will not be examined during the period that the TRDA is in effect.

**7)** Results in the mailing of a notice and demand to employer for the employer's portion of FICA taxes on unreported tips determined for the six month period used to set the tip rate(s).

**8)** Prevents employer (only) assessments during the period that the agreement is in effect.

## TRAC

**1)** Does not require that a tip rate be established, but it does require the employer to:
  **a)** Establish a procedure where a directly tipped employee is provided (no less than monthly) a written statement of charged tips attributed to the employee.
  **b)** Implement a procedure for the employee to verify or correct any statement of attributed tips.

      **c)** Adopt a method where an indirectly tipped employee reports his or her tips (no less than monthly). This could include a statement prepared by the employer and verified or corrected by the employee.

      **d)** Establish a procedure where a written statement is prepared and processed (no less than monthly) reflecting all cash tips attributable to sales of the directly tipped employee.

**2)** Does not require an agreement between the employee and the employer.

**3)** Affects all (100%) of the employees.

**4)** Provides that if the tip rate does not improve collectively, the TRAC may be revoked. If revoked, the employer could be subject to a TRDA or tip examination.

**5)** Includes a commitment by the employer to educate and reeducate quarterly all directly and indirectly tipped employees and new hires of their statutory requirement to report all tips to their employer.

**6)** Participation assures the employer that prior periods will not be examined during the period that the agreement is in effect.

**7)** Prevents employer (only) assessments during the period that the agreement is in effect.

## Instituting the Program

To enter into one of the arrangements, an employer should submit an application letter to the area IRS Chief, Examination/Compliance Division, Attn: Tip Coordinator. The Tip Coordinator can provide a letter format as well as extensive information on the two separate arrangements.

All employers with establishments where tipping is customary should review their operations. Then, if it is determined that there is or has been an underreporting of tips, the employer should apply for one of the two arrangements under the TRD/EP. Employers currently with the TRDA in effect may revoke the arrangement and simultaneously enter into a TRAC.

The particular advantage to the employer who adopts one of these programs is that no subsequent tip examination is imposed as long as terms of the arrangement have been met and all tips have been reported.

## BASIC RULES RELATING TO TIP INCOME REPORTING

The following discussion concerns how tip income is taxed and how it should be reported to the IRS on the federal income tax return. The employees of food and beverage companies are the main subjects of this review; the record keeping rules and other information also apply to other workers who receive tips.

As pointed out earlier, all tips that are received by employees are taxable income and are subject to federal income taxes. Employees must include in gross income all tips received directly from customers, and tips from charge customers paid to the employer, who must pay them to the employee. In addition, cash tips of $20 or more that an employee receives in a month while working for any one employer are subject to withholding of income tax, social security retirement tax, and Medicare tax. The employee should report tips to the employer in order to determine the correct amount of these taxes.

Tips and other pay are used to determine the amount of social security benefits that an employee receives when he or she retires, becomes disabled, or dies. Noncash tips are not counted as wages for social security purposes. Future Social Security Administration (SSA) benefits can be figured correctly only if the SSA has the correct information. To make sure that an employee has received credit for all his or her earnings, the employee should request a statement of earnings from the SSA at least every other year. The SSA will send the person a statement that should be carefully checked to be sure it includes all of the employee's earnings.

Every large food and beverage business must report to the IRS any tips allocated to the employees. Generally, tips must be allocated to be paid by employees when the total tips reported to an employer by employees are less than 8% of the establishment's food and beverage sales of that employee. This necessitates the employer and employees keeping accurate records of the employee's tip income.

## Daily Tip Record

The employee must keep a daily tip record so he or she can:

1) Report tips accurately to the employer.
2) Report tips accurately on a tax return.
3) Prove tip income if the taxpayer's return is ever questioned.

There are two ways to keep a daily tip record:

1) The employee can keep a daily "tip diary."
2) The employee should keep copies of documents that show the tips, such as restaurant bills and credit card charge slips.

The employee can start record keeping by writing his or her name, the employer's name, and the name of the business if it is different from the employer's name. Each workday, the employee should write and date the following information in a tip diary.

1) Cash tips received directly from customers or other employees.

2) Tips from credit card charge customers that the employer pays the employee.

3) The value of any noncash tips received, such as tickets, passes, or other items of value.

4) The amount of tips the employee paid out to other employees through tip pools, tip splitting, or other arrangements, and the names of the employees to whom tips were paid.

## Reporting Tips to the Employer

The employee must report tips to the employer so that:

1) The employer can withhold federal income tax, social security taxes, and Medicare taxes.

2) The employer can report the correct amount of the employee's earnings to the Social Security Administration. This will affect the employee's benefits when the employee retires or becomes disabled, or the family's benefits upon the employee's death.

## What Tips to Report

Only cash, check, or credit card tips should be reported to the employer. If the total tips for any one month from any one job are less than $20, they should not be reported to the employer. The value of any noncash tips, such as tickets or passes, is not reported to the employer because the employee does not have to pay social security and Medicare taxes on these tips. The employee will, however, report them on his or her individual tax return. The following information should be written on the report to be given to the employer:

1) Name, address, and social security number.

2) The employer's name, address, and business name if it is different from the employer's name.

3) The month, or the dates of any shorter period, in which the tips are received.

4) The total amount of tips the employee received.

The employee must sign and date the report and give it to the employer. The employee should keep a copy of the report for his or her personal records. The report is to be completed each month and given to the employer by the tenth of the next month.

## Employer Records for Tip Allocation

Large food and beverage establishments are required to report certain additional information about tips to the IRS. To make sure that employees are reporting tips correctly, employers must keep records to verify amounts reported by employees. Certain employers must allocate tips if the percentage of tips reported by employees falls below a required minimum percentage of gross sales. To allocate tips means to assign an additional amount as tips to each employee whose reported tips are below the required percentage. The rules apply to premises in which:

1) Food and beverages are provided for consumption on the premises.
2) Tipping is customary.
3) The employer normally employed more than ten people on a typical business day during the preceding calendar year.

Tip allocation rules do not apply to food and beverage establishments where tipping is not customary such as:

1) A cafeteria or fast food restaurant.
2) A restaurant that adds a service charge of 10% or more to 95% or more of its food and beverage sales.
3) Food and beverage establishments located outside the United States.

The rules apply only if the total amount of tips reported by all tipped employees to the employer is less than 8%, or some lower acceptable percentage of the establishment's total food or beverage sales, with some adjustments. If reported tips total less than 8% of total sales, the employer must allocate the difference between 8% of total sales, or some lower acceptable percentage approved by the IRS, and the amount of tips reported by all tipped employees. The employer will exclude carryout sales, state and local taxes, and sales with a service charge of 10% or more when figuring total sales.

Usually, the employer will allocate to all affected employees their share of tips every payroll period. However, the employer should not withhold any taxes from the allocated amount. No allocation will be made to the employee if the employee reports tips at least equal to the employee's share of 8% of the establishment's total food and beverage sales.

## Penalty for Not Reporting Tips

If the employee does not report tips to his or her employer as required, the employee can be subject to a penalty equal to 50% of the social security and Medicare taxes owed. The penalty amount is in addition to the taxes owed. The penalty can be avoided if the employee can show reasonable cause for not reporting the tips to the employer. A statement should be attached to the tax return explaining why the tips were not reported to the employer. If an employee's regular pay is not enough for the employer to withhold all the taxes owed on the regular pay plus reported tips, the employee can give the employer money to pay the rest of the taxes, up to the close of the calendar year.

If the employee does not give the employer enough money, the employer will apply the regular pay and any money given by the employee in the following order:

1) All taxes on the employee's regular pay.
2) Social security and Medicare taxes on the reported tips.
3) Federal, state, and local income taxes on the reported tips.

Any taxes that remain unpaid can be collected by the employer from the employee's next paycheck. If withholding taxes remain uncollected at the end of the year, the employee must make an estimated tax payment. To report these taxes, a return must be filed even if the employee would not otherwise have to file. If the employer could not collect all the social security and Medicare taxes owed on the tips reported to the employer, the uncollected taxes must be shown by the employer on a Form W-2. The employee must then also report these uncollected taxes on his or her return.

## Tip Rates

Depending on the Occupational Category and the employer's business practices, tips can be *measured* in different ways.

1) *Actual tips* generally apply to Employees in Occupational Categories (O.C.) where pooling of tips is common. The tips are pooled during a shift and the total is split among the employees of the O.C. who worked the shift.
2) *Tip rates* generally apply to employees in O.C. where pooling of tips is not common. The rate may be a percentage of sales, a dollar amount, or other accurate basis of measurement per hour or shift, a dollar amount per drink served, a dollar amount per working hour, or other accurate measurement.

### Methods for Determining Tip Rates

The employer will determine tip rates for the O.C. based on information available to the employer, historical information provided by the district director, and generally accepted accounting principles (GAAP). The rates will specify whether the tips are received as a percentage of sales, a dollar amount per hour or shift, a dollar amount per drink served, a dollar amount per dealing hour in a casino, or on another basis.

## Initial Tip Rate

The initial tip rate for each O.C. is shown where pool and split tips methods are used by the employees.

## ANNUAL REVIEW

The employer will review annually, on a calender year basis, changes in the tip rates assigned to its O.C. In connection with the review, the employer can review its O.C. The initial rates for each O.C. will apply to the first full calendar year of the review.

## Employer Submission

If the employer believes that a revision of one or more rates or O.C. is appropriate, the employer will submit proposed revisions to the District Director by September 30. If the employer fails to submit a proposed rate revision by September 30 of the taxable year, the employee will be treated as having submitted the rate in effect for the current year.

## District Director Review

The district director will review the proposed rates and notify the employer in writing of the approval or disapproval by November 30. If the District Director does not approve one or more proposed rates, the existing rate or rates will be continued until no later than the last day of the following February.

The effective date of revised rates and O.C. will become effective on the later of January 1 of the calendar year, or on the first day of the month following the date the employer and the district director agree upon a revised rate. The district director can examine a participating employee's tip income for any period if an employee reports tips at a rate less than the tip rate for the employee's occupational category.

These amounts must be an additional tax on the employee's tax return. The employee may have uncollected taxes if his or her regular pay was not enough for the employer to withhold all the taxes the taxpayer owed, but did not give the employer enough money to pay the rest of the taxes. The employee must report these uncollected taxes on a return.

## ALLOCATED TIPS

Allocated tips are tips that the employer assigned to an employee in addition to the tips the employee reported to the employer for the year. The employer will have done this only if the employee worked in a restaurant, cocktail lounge, or similar business that must allocate tips to employees, and the reported tips were less than the employee's share of 8% of food and drink sales. If allocated tips are shown on a return, and if social security and Medicare taxes were not withheld from the allocated tips, these taxes must be reported as additional tax on a return.

## Allocation Formula

The allocation can be done either under a formula agreed to by both the employer and the employees or, if they cannot reach an agreement, under a formula prescribed by IRS regulations. The allocation formula in the regulations provides that tip allocations are made only to directly tipped employees. If tips are received directly from customers, the employees are directly tipped employees, even if the tips are turned over to a tip pool. Waiters, waitresses, and bartenders are usually considered directly tipped employees. If tips are not normally received directly from customers, the employee is an indirectly tipped employee. Examples are busboys, service bartenders, and cooks. If an employee receives tips both directly and indirectly through tip splitting or tip pooling, the employee is treated as a directly tipped employee.

If customers of the establishment tip less than 8% on average, either the employee or a majority of the directly tipped employees can petition to have the allocation percentage reduced from 8%. This petition is made to the district director for the IRS district in which the establishment is located. The percentage cannot be reduced below 2%.

A fee is required to have the IRS consider a petition to lower the tip allocation percentage. The fee must be paid by check or money order made out to the Internal Revenue Service. (The user fee amount for 1998 is $275; the district director in the taxpayer's area will know if this amount has changed.)

The employees' petition to lower the allocation percentage must be in writing, and must contain enough information to allow the district director to estimate with reasonable accuracy the establishment's actual tip rate. This information might include the changed tip rate, type of establishment, menu prices, location, hours of operation, amount of self-service required, and whether the customer receives the check from the server or pays the server for the meal. If the employer possesses any relevant information, the employer must provide it to the district upon request of the employees or the district director.

The employees' petition must be consented to by more than one-half of the directly tipped employees working for the establishment at the time the petition is filed. If the petition covers more than one establishment, it must be consented to by more than one-half of the total number of directly tipped employees of the covered establishments. The petition must state the total number of directly tipped employees of the establishment(s) and the number of directly tipped employees consenting to the petition.

The petition may cover two or more establishments if the employees have made a good faith determination that the tip wages are essentially the same and if the establishments are:

1) Owned by the same employer.
2) Essentially the same type of business.
3) In the same Internal Revenue Service region.

A petition that covers two or more establishments must include the names and locations of the establishments and must be sent to the district director for the district in which the greatest number of covered establishments are located. If there is an equal number of covered establishments in two or more districts, the employees can choose which district to petition. Employees who file a petition must promptly notify their employer of the petition. The employer must then promptly furnish the district director with an annual information return form showing the tip income and allocated tips filed for the establishment for the three immediately preceding calendar years.

The employer will report the amount of tips allocated to employees on the employees' Form W-2 separately from wages and reported tips. The employer bases withholding only on wages and reported tips. The employer should not withhold income, social security, and Medicare taxes from the allocated amount. Any incorrectly withheld taxes should be refunded to the employee by the employer.

If an employee leaves a job before the end of the calendar year and requests an early Form W-2, the employer does not have to include a tip allocation on the Form W-2. However, the employer can show the actual allocated amount if it is known, or show an estimated allocation. In January of the following year, the employer most provide Form W-2 if the early Form W-2 showed no allocation and the employer later determined that an allocation was required, or if the estimated allocation shown was wrong by more than 5% of the actual allocation.

If an employee does not have adequate records for his or her actual tips, the employee must include the allocated tips shown on the Form W-2 as additional tip income on the tax return. If the employee has records, allocated tips should not be shown on the employee's return. Additional tip income is included only if those records show more tips received than the amount reported to the employer.

# Chapter 15

## Reporting Cash Payments of Over $10,000

Often smugglers and drug dealers use large cash payments to "launder" money from illegal activities. Laundering means converting "dirty" money or illegally gained money to "clean" money. Congress passed the Tax Reform Act of 1984 and the Anti-Drug Abuse Act of 1988 requiring the payment of certain cash payments of over $10,000 to be reported to the Internal Revenue Service. Any person in a trade or business who receives more than $10,000 in a single transaction or in related transactions must report the transaction to the IRS. The government can often trace the laundered money through payments that are reported. Compliance with the law provides valuable information that can stop those who evade taxes and those who profit from the drug trade and other criminal activities.

A "person" includes an individual, a company, a corporation, a partnership, an association, a trust, or an estate. A report does not have to be filed if the entire transaction, including the receipt of cash, takes place outside of:

1) The 50 states.
2) The District of Columbia.
3) Puerto Rico.
4) A possession or territory of the United States.

However, a report must be filed if the transaction, including the receipt of cash, occurs in Puerto Rico or a possession or territory of the United States and the person is subject to the Internal Revenue Code.

A transaction occurs when:

1) Goods, services, or property are sold.
2) Property is rented.
3) Cash is exchanged for other cash.
4) A contribution is made to a trust or escrow account.
5) A loan is made or repaid.
6) Cash is converted to a negotiable instrument such as a check or bond.

Payments to be reported include:

1) A sum over $10,000.
2) Installment payments that cause the total cash received within one year of the initial payment to total more than $10,000.
3) Other previously unreportable payments that cause the total cash received within a 12-month period to total more than $10,000.
4) Those received in the course of a trade or business.
5) Those received from the same buyer or agent.
6) Those received in a single transaction or in related transactions.

## A DESIGNATED REPORTING TRANSACTION

A designated reporting transaction is the retail sale of any of the following:

1) A consumer durable, such as an automobile or boat. A consumer durable is property other than land or buildings that is suitable for personal use and can reasonably be expected to last at least one year under ordinary usage.
2) Has a sales price of more than $10,000.
3) Tangible property.
4) A "collectible," including works of art, rugs, antiques, gems, stamps, coins.
5) Travel or entertainment, if the total sales price of all items sold for the same trip or entertainment event in one transaction, or related transactions, is more than $10,000. The sales price of items such as air fare, hotel rooms, and admission tickets are all included.

## RETAIL SALES

The term "retail sales" means any sale made in the course of a trade or business that consists mainly of making sales to ultimate consumers. Thus, if a business consists mainly of making sales to ultimate consumers, all sales made in the course of that business are retail sales. This includes sales of items that will also be resold.

## DEFINITION OF CASH

In this context, cash is considered to be:

1) The coins and currency of the U.S. and any other recognized country.
2) Cashier's checks, bank drafts, traveler's checks, and money orders received if they have a face value of $10,000 or less and were received in:
   a) A designated reporting transaction.
   b) Any transaction in which the receiver knows the payer is trying to avoid the reporting of the transaction.

A check drawn on an individual's personal account is not considered cash; however, a cashier's check, even when labeled a "treasurer's check" or "bank check," is considered cash.

## EXCEPTIONS TO DEFINITION OF CASH

A cashier's check, bank draft, traveler's check, or money order received in a designated transaction is not treated as cash if:

1) It is the proceeds from a bank loan. As proof that it is proceeds from a bank loan, a copy of the loan document, a written statement or lien instructions from the bank, or similar proof are acceptable as evidence,
2) If received in payment on a promissory note or an installment sales contract, including a lease that is considered a sale for federal tax purposes. This exception applies if:
   a) The receiver uses similar notes or contracts in other sales to ultimate consumers in the ordinary course of trade or business.
   b) Total payments for the sale are received on or before the 60th day after the sale, and are 50% or less of the purchase price.
3) For certain down payment plans in payment for a consumer durable or collectible, or for travel and entertainment, and *all three* of the following statements are true:

**a)** It was received under a payment plan requiring one or more down payments, and payment of the remainder before receipt of goods or service.

**b)** It was received more than 60 days before final payment was due.

**c)** Similar payment plans are used in the normal course of the trade or business.

## TAXPAYER IDENTIFICATION NUMBER (TIN)

The receiver must furnish the correct TIN of the person or persons from whom the cash is received. If the transaction is conducted on behalf of another person or persons, the receiver must furnish the TIN of that person or persons. There are three types of TINs:

**1)** The TIN for an individual, including a sole proprietor, is the individual's social security number (SSN).

**2)** The TIN for a nonresident alien individual who needs a TIN, but is not eligible to get an SSN, is an IRS individual taxpayer identification number (ITIN). An ITIN has nine digits, similar to an SSN.

**3)** The TIN for other persons, including corporations, partnerships, and estates, is the employer identification number.

A nonresident alien individual or a foreign organization does not have to have a TIN, and so a TIN does not have to be furnished for them, if *all* the following are true:

**1)** The individual or organization does not have income effectively connected with the conduct of a trade or business in the United States, or an office or place of business or a fiscal or paying agent in the United States, at any time during the year.

**2)** The individual or organization does not file a federal tax return.

**3)** In the case of a nonresident alien individual, the individual has not chosen to file a joint federal income tax return with a spouse who is a U.S. citizen or resident.

## RELATED TRANSACTIONS

Any transaction between a buyer, or an agent of the buyer, and a seller that occurs within a 24-hour period are related transactions. If a person receives over $10,000 in cash during two or more transactions with one buyer in a 24-hour period, he or she must treat the transactions as one transaction and report the payments. For example, if two products are sold for $6,000 each to the same customer in one day, and the customer pays the seller in cash, they are related transactions. Because they total $12,000, they must be reported.

Transactions can be related if they are more than 24 hours apart if the person knows, or has reason to know, that each is one of a series of connected transactions. For example, a travel agent receives $8,000 from a client in cash for a trip. Two days later, the same client pays the agent $3,000 more in cash to include another person on the trip. These are related transactions and must be reported.

When a person receives $10,000 or less in cash, the person may voluntarily report the payment if the transaction appears to be suspicious. A transaction is suspicious if it appears that a person is trying to cause the receiver not to report, or is trying to cause a false or incomplete report, or if there is a sign of possible illegal activity.

The amount received and when it was received determines when it must be reported to the IRS. Generally, a report must be filed within 15 days after receiving payment. If the first payment is not more than $10,000, the seller must add the first payment and any later payments made within one year of the first payment. When the total cash payments are more than $10,000, the buyer must file within 15 days. After a report is filed, a new count of cash payments received from that buyer within a 12-month period must be reported to the IRS within 15 days of the payment that causes the additional payments to total more than $10,000. The report can be filed in the seller's local IRS office.

A written statement must be given to each person named on the report to the IRS. The statement must show the name and address of the person who receives the payment, the name and telephone number of a contact person, and the total amount of reportable cash received from the person during the year. It must state that the information is being reported to the IRS. The statement must be sent to the buyer by January 31 of the year after the year in which the seller receives the cash that caused the information to be filed with the IRS. The individual making the report must keep a copy of every report filed for five years.

## PENALTIES

There are civil penalties for failure to:

1) File a correct report by the date it is due.
2) Provide the required statement to those named in the report.

**3)** If the person receiving the cash payment intentionally disregards the requirement to file a correct form by the date it is due, the penalty is the larger of:

**a)** $25,000.

**b)** The amount of cash the person received and was required to report, up to $100,000.

There are criminal penalties for:

**1)** Willful failure to file a report.

**2)** Willfully filing a false or fraudulent report.

**3)** Stopping or trying to stop a report from being filed.

**4)** Setting up, helping to set up, or trying to set up a transaction in a way that would make it seem unnecessary to file a report.

Interference with or prevention of the filing of a report as well as actual willful failure to file a report may result in a substantial fine, imprisonment, or both. The fine can be up to $250,000 ($500,000 for corporations). An individual may also be sentenced to up to five years in prison. Both a fine and a prison sentence may be imposed.

The penalties for failure to file can also apply to any person, including a payer, who attempts to interfere with or prevent the seller, or business, from filing a correct report. This includes any attempt to *structure* the transaction in a way that would make it seem unnecessary to file a report by breaking up a large cash transaction into small cash transactions.

# Chapter 16

# Derivatives: Everyone Has an Opinion, and the Securities and Exchange Commission Acts

There is little doubt that Derivatives is the '90s buzz word in the areas of accounting, finance, banking, and investments. The SEC, the AICPA, the FASB, the GASB, the GAO, the FEI, the AIMR, the IASC, IOSCO, CBOT and myriad other worthy organizations have all jumped into the fray to attempt to prevent another Orange County, California-type debacle from occurring. The losses of Procter and Gamble, other large companies, and banks had raised concern, but the fiasco of a public body so obviously misusing derivatives—and being caught—called for drastic action. How best to guard against anything like this happening again?

The Financial Accounting Standard Board's FASB 119, *Disclosures About Derivative Financial Instruments and Fair Value of Financial Instruments,* was a giant step in the right direction as far as disclosure was concerned, but it was not enough. (See *ADB* Chapter 10.) After 10 years of wresting with the derivatives problem, the Board adopted FASB 133, *Accounting for Derivative Instruments and Hedging Activities.* This new Standard supersedes FASBs 80, 105, and 119 and also amends FASBs 52 and 107.

Various private sector entities highlighted, pinpointed, and underlined problems associated with disclosures about these market risk sensitive instruments, as identified by users of financial reports. The Securities and Exchange Commission's study, preceding the release (in March, 1996) of their proposals for amendments to regulations governing disclosure information about derivatives and other financial instruments and the issuance in February 1977 of amendments to SEC rules, took into consideration concerns by many organizations. For example, the Association for

Investment Management and Research (AIMR), an organization of financial analysts, in a paper discussing financial reporting in the 1990s and on into the next century, noted that users are confounded by the complexity of financial instruments.

After considerable investigation into the needs of investors and creditors, the American Institute of Certified Public Accountants' (AICPA) Special Committee on Financial Reporting confirmed in a study completed in 1994 that users are confused. The users complained that business reporting is not meeting their needs in answering difficult but important questions about innovative financial instruments that companies may have entered into. They felt they needed more specific information about how companies account for those instruments, how that accounting affects the financial statements, and how risk is handled.

Other organizations have made recommendations about how to improve such disclosures on market risk sensitive instruments. These organizations include regulators, such as the Group of Ten Central Bankers, the Federal Reserve Bank of New York, the Basle Committee and the Technical Committee of the International Organization of Securities Commissions (IOSCO), and private sector bodies, such as the Group of Thirty and a task force of the Financial Executives Institute (FEI).

The SEC study found that, in general, these organizations have stressed the need to make more understandable the risks inherent in market risk sensitive instruments. In particular, they have called for additional quantitative and qualitative disclosures about market risk. For example, the Federal Reserve Bank of New York recommended a new financial statement providing quantitative information about the overall market risk of an entity. In addition, the FEI task force recommended that companies disclose some type of information that conveys overall exposure to market risk. In this regard, the FEI task force suggested two distinct approaches. One approach is to provide a high-level summary of relevant statistics about outstanding activity at period end. The second approach is to communicate the potential loss which could occur under specified conditions using either a value at risk or another comprehensive model to measure market risk.

## FASB STATEMENT 119

FASB 119 prescribed, among other things, disclosures in the financial statements about the policies used to account for derivative financial instruments, and a discussion of the nature, terms, and cash requirements of derivative financial instruments. It also encouraged, but did not require, disclosure of quantitative information about an entity's overall market risk. As mentioned earlier, this was a first decisive step in the right direction, but further standards, particularly relating to *accounting* for derivatives and hedging, were considered necessary.

Standards similar to FASB 119 have been adopted by the International Accounting Standards Committee, IAS 32; the Canadian Institute of Chartered Accountants; and the Australian Accounting Standards Board. Whether all of these bodies will endeavor to expand upon the requirements in these standards remains to be seen. However, the IASC does have two committees working on a temporary as well as a more long-range standard relating to financial instruments including derivatives. An ED of the former dealing with recognition and measurement is scheduled for release in the fall of 1998.

During 1994, in response, in part, to the concerns of investors, regulators, and private sector entities, the SEC staff reviewed the annual reports of approximately 500 registrants. In addition, during 1995, annual reports were reviewed by the SEC staff to assess the effect of FASB 119 on disclosures about market risk sensitive instruments. As a result of these reviews, the SEC staff observed that FASB 119 did have a positive effect on the quality of disclosures about derivative financial instruments. However, the SEC staff also concluded there was a need to improve disclosures about them, other financial instruments, and derivative commodity instruments. In particular, the SEC staff had identified the following three primary disclosure issues which should be considered when following the new rules.

## FURTHER DISCLOSURE MEASURES NEEDED

1)  Footnote disclosures of accounting policies for derivatives often are too general to convey adequately the diversity in accounting that exists for derivatives. As a result, it is often difficult to determine the impact of derivatives on registrants' statements of financial position, cash flows, and results of operations.

2)  Disclosures frequently focus on derivatives and other financial instruments only in isolation. For this reason, it may be difficult to assess whether these instruments increase or decrease the net market risk exposure of a registrant.

3)  Disclosure about financial instruments, commodity positions, firm commitments, and other anticipated transactions, *reported items*, in the footnotes to the financial statements, Management's Discussion and Analysis (MD&A), schedules, and selected financial data may not reflect adequately the effect of derivatives on such reported items. Without disclosure about the *effects* of derivatives, information about the reported items may be incomplete or perhaps misleading.

## For Study and Consideration

For one and one-half years, members of the SEC staff researched derivatives, related risk management activities, and alternative disclosure approaches to make these activities less a mystery to investors, the general public, and even many professionals who actually deal with these activities in one capacity or another, before drawing up proposals for consideration. In addition, during this period, the SEC and its staff developed a list of guiding principles to provide a foundation for proposed amendments and recommendations.

1) Disclosures should make it possible for investors to understand better how derivatives affect a registrant's statements of financial position, cash flows, and results of operations.

2) Disclosures should provide information about market risk.

3) Disclosures should clearly explain for the investor how market risk sensitive instruments are used in the registrant's business.

4) Disclosures about market risk should not focus on derivatives in isolation, but rather should point out the "opportunity" for loss inherent in all market risk sensitive instruments.

5) Disclosure requirements about market risk should be flexible enough to accommodate different types of registrants, different degrees of market risk exposure, and different ways of measuring market risk.

6) Disclosures about market risk should highlight, where appropriate, special risks relating to leverage, option, or prepayment features.

7) New disclosure requirements should build on existing disclosure requirements, where possible, to simplify the learning process for additional procedures and to minimize compliance costs to registrants.

## Derivatives—Good and Bad

During the last several years, there has been substantial growth in the use of derivative financial instruments, other financial instruments, and derivative commodity instruments. The SEC agrees that these instruments can be effective tools for managing registrants' exposures to market risk. After all, grain futures, hedging, and the commodity market are all good heartland, conservative agricultural measures undertaken as risk prevention, not as flyers in a volatile market. However, what was an ordered, conservative approach to hedging in the 1800s began developing rapidly and spectacularly in some areas as wild speculation in the late 1900s. During 1994, some investors and registrants experienced significant, and sometimes unexpected, losses in market risk sensitive instruments due to, among other things, changes in interest rates, foreign currency exchange rates, and commodity prices. In light of these losses and the substantial growth in the use of market risk sensitive instruments, public disclosure about these instruments has emerged as an important issue in financial markets.

As mentioned, a portion of the SEC study on derivatives during 1994 and 1995 was a review of annual reports filed by approximately 500 registrants. The avowed purpose was to assess the quality of disclosures relating to market risk sensitive instruments and to determine what, if any, additional information was needed to improve disclosures about derivatives. They determined that partly because of FASB 119, disclosures reviewed in 1995 were more informative than those reviewed in 1994.

## THREE BASIC PROPOSALS

It was the opinion of those reviewing the situation that the three aforementioned significant disclosure issues remain as problems. To address these specific disclosure issues, the SEC proposed guidance reminders and amendments to their basic regulations, and it is these specific proposals that have led to the new amendments to the SEC regulations:

1) Amendments to Regulation S-X requiring enhanced descriptions in the footnotes to the financial statements of accounting policies for derivative financial instruments and derivative commodity instruments. These disclosures would be required unless the registrant's derivative activities are not material. The materiality of derivatives activities would be measured by the fair values of derivative financial instruments and derivative commodity instruments at the end of each reporting period and the fair value of those instruments during each reporting period.

2) Amendments creating a new item within Regulation S-K requiring disclosure outside the financial statements of qualitative and quantitative information about derivative financial instruments, other financial instruments, and derivative commodity instruments. These disclosures would be required if the fair values of market risk sensitive instruments outstanding at the end of the current reporting period were material or the potential loss in future earnings, fair values, or cash flows of market risk sensitive instruments from reasonably possible market movements appeared likely to be material.

3) Reminders to registrants that when they provide disclosure about financial instruments, commodity positions, firm commitments, and other anticipated transactions, such disclosure must include information about derivatives that affect directly or indirectly such reported items, to the extent the effects of such information is material and

necessary to prevent the disclosure about the reported item from being misleading. For example, when information is required to be disclosed in the footnotes to the financial statements about interest rates and repricing characteristics of debt obligations, registrants should include, when material, disclosure of the effects of derivatives. Similarly, summary information and disclosures in MD&A about the cost of debt obligations should include, when material, disclosure of the effects of derivatives.

## THE SEC TAKES ACTION

*Disclosure of Accounting Policies for Derivative Financial Instruments and Derivative Commodity Instruments and Disclosure of Quantitative and Qualitative Information About Market Risk Inherent in Derivative Financial Instruments, Other Financial Instruments, and Derivative Commodity Instruments*

From the title of the rules released on February 3, 1997, it would almost appear that the Securities and Exchange Commission feels the ills of the "derivatives problem" can be solved if someone can just come up with the right disclosure and accounting policy formulas to make everything clear to the naive, as well as the sophisticated, investor and end user. At least they tried very hard to find that formula for the disclosure part, and appeared to have faith that the FASB would soon come up with the accounting part.

Thus, the Commission has amended rules and forms for domestic and foreign issuers to clarify and expand existing disclosure requirements for "market risk sensitive instruments." The amendments require enhanced disclosure of accounting policies for derivative financial instruments and derivative commodity instruments (derivatives) in the *footnotes* to the financial statements. In addition, the amendments expand existing disclosure requirements to include quantitative and qualitative information about market risk inherent in market risk sensitive instruments. The required quantitative and qualitative information should be disclosed *outside the financial statements and footnotes.* In addition, the quantitative and qualitative information will be provided safe harbor protection under a new Commission rule.

Disclosures about financial instruments, commodity positions, firm commitments, and anticipated transactions (reported items) must include disclosures about derivatives that *directly* or *indirectly* affect such reported items, to the extent such information is material and necessary to prevent the disclosures from being misleading. The amendments are designed to provide additional information about market risk sensitive instruments, which investors can use to better understand and evaluate the market risk exposures of a registrant.

## Planned Reconsideration

The Commission recognizes the evolving nature of market risk sensitive instruments, market risk measurement systems, and market risk management strategies and, thus, intends to continue considering how best to meet the information needs of investors. In this regard, the Commission expects to monitor continuously the effectiveness of these new rules and final disclosure items, as well as the need for additional proposals.

Specifically, the Commission expects to reconsider these amendments after each of the following:

1) The FASB issues a new accounting standard for improving accounting recognition, measurement, and related discoveries for derivatives. (This should be underway with the adoption of FASB 133.)
2) Development in the marketplace of new generally accepted methods for measuring market risk.
3) A period of three years from the initial effective date of Item 305 of Regulation S-K and Item 9A of Form 20-F.

## Effective Dates

The amendments became effective over a period of several months to provide registrants with time to respond to the new disclosure requirements. Some compliance dates were staggered depending upon the type of entity and its capitalization. For registrants that were likely to have experience with measuring market risk, less lead time was provided. The schedule was as follows:

1) Item 10(g) of Regulation S-B was effective for filings with the Commission 60 days after the rules were published in the Federal Register.
2) 210.4-08(n) of Regulation S-X and the amendment to Item 310 of Regulation S-B is effective, and disclosures under that rule required for filings with the Commission that include financial statements for fiscal periods ending after June 15, 1997. This requires enhanced descriptions of accounting policies for derivatives in the *footnotes* to the financial statements. These disclosure requirements are applicable only to derivatives; the requirements do not relate to other financial instruments. Accounting policy disclosure requirements for other financial instruments are prescribed by existing GAAP—APB 22—for example, and Commission guidance.
3) For bank and thrifts, and nonbank and nonthrifts with market capitalizations on January 28, 1997, in excess of $2.5 billion, Item 30 of Regulation S-K and Item 9A of Form 20-F are effective; and disclosures under those items required for filings with the Commission that in-

clude annual financial statements for fiscal years ending after June 15, 1997.

4) For nonbank and nonthrift registrants with market capitalizations on January 28, 1997, of $2.5 billion or less, Item 305 of Regulation S-K and Item 9A of Form 20-F are effective, and disclosures under those items required for filings with the Commission that include annual financial statements for fiscal years ending after June 15, 1998.

5) Under Item 305 of Regulation S-K and Item 9A of Form 20-F, interim information is required after the first fiscal year end in which Item 305 of Regulation S-K and Item 9A of Form 20-F are effective.

## Provisions of Items 305 and 9A

The amendments to Regulation S-K to add Item 305, and Form 20F to add Item 9A, require disclosure of *quantitative* and *qualitative* information about market risk for derivatives and other financial instruments, and require that those disclosures be presented *outside the financial statements.* Items 305 and 9A do not pertain solely to derivatives, but also to other financial instruments. Thus, disclosures under those Items are required for registrants that have material amounts of other financial instruments, even when they have no derivatives.

These Items also *encourage* registrants to include other market risk sensitive instruments, positions, and transactions (such as commodity positions, derivative commodity instruments that are not permitted by contract or business custom to be settled in cash or with another financial instrument, and cash flows from anticipated transactions) within the scope of their quantitative and qualitative disclosures about market risk. Registrants that select the sensitivity analysis or value at risk disclosure alternatives and voluntarily include those other market risk sensitive instruments, positions, and transactions within their quantitative disclosures about market risk are permitted to present comprehensive market risk disclosures, which reflect the combined effect of both the required and voluntarily selected instruments, positions, and transactions.

Finally, if those other market risk sensitive instruments, positions, and transactions are not voluntarily included in the quantitative disclosures about market risk and, as a result, the disclosures do not fully reflect the net market risk exposures of the registrant, Items 305(a) and 9A(a) require that registrants discuss the absence of those items as a limitation of the disclosed market risk information.

## Quantitative Information

Items 305(a) and 9A(a) require registrants to disclose quantitative information about market risk sensitive instruments using one or more of the following alternatives:

1) Tabular presentation of fair value information and contract terms relevant to determining future cash flows, categorized by expected maturity dates.

2) Sensitivity analysis expressing the potential loss in future earnings, fair values, or cash flows from selected hypothetical changes in market rates and prices.

3) Value at risk disclosures expressing the potential loss in future earnings, fair values, or cash flows from market movements over a selected period of time and with a selected likelihood of occurrence.

Preparation of this quantitative information also requires the registrants to categorize market risk sensitive instruments into instruments entered into for trading purposes, and instruments entered into for purposes other than trading. Within both the trading and other than trading portfolios, separate quantitative information should be presented for each market risk exposure category (i.e., interest rate risk, foreign currency exchange rate risk, commodity price risk, and other relevant market risks, such as equity price risk), to the extent material.

Registrants may use different disclosure alternatives for each of the separate disclosures.

## Qualitative Information

In addition to the quantitative information, Items 305(b) and 9A(b) also require registrants to disclose qualitative information about market risk. These items require disclosure of:

1) A registrant's primary market risk exposures at the end of the current reporting period.

2) How the registrant manages those exposures (such as a description of the objectives, general strategies, and instruments, if any, used to manage those exposures).

3) Changes in either the registrant's primary market risk exposures or how those exposures are managed, when compared to the most recent reporting period and what is known or expected in future periods.

## Requirements for Small Business Issuers

Small companies and registered investment companies are exempt from a portion of the new requirements. The amendments in Rule 4–08(n) of Regulation S-X and Item 310 of Regulation S-B, relating to accounting policy disclosures, apply to registered investment companies and small business issuers, along with other registrants. However, Item 305 and Item

9A do not apply to registered investment companies and small business issuers.

The Commission believes that because of the evolving nature of the disclosures and the relative costs of compliance for small business issuers, it is appropriate, at this time, to exempt them from disclosing quantitative and qualitative information about market risk. Furthermore, they will not be required to provide these market risk disclosures whether or not they file on specially designated small business forms. In addition, the Commission has extended the safe harbor for forward-looking information to Item 305 disclosures that are made voluntarily by small business issuers.

Accordingly, at this time, the Commission is not adopting amendments to Regulation S-B to incorporate an item similar to Item 305. Small business issuers, however, are required to comply with the amendment regarding accounting policies disclosures for derivatives, to comply with Rule 12b-20 under the Exchange Act and Rule 408 under the Securities Act. These rules require registrants to provide additional information about the material effects of derivatives on other information expressly required to be filed with the Commission, and to the extent market risk represents a known trend, event, or uncertainty, to discuss the impact of market risk on past and future financial condition and results of operations, pursuant to Item 303 of Regulation S-B.

## Application to Foreign Private Issuers

As the interest in international securities and investment grows, it is important to keep in mind that the SEC also is charged with the responsibility of seeing that the investor has adequate information about the financial status of foreign entities.

Item 9A of Form 20-F requires disclosure by all foreign private issuers of quantitative and qualitative information about market risk. In addition, foreign private issuers that prepare financial statements in accordance with Item 18 of Form 20-F are required to provide all information required by U.S. GAAP and Regulation S-X, including descriptions in the footnotes to the financial statements of the policies used to account for derivatives.

## Lack of Direction Noted

The SEC study revealed that in the absence of comprehensive requirements for accounting for derivatives, registrants had been developing accounting practices for options and complex derivatives by piecemeal application of the various APB Opinions, FASB Statements, EITF Issues, and the limited amount of such literature that did exist.

The varied applications were complicated because existing derivative literature referred to at least three distinctly different methods of accounting for derivatives: fair value accounting, deferral accounting, and accrual accounting. Further, the underlying concepts and criteria used in determining the applicability of these accounting methods were not consistent.

To illustrate: Under the fair value method, derivatives were carried on the balance sheet at fair value with changes in that value recognized in earnings or stockholders' equity. Under the deferral method, gains and losses from derivatives were deferred on the balance sheet and recognized in earnings in conjunction with earnings of designated items. Under the accrual method, each net payment or receipt due or owed under the derivative was recognized in earnings during the period to which the payment or receipt related; there was no recognition on the balance sheet for changes in the derivative's fair value.

All that is now so much history. All derivative instruments are subject to fair value accounting. And hedging rules have been clearly spelled out so that there is no longer the tug-of-war between accounting applications suggested in FASB 52, *Foreign Currency Translation* (amended by FASB 133), and FASB 80, *Accounting for Futures Contracts* (superseded by FASB 133). Various other interpretations and opinions have also been superseded in an attempt to bring uniformity to accounting for derivatives.

As a result of lack of consistent direction during its 1994–1995 reviews of filings, the SEC staff observed that registrants, in attempting to interpret the literature, were accounting for the same type of derivative in many different ways. (We assume that it remained a moot question as to whether the interpretation was based on evidence of advantage to the registrant.) Thus, it was difficult to compare the financial statement effects of derivatives across registrants.

## Building on FASB 119

In order to provide a better understanding of the accounting for derivative financial instruments, FASB 119 required disclosure of the policies used to account for such instruments, in line with the requirements of APB 22. Specifically, FASB 119 emphasized the disclosure of policies for recognizing, or not recognizing, and measuring derivative financial instruments. When recognized, the location of where those instruments and related gains and losses were reported in the statements of financial position and income must be clearly indicated.

However, FASB 119 did not provide explicit instruction concerning what must be disclosed in accounting policies footnotes to make more understandable the effects of derivatives on the statements of financial position, cash flows, and results of operations; and it does not address disclosure of accounting policies for derivative commodity instruments. Thus, to facilitate a more informed assessment of the effects of derivatives on financial statements, the amendments make explicit the items to be disclosed in the accounting policies footnotes for derivative financial instruments and derivative commodity instruments. At this time, the SEC was still very hopeful that the FASB would come up with a more effective answer to the *accounting* problem as they attempted to deal with the disclosure problem. Possibly their faith will be justified by results from FASB 133.

## Disclosure Rule in Regulation S-X

The SEC's amendments to Regulation S-X require enhanced descriptions in the footnotes to the financial statements of accounting policies for derivative financial instruments and derivative commodity instruments. These disclosures are required unless the registrant's derivative activities are not material. The materiality of derivatives' activities is to be measured by the fair values of derivative financial instruments and derivative commodity instruments at the end of each reporting period, and the fair value of those instruments during each reporting period.

The amendments pertaining to accounting policies add a new paragraph to Regulation S-X to require disclosure in the footnotes to the financial statements relating:

1) Each method used to account for derivatives.
2) Types of derivatives accounted for under each method.
3) The criteria required to be met for each accounting method used (e.g., the manner in which risk reduction, correlation, designation, and/or effectiveness tests are applied).
4) The accounting method used if the specified criteria are not met.
5) The accounting for the termination of derivatives designated as hedges or used to affect directly or indirectly the terms, fair values, or cash flows of a designated item.
6) The accounting for derivatives if the designated item matures, or is sold, extinguished, terminated, or, if related to an anticipated transaction, is no longer likely to occur.
7) Where and when derivatives and their related gains and losses are reported in the statements of financial position, cash flows, and results of operations.

The amendments require registrants to distinguish between accounting policies used for derivatives entered into for trading purposes, and those that are entered into for purposes other than trading.

Disclosure of accounting policies for derivatives are required unless the registrant's derivative activities are not material. The materiality of derivatives activities is to be measured by the fair values of derivative financial instruments and derivative commodity instruments at the end of each reporting period, and the fair value of those instruments during each reporting period. In essence, the amendments clarified the application of the accounting policy disclosure requirements that had been set forth in FASB 119 for derivative financial instruments. They also extended those requirements to the disclosure of accounting policies for derivative commodity instruments.

## Disclosure of Quantitative and Qualitative Information About Market Risk in Regulation S-K and Elsewhere

The amendments create a new item in Regulation S-K, requiring disclosure outside the financial statements of *quantitative* and *qualitative* information about derivative financial instruments, other financial instruments, and derivative commodity instruments. If any of the following items are material, these disclosures are required:

1) The fair values of market risk sensitive instruments outstanding at the end of the current reporting period.

2) The potential loss in future earnings, fair values, or cash flows of market risk sensitive instruments from reasonably possible market movements.

In complying with the proposed amendments requiring disclosure of quantitative information about market risk, registrants would be permitted to select any one of the three disclosure alternatives listed above as well as the necessary qualitative information. However, it must be remembered that market risk is inherent in *both derivative and nonderivative* instruments, including:

1) Other financial instruments, comprised of nonderivative financial instruments such as investments, loans, structured notes, mortgage-backed securities, indexed instruments, interest-only and principal-only obligations, deposits, and other debt obligations.

2) Derivative financial instruments—futures, forwards, swaps, options, and other financial instruments with similar characteristics.

3) Derivative commodity instruments that are reasonably possible to be settled in cash or with another financial instrument including commodity futures, commodity forwards, commodity swaps, com-

modity options, and other commodity instruments with similar characteristics, to the extent such instruments are not derivative financial instruments.

Generally accepted accounting principles (GAAP) and SEC rules require disclosure of certain *quantitative* information about some of these derivative financial instruments. For example, registrants are currently required to disclose notional amounts of derivative financial instruments and the nature and terms of debt obligations. However, this information is often abbreviated, is presented piecemeal in different parts of the financial statements, and does not apply to all market risk sensitive instruments. Thus, investors often are unable to determine whether, if, or how particular financial and commodity instruments actually affect a registrant's net market risk exposure. FASB 119 encouraged, but did not require, disclosure of quantitative information about the overall market risk inherent in derivative financial instruments and other instruments subject to market risk. Therefore, implementation of this portion of the amendments is spelled out in detail for both quantitative and qualitative disclosure.

## General Considerations on Quantitative Disclosure

In addition to selecting and using one of the three alternative quantitative market risk disclosure methods, registrants are required to discuss material limitations that could cause that information not to reflect the overall market risk of the entity. This discussion necessarily includes descriptions of each limitation, and if applicable, the instruments' features that are not reflected fully within the selected quantitative market risk disclosure alternative.

Registrants are also required to summarize information for the preceding fiscal year, and discuss the reasons for any material changes in quantitative information about market risk when compared to the information reported in the previous period. Provision is made for companies to change their method of presentation of the quantitative information from one to another of the three alternatives. However, if they do change, they should explain why they changed, and summarize comparable information under the new method for the year preceding the year of the change.

## Qualitative Information About Market Risk

A *qualitative* discussion of a registrant's market risk exposures, and how those exposures are managed, is important to an understanding of a registrant's market risk. Such qualitative disclosures help place market risk management activities in the context of the business and, therefore, are a useful complement to quantitative information about market risk. FASB 119 required that certain qualitative disclosures be provided about market risk management activities associated with derivative financial instruments held or issued for purposes other than trading. In particular, it required disclosure of the entity's objectives for holding or issuing the derivative financial instruments, the context needed to understand those objectives, and its general strategies for achieving those objectives. In addition, Statement 119 required separate disclosures about derivative financial instruments used as hedges of anticipated transactions. As indicated above, these requirements applied only to certain derivatives held or issued for purposes other than trading.

In essence, the qualitative disclosure requirements created a new requirement in Regulation S-K, which expanded certain FASB 119 disclosures to:

1) Encompass derivative commodity instruments, other financial instruments, and derivative financial instruments entered into for trading purposes.

2) Require registrants to evaluate and describe material changes in their primary risk exposures, and material changes in how those exposures are managed.

In particular, the amendments require narrative disclosure outside the financial statements of:

1) A registrant's primary market risk exposures.

2) How those exposures are managed; e.g., a description of the objectives, general strategies, and instruments, if any, used to manage those exposures.

In preparing the qualitative disclosures about market risk, the Commission expects registrants to describe their primary market risk exposures as they exist at the end of the current reporting period, and how those risks currently are being managed. Registrants also are asked to describe material changes in their primary market risk exposures and material changes in how these risks are managed as compared to what was in effect during the most recent reporting period, and what is known or expected to be in effect in future reporting periods.

These qualitative disclosure requirements apply to derivative financial instruments, other financial instruments, and derivative commodity instruments. As in the case with respect to the quantitative disclosures about market risk, the qualitative disclosures are presented separately for market risk sensitive instruments that are entered into for trading purposes, and those that are entered into for purposes other than trading. In addition, qualitative information about market risk is presented separately for those instruments used to manage risks inherent in anticipated transactions.

Finally, to help make disclosures about market risk more comprehensive, as is the case with the quantitative disclosures, the Commission also is encouraging registrants to disclose qualitative information about market risk relating to other items, such as derivative commodity instruments not reasonably possible to be settled in cash or with another financial instrument, commodity position, cash flows from anticipated transactions, and operating cash flows from nonfinancial and noncommodity instruments, e.g., cash flows generated by manufacturing activities.

# Chapter 17

## The Securities and Exchange Commission: Private Securities Litigation Reform Act of 1995

To reduce the number of frivolous class action lawsuits, Congress passed the Private Securities Litigation Reform Act of 1995 (the Act). The Act revises the securities laws that professional investors and class action lawyers have used against corporations, accountants, and securities underwriters to win billions of dollars in damages. A safe harbor provision now protects companies from the legal liability for forecasts that subsequently proved to be incorrect, as well as for statements that were inaccurate when they were made. Key personnel of a large number of national CPA firms and various state CPA associations urged members of Congress to support reforms in the bill; the passage of the bill is considered to be significantly helpful to business corporations and the accounting and investment banking professions. The law encourages the dissemination of forward-looking information and forecasts, using easily understood language that lessens the possibility of frivolous lawsuits by the users of financial statements. The Act's fundamental purpose is to address concerns, raised in a number of Congressional hearings over a four-year period, that the securities litigation system was misaligned in a way that overcompensated weak cases to the detriment of strong cases, and that served investor interests poorly. As the Statement of Managers accompanying the Conference Report explained:

"The private securities litigation system is too important to the integrity of American capital markets to allow this system to be undermined by those who seek to line their own pockets by bringing abusive lawsuits. Private securities litigation is an indispensable tool with which defrauded investors can recover their losses without having to rely upon government

250

action. Such private lawsuits promote public and global confidence in our capital markets, help to deter wrongdoing, and guarantee that corporate officers, auditors, directors, lawyers, and others perform their jobs properly. This legislation seeks to return the securities litigation system to that high standard."

## PROVISIONS OF THE ACT

The following are some of the Act's provisions:

1) The Act implements a system of proportionate liability in which peripheral defendants pay only their fair share of a judgment. Less accountable defendants will pay a proportionate share of the damages, but parties that knowingly engage in fraudulent actions are still subject to the fullest extent of joint and several liability. Proponents of the bill argued that joint and several liability in the previous law caused plaintiffs' lawyers to target rich defendants.

   The proportionate liability of proportionately liable defendants can exceed their percentage of responsibility in two respects. First, if the liability share of any codefendant is found to be uncollectible within six months of entry of the judgment, proportionately liable defendants will be liable for the uncollectible portion in proportion to their share of responsibility, up to 50 % of each covered person's proportionate share. Second, plaintiffs with net worth of under $200,000 and who incur damages equal to more than 10% of their net worth could still enforce their judgment against all defendants jointly and severally.

   The Act also clarifies a number of open issues concerning the operation of rights of contribution among codefendants. A defendant who settles a private action is discharged from all claims of contribution brought by other persons, and any subsequent judgment in the action is reduced by the greater of the percentage of responsibility of the settling defendant or the amount paid to the plaintiff by the settling defendant. A defendant against whom a judgment is not collectible is subject to contribution and to continuing liability to the plaintiff. A proportionate share of responsibility has a contribution claim against other defendants, except settling defendants, or any other person responsible for the conduct. All claims for contribution are to be determined based on the percentage of responsibility of the claimant and of each person who would have been liable if joined in the original action. Contribution claims are subject to a six-month statute of limitations.

2) A significant part of the Act for the various professions is its system of proportionate liability which the professions had urged Congress to adopt as part of the legislation. For example, a defendant who is found only to have acted carelessly, and did not *knowingly* commit fraud, would be responsible for a proportionate amount of the damages instead of for the fullest amount of money possible as under the old law.

3) All defendants involved in the action remain jointly and severally liable to investors with a net worth under $200,000 who lost more than 10% of their net worth. Defendants liable for their proportionate share are also liable for up to an additional 50% of their share to help pay for insolvent codefendants.

4) The Act encourages voluntary disclosure of forward-looking information to investors by establishing a carefully designed safe harbor rule. The safe harbor protects statements made and meaningful cautionary risk disclosures that identify factors that could alter actual results.

5) Language was added to the safe harbor provision to make certain that forward-looking information has meaningful support behind it. The safe harbor does not protect those who knowingly make a false or misleading statement.

6) The 1995 Act requires that auditors immediately disclose illegal acts discovered in the course of an audit. Auditors must notify the SEC of illegal acts ignored or improperly considered by management. This puts a time limit on when illegal acts must be reported to the SEC. The board of directors has *one* business day to report to the SEC that the independent auditor has reported a material illegal act, and the auditor has determined that senior management and the board of directors have not taken appropriate actions, or are not expected to take appropriate action. If the independent auditor does not receive a copy of the board of directors' report to the SEC within the one business day period, the independent auditor must resign from the engagement or furnish the SEC with a copy of the original fraud report. This requirement ensures immediate reporting of illegal acts.

7) The Act gives the SEC the power to sue people or companies for aiding and abetting others who commit fraud. The provision is designed to ensure the SEC's enforcement authority which prevents aiding and abetting from not being considered an actionable offense in private securities fraud lawsuits.

8) The law does not require the loser of a case to pay all attorneys' fees, but it does impose sanctions against attorneys who file frivolous lawsuits. If a court finds that either the plaintiff's or the defendant's attorneys made arguments that were legally irrelevant or lacking evidentiary support, the court must impose sanctions unless it is a trifling violation. Reasonable

attorneys' costs and fees are presumed to be adequate reimbursement. The statute of limitations is not changed with respect to the three-year time limit for filing securities fraud lawsuits. Current law permits actions to be brought within one year after discovery of an alleged violation, and no more than three years after the alleged violation occurred.

## CERTIFICATION FILED WITH COMPLAINT

Each plaintiff seeking to serve as a representative party on behalf of a class must provide a sworn certification, which shall be personally signed by the plaintiff and filed with the complaint, that states that the plaintiff has reviewed the complaint and authorized this filing, and states that the plaintiff did not purchase the security that is the subject of the complaint at the direction of plaintiff's counsel or in order to participate in any private action.

## NONWAIVER OF ATTORNEY PRIVILEGE

The certification filed shall not be construed to be a waiver of the attorney-client privilege.

## APPOINTMENT OF LEAD PLAINTIFF

No later than 20 days after the date on which the complaint is filed, the plaintiff or plaintiffs shall cause to be published, in a widely circulated national business-oriented publication or wire service, a notice advising members of the purported plaintiff class of the action, and the claims asserted therein. Not later than 60 days after the date on which the notice is published, any member of the purported class may move the court to serve as lead plaintiff of the purported class.

No later than 90 days after the date on which a notice is published, the court shall consider any motion made by a class member who is not individually named as a plaintiff in the complaint or complaints, and shall appoint as lead plaintiff the member or members of the purported plaintiff class that the court determines to be most capable of adequately representing the interests of class members who is referred to as the *most adequate plaintiff.*

## ADDITIONAL NOTICES REQUIRED UNDER FEDERAL RULES

Notice required under the early notice requirement should be in addition to any other required notice.

## CONSOLIDATED ACTIONS

If more than one action on behalf of a class asserts substantially the same claim or claims for pretrial purposes or trial, the court will appoint the most adequate plaintiff as lead plaintiff for the consolidated actions.

## REBUTTABLE PRESUMPTION

The court shall adopt a presumption that the most adequate plaintiff in any private action is the person or group of persons who has either filed the complaint, or made a motion in response to a notice in the determination of the court, and has the largest financial interest in the relief sought by the class.

## DISCOVERY

Discovery relating to whether a member or members of the purported plaintiff class is the most adequate plaintiff can be conducted by a plaintiff only if the plaintiff first demonstrates a reasonable basis for a finding that the presumptively most adequate plaintiff is incapable of adequately representing the class.

## SELECTION OF LEAD COUNSEL

The most adequate plaintiff will, subject to the approval of the court, select and retain counsel to represent the class.

## RESTRICTIONS ON PROFESSIONAL PLAINTIFFS

A person may be a lead plaintiff, or an officer, director, or fiduciary of a lead plaintiff, in no more than five securities class actions brought as plaintiff class actions.

## RECOVERY BY PLAINTIFFS

The share of any final judgment or of any settlement that is awarded to a representative party serving on behalf of a class shall be equal, on a per share basis, to the portion of the final judgment or settlement awarded to all members of the class. However, the court may permit lead plaintiffs to recover reasonable costs and expenses, including lost wages.

## RESTRICTIONS ON SETTLEMENTS UNDER SEAL

The terms and provisions of any settlement of a class action should not be filed under seal, except that on motion of any party to the settlement, the court can order filing under seal for those portions of a settlement agreement as to which good cause is shown for a filing under seal.

## RESTRICTIONS ON PAYMENT OF ATTORNEYS' FEES AND EXPENSES

Total attorneys' fees and expenses awarded by the court to counsel for the plaintiff class shall not exceed a reasonable percentage of the amount of any damage and prejudgment interest actually paid to the class.

## DISCLOSURE OF SETTLEMENT TERMS TO CLASS MEMBERS

Any proposed or final settlement agreement that is published or otherwise disseminated to the class will include a cover page summarizing the information contained in the following statements:

*Statement of plaintiff recovery.* The amount of the settlement proposed to be distributed to the parties to the action, is determined in the aggregate and on an average per share basis.

*Agreement of the amount of damages.* If the settling parties agree on the average amount of damages per share that would be recoverable if the plaintiff prevailed on each claim alleged, a statement concerning the average amount of such potential damages per share, and a statement from each settling party should be made.

*Disagreement on the amount of damages.* If the parties do not agree on the average amount of damages per share that would be recoverable if the plaintiff prevailed on each claim alleged, a statement from each settling party must be made concerning the issue or issues on which the parties disagree.

*Inadmissibility for certain purposes.* A statement made concerning the amount of damages shall not be admissible in any federal or state judicial action or administrative proceeding, other than an action or proceeding arising out of such statement.

*Statement of attorneys' fees or costs sought.* If any of the settling parties or their counsel intend to apply to the court for an award of attorneys' fees or costs from any fund established as part of the settlement, a statement indicating which parties or counsel intend to make such an application, the amount of such fees and costs determined on an average per share basis, and a brief explanation supporting the fees and costs sought is required. Such information will be clearly summarized on the cover page of any notice to a party of any proposed or final settlement agreement.

*Identification of lawyers' representatives.* The name, telephone number, and address of one or more representatives of counsel for the plaintiff class who will be reasonably available to answer questions from the class.

*Reasons for settlement.* A brief statement explaining the reasons why the parties are proposing the settlement must be made.

*Other information.* Information that might be required by the court.

## ATTORNEY CONFLICT OF INTEREST

If a plaintiff class is represented by an attorney who directly owns or otherwise has a beneficial interest in the securities that are the subject of a litigation, the court shall make a determination of whether such ownership or other interest constitutes a conflict of interest sufficient to disqualify the attorney from representing the plaintiff class.

## SECURITY FOR PAYMENT OF COSTS IN CLASS ACTIONS

In any private action that is certified as a class action, the court may require an undertaking from the attorneys for the plaintiff class, the plaintiffs' class, or both, in such proportions and at such times as the court determines are just and equitable for the payment of fees and expenses that may be awarded.

The Act does permit a court to require plaintiffs, defendants, or their attorneys to post a bond for the payment of fees and expenses that may be awarded.

## MISLEADING STATEMENTS AND OMISSIONS

In actions in which the plaintiff alleges that the defendant made an untrue statement of a material fact, or omitted a material fact necessary to prevent the statements from being misleading, the complaint must specify the following:

1)  Each statement alleged to have been misleading,
2)  The reason or reasons why the statement is misleading, and

3) If an allegation regarding the statement or omission is made on information and belief, the complaint should state the specific facts on which that belief is based.

## REQUIRED STATE OF MIND

In any private action in which the plaintiff may recover money damages only on proof that the defendant acted with a particular state of mind, the complaint shall state specifically which facts give rise to a strong inference that the defendant acted with the required state of mind.

## SANCTION FOR WILLFUL VIOLATION

A party aggrieved by the willful failure of an opposing party to comply with this Act may apply to the court for an order awarding appropriate sanctions.

## CAUSATION OF LOSS

In any private action, the plaintiff shall have the burden of proving that the act or omission of the defendant alleged to violate this Act caused the loss for which the plaintiff seeks to recover damages.

## LIMITATION ON DAMAGES

Stock prices frequently have a tendency to recover part of their market price after the initial price adjustment to adverse news about a company. If a security recovers some or all of its market price during the 90-day period after the dissemination of information correcting the misstatement or omission that is the basis for the action, damages will be capped at the difference between the price paid for the security and the mean trading price of the security during the 90-day period.

If the plaintiff sells or repurchases the subject security prior to the expiration of the 90-day period, the plaintiff's damages shall not exceed the difference between the purchase or sale price paid or received, as appropriate, by the plaintiff for the security and the mean trading price of the security during the period beginning immediately after dissemination of information correcting the misstatement or omission and ending on the date on which the plaintiff sells or repurchases the security. For the purposes of this rule, the *mean trading price* of a security shall be an average of the daily trading price of that security, determined as of the close of the market each day during the 90-day period.

## Private Class Actions

The provisions of this Act shall apply in each private action arising that is brought as a plaintiff class action.

## Multiple Actions

If more than one action is filed on behalf of a class asserting substantially the same claim or claims, only the plaintiff or plaintiffs in the first filed action will be required to cause notice to be published.

## Presumption in Favor of Attorneys' Fees and Costs for Abusive Litigation

The court shall adopt a presumption that the appropriate sanction for failure of any responsive pleading, or dispositive motion to comply with any requirement of the court, is an award to the opposing party of the reasonable attorneys' fees and other expenses incurred as a direct violation.

## Rebuttal Evidence for Sanctions Against Abusive Litigation

The presumption may be rebutted only upon proof by the party, or attorney against whom sanctions are to be imposed, that the award of attorneys' fees and other expenses will impose an unreasonable burden on that party or attorney and would be unjust, and the failure to make such an award would not impose a greater burden on the party in whose favor sanctions are to be imposed. If the party or attorney against whom sanctions are to be imposed meets its burden, the court shall award the sanctions that the court deems appropriate.

## Availability of Documents

Any document filed with the Commission or generally disseminated shall be deemed to be readily available.

## STAY PENDING DECISION ON MOTION EXEMPTION AUTHORITY

In any private action, the court shall stay discovery, other than discovery that is specifically directed to the application of an exemption, during the tendency of any motion by a defendant for summary judgment that is based on the ground that the statement or omission upon which the complaint is used is a forward-looking statement, and the exemption provided precludes a claim for relief.

## EXEMPTION AUTHORITY

The Commission may provide presumptions from any provision of this Act that is consistent with the public interest and the protection of investors as determined by the Commission.

## EFFECT ON OTHER AUTHORITY OF THE COMMISSION

Nothing in the Act limits, either expressly or by implication, the authority of the Commission to exercise similar authority or to adopt similar rules and regulations with respect to forward-looking statements under any other statute under which the Commission exercises rule-making authority.

## DEFINITION OF FORWARD-LOOKING STATEMENTS

*Forward-Looking Statement.* The term means a statement containing a projection of revenues, income including income loss, earnings including earnings loss per share, capital expenditures, dividends, capital structure, or other financial items. These could include, but are not limited to, the following:

- A statement of the plans and objectives of management for future operations, including plans or objectives relating to the products or services of the issuer.
- A statement of future economic performance, including any such statement contained in a discussion and analysis of financial condition by the management or in results of operations included pursuant to the rules and regulations of the Commission.
- Any statement of the admissions underlying or relating to any other statement.

- Any report issued by an outside reviewer retained by an issuer, to the extent that the report assesses a forward-looking statement made by the issuer.

- A statement containing a projection or estimate of such other items as may be specified by rule or regulation of the Commission.

## SAFE HARBOR FOR FORWARD-LOOKING STATEMENTS

Liability for forward-looking statements such as earnings or sales forecasts has had the undesirable effect of discouraging companies from sharing such information with investors, despite keen market interest in this information. This has become a particular concern for high technology companies which tend to have volatile stock prices, and therefore are frequent targets of class action lawsuits when projections are not realized. While the primary beneficiaries of the safe harbor are issuers and their officers, the Act also offers useful protection to broker-dealers in their roles as underwriters and analysts. The safe harbor is offered to:

1) An issuer who, at the time that the statement is made, is subject to the reporting requirements of the Exchange Act.
2) A person acting on behalf of such issuer.
3) An outside reviewer retained by such issuer making a statement on behalf of such issuer.
4) An underwriter, with respect to information provided by such issuer or information derived from information provided by the issuer.

In addition, the safe harbor excludes certain categories of issuers and transactions, most notably issuers who have been subject to criminal or SEC enforcement sanctions within the preceding three years, issuers that are investment companies, and statements made in connection with a tender offer or initial public offering, or that are included in an audited financial statement. The safe harbor generally applies to a forward-looking statement if it is identified as a forward-looking statement, and is accompanied by meaningful cautionary statements identifying important factors that could cause actual results to differ materially from those in the forward-looking statement; or is immaterial; or the plaintiff fails to prove the forward-looking statement was made with actual knowledge; or if made by a business entity was made by and with the approval of an executive officer of that entity, and made or approved by such officer with actual knowledge by that officer that the statement was false or misleading.

Oral statements made by an issuer, or by a person acting on behalf of such issuer, can also be covered under a corollary formulation of the safe harbor. Under the corollary, an oral statement qualifies for the safe harbor if the oral statement is accompanied by a cautionary statement pointing out that the oral statement is a forward-looking statement, that actual results may vary, and identifying an available written document setting out the meaningful cautionary statements identifying important factors that could cause actual results to differ that are required by the primary safe harbor.

The safe harbor was drafted in such a way that even if a forward-looking projection or estimate did not contain adequate cautionary language, a plaintiff would still have to prove that the speaker had actual knowledge that the statement was false or misleading. The safe harbor directs courts to stay all discovery, except for discovery directed at the applicability of the safe harbor, while a motion to dismiss based on the safe harbor is pending.

## Class Action Reforms

The Act creates a procedure for the court to appoint as lead plaintiff the plaintiff with the largest financial interest. The Act also adopts other class action reforms, such as prohibiting the payment of referral fees to securities brokers.

## Proportionate Liability and Contributions

The Act generally limits joint and several liability to persons who knowingly commit a violation of the securities laws. The Act requires a defendant to pay 50% more than its proportionate share of damages in certain cases where other defendants' shares are uncollectible, and preserves joint and several liability for plaintiffs with a net worth under $200,000 whose damages exceed 10% of their net worth. The Act clarifies certain issues regarding the operation of rights of contribution.

## Reduction of Damage

The Act provides that a defendant can reduce damages by proving that all or part of the decline in the value of the securities was caused by factors other than the alleged misstatement or material omission in the prospectus.

## Right of Rescission

The Act provides a right of rescission to the buyer of a security if the security was sold in violation of the registration or prospectus delivery requirements, or if it was offered or sold by means of a prospectus or oral communication which included an untrue statement of a material fact or omitted to state a material fact.

## AIDING AND ABETTING

The Act gives the SEC (but not private plaintiffs) authority to bring civil injunctive actions and to seek civil money penalties against any person who knowingly provides substantial assistance to another person in violation of the Exchange Act to the same extent as the person to whom such assistance is provided.

## STAY OF DISCOVERY AND PRESERVATION OF EVIDENCE

A stay of discovery is required while a motion to dismiss is pending, other than a particular discovery needed to preserve evidence. Any party to the action with actual notice of the allegations contained in the complaint shall treat all documents, data compilation, and tangible objects that are in the custody or control of such person and that are relevant to the allegations, as if they were the subject of a continuing request for production of documents from an opposing party. A party aggrieved by the willful failure of an opposing party to comply with this requirement may apply to the court for sanctions. The use of the term *willful failure* should give protection from liability for inadvertent violations.

## PROTECTIONS FOR SENIOR CITIZENS AND QUALIFIED INVESTMENT RETIREMENT PLANS

The SEC must determine whether senior citizens or qualified retirement plans have been adversely impacted by abusive securities fraud litigation and whether they are adequately protected from such litigation by the Act. If the SEC finds any such adverse impact or lack of adequate protection, it is to submit to Congress a report containing recommendations for protection from securities fraud, or for protection from abusive litigation.

## RACKETEER INFLUENCED AND CORRUPT ORGANIZATION ACT (RICO)

The Act eliminates private RICO liability, with its accompanying exposure to treble damages, for conduct that would have been actionable as fraud in the purchase or sale of securities. This does not apply to an action against any person who is criminally convicted in connection with the fraud, in which case the statute of limitations will begin to run from the date the conviction becomes final.

## PROPORTIONATE LIABILITY

Major accounting firms argued that joint and several liability under the anti-fraud provisions of the securities laws had created an unjustifiable liability exposure in cases where their role was relatively peripheral, but their potential deep-pocket liability for the more culpable conduct of others was enormous. Accounting firms argued that this disproportionate liability exposure was forcing them to curtail audit services for companies that were regarded as high risks for potential litigation, particularly start-up firms and firms with volatile stock prices in the high technology sectors. In place of joint and several liability, accounting firms sought a limited system of proportionate liability, so that the liability of less culpable defendants would bear some relationship to their degree of responsibility for the damages incurred.

The Act provides that a defendant in an action is jointly and severally liable only if the person who tries the facts specifically finds that the defendant *knowingly committed* a violation of the securities laws. The provision provides an extensive clarification of the term, which essentially requires that the defendant engaged in conduct with actual knowledge of the facts and circumstances that make the conduct a violation of the securities laws. The Act also expressly provides that *reckless conduct* will not be construed to constitute a knowing commission of a violation of the securities laws. The Act also takes pains to avoid supporting the argument that recklessness is a sufficient standard for anti-fraud liability by providing that nothing in the Act should be construed to create, affect, or in any manner modify, the standard of liability associated with any action arising under the securities laws. For defendants who are not found to have committed a knowing violation of the securities laws, the Act offers a qualified form of proportionate liability. Such a defendant is only liable for the portion of the judgment that corresponds to its percentage of responsibility. In determining the percentage of responsibility for each defendant, the person examining the facts must consider:

1) The nature of the conduct of each covered person found to have caused or contributed to the loss incurred by the plaintiff or plaintiffs.

2) The nature and extent of the causal relationship between the conduct of each such person and the damages incurred by the plaintiff or plaintiffs.

## INDEMNIFICATION AGREEMENTS

The indemnification agreement expressly permits a defendant to recover attorneys' fees and costs incurred in connection with an action in which the defendant prevails. The Act does not change the enforceability of indemnification contracts in the event of settlement.

## RULE OF CONSTRUCTION

The Act clarifies two points:

1) Nothing in the Act is to be deemed to prevent the SEC from restricting or otherwise regulating private actions under the Exchange Act.
2) Nothing in the Act is to be deemed to create or ratify any implied right of action.

## THE ACT'S EXCEPTION PROVISION

The Act's exception for material of little value could alleviate a concern about the Act's use of the term *substantial* in relation to complaints. The word *substantial* might be used to argue that plaintiffs' complaints are to be subjected to a less rigorous scrutiny than papers filed by other parties. The ability to rebut any finding of a violation by showing that the finding was of little value suggests that the standard probably will be the same for both plaintiffs and defendants. Although it is not clear whether there is some distinction intended between substantial and irrelevancy, *the exception provision* in the Act was not the intention of Congress to hold defendants to a more stringent standard than plaintiffs.

## CONCLUSION

The Act reforms many of the procedures that govern private class actions. It is intended to address a number of concerns about securities class actions, such as the race to the courthouse to file cases within days or even hours of a sharp stock price decline; the ability of attorneys to select plaintiffs with nominal holdings to bring a class action case; the lack of opportunities for institutional investors to participate in litigation brought on their behalf; and the lack of effective notice to investors of the terms of class action settlements. Institutional investors are encouraged to take a more active role in securities class action lawsuits. Within 20 days of filing a class action lawsuit, the plaintiff must provide notice to members of the purported class. The notice is to identify the claims alleged in the lawsuit and indicate that potential members have 60 days from publication to file a motion to seek to serve as lead plaintiff. If more than one action is filed, only the plaintiff in the first action is required to file the notice. The notice must be filed in a widely circulated business publication.

Once designated by the court, the lead plaintiff is authorized to select and retain counsel for the class. It is unclear whether this provision would encompass other related powers, such as to replace counsel, to direct litigation strategy, or to reject or give preliminary approval to settlements. The amount of autonomy that courts actually give to lead plaintiffs to manage the case could have a significant impact on whether institutional investors will avail themselves of this new procedure.

# Chapter 18

# Y2K: U.S. Securities and Exchange Commission and International Organization of Securities Commissions

## PREPARE FOR THE YEAR 2000 (Y2K)

All of the concern, cajoling, scare tactics, threats, warnings, cautions, plans, and provisions about the Year 2000 problem may turn out to be a good thing in preventing complete chaos worldwide, or it may have been overplayed.

On the other hand, when one thinks of the global extent of the use of computers by governments, banks, stock exchanges, commodity markets—down to the smallest factory or business in a developing economy—maybe it's impossible to overstate the threat. After all, computer links do "link" a chain which could snap at any juncture. Regardless, we can all blame it on the '60s for being penny wise and pound foolish in designing and developing computer programs using only two digits to identify a year in the date field without considering the impact of the upcoming change in the century.

## Y2K FIASCO?

If not corrected, those computer applications using two digits rather than four could fail or create erroneous results by, or at, the Year 2000. The Year 2000 issue affects virtually all companies and organizations.

As most of us are aware by now, the problem results from the inability of computer hardware and software operating on a two-digit year to cope with the end of the century. The digits 00 may be misinterpreted, for example, as 1900, as some special code, or a glitch in the system, with the distinct possibility of causing errors or operational failure of the computer systems. The impact is evidently not easy to predict, because even though the basic Year 2000 issue is well publicized, there are many areas in which even the computer experts disagree on how it should be handled. The two most widely used spreadsheet programs attack the problem in different ways. And what about the year-formatted data imported from other spreadsheets, accounting software databases, or an Internet Web site? Yes, it would be wise to look ahead.

The Year 2000 issue may manifest itself before, on, or after January 2000, and its effects on financial reporting and operations may range from inconsequential errors to business failure. Obviously, this is a major concern to all accountants, auditors, and the general business community.

## SECURITIES AND EXCHANGE COMMISSION'S CAUTIONARY MEASURES

Almost any organization dealing with accounting and finance has issued a pronouncement of one sort or another dealing with Y2K. The U.S. Securities and Exchange Commission is facing the problem on several fronts. Wanting to be sure that an entity's need for and cost of preparing computer adjustments to face the new millennium is out in the open and readily apparent to the investing public, the SEC recently updated Staff Legal Bulletin No. 5 (CF/IM). This report was prepared by the Divisions of Corporation Finance and of Investment Management.

The bulletin reminds public operating companies, investment advisers, and investment companies to consider their disclosure obligations relating to anticipated costs, problems, and uncertainties associated with the Year 2000 issue. Originally issued in October 1997, the bulletin was revised in January 1998. Its purpose is to emphasize the importance of the Year 2000 issue and provide specific *guidance* relating to *existing* Commission rules and regulations. (Uncertainty had been expressed by members of the accounting and legal professions regarding just what should be disclosed.)

The announcement cautions that this bulletin is not a rule, regulation, or statement of the SEC, but represents the Divisions staffs' views of how the concerns should be handled. The Commission has not approved or disapproved the content.

## Disclosure by Public Companies Regarding the Y2K Issue

The disclosure provisions of the rules and forms applicable to public companies are intended to provide information that will enable the investing public to make informed investment and voting decisions. Taking this into consideration, the Division of Corporation Finance decided that, as they currently stand, the provisions are adequate with respect to companies whose filings are processed by that Division. Since they believe that the rules are adequate, the Division has given guidance to companies about the extent to which Year 2000 compliance issues should be disclosed in their public filings.

Legal Bulletin No. 5 points out that each company's potential costs and uncertainties will depend on a number of factors, including its software and hardware and the nature of the particular business or industry. Companies must also coordinate with other entities with which they electronically interact, both domestically and globally, including suppliers, customers, creditors, borrowers, and financial service organizations.

If an entity fails to address the situation successfully, it may face material adverse consequences. Companies should review, on an ongoing basis, whether they need to disclose anticipated costs, problems, and uncertainties associated with Y2K, particularly in their filings with the Commission. Public companies may have to disclose this information in Commission filings because:

1) The form or report may require the disclosure.

2) In addition to the information that the company is specifically required to disclose, the disclosure rules require disclosure of any further material information necessary to make the required disclosure *not misleading.*

3) Anti-fraud requirements of the Securities Act and the Exchange Act apply to statements and omissions both in Commission filings and outside of Commission filings.

### Disclosure: How, why, when and where.

1) Companies should include disclosure in their "Management's Discussion and Analysis of Financial Condition and Results of Operations" (MD&A), which appears in companies' annual reports and quarterly reports filed with the Commission, as well as in many registration statements, if:

   a) The cost of addressing the Year 2000 issue is a material event or there is uncertainty that would cause reported financial information *not* to be necessarily indicative of future operating results or financial condition.

   b) The costs and/or the consequences of incomplete or untimely resolution of their Year 2000 concerns represent a known material event or uncertainty that is reasonably expected to affect their future financial results, or cause their reported financial information not to be necessarily indicative of future operating results or future financial condition.

The Division noted in its Current Issues Outline that companies may be undertaking major research and development projects in order to address the problem. However, to the extent the problem is not successfully addressed, material adverse consequences could follow. Furthermore, if they have not disclosed their uncertainty, they could well be in trouble with the SEC as well as with investors and creditors.

**2)** If Year 2000 issues materially affect a company's products, services, or competitive conditions, companies may need to disclose this in their "Description of Business," item 101 of SEC regulations S-K and S-B. In their determination of whether to include disclosure, companies should consider the effects of the Year 2000 issue on *each* of their reportable segments. (Some may be much more susceptible to problems than others.)

**3)** A company's Y2K costs or consequences may reach a level of importance that prompts it to consider filing a Form 8-K. At their option, companies would file these reports under Item 5 of Form 8-K. In considering whether to file a Form 8-K, companies should be particularly mindful of the accuracy and completeness of information in registration statements filed under the Securities Act that incorporate by reference Exchange Act reports, including Form 8-Ks.

**4)** The Emerging Issues Task Force (EITF) considered the issue of how to account for the costs of modifying computer software for Year 2000 projects in the financial statements. In July 1996, the EITF concluded that these costs should be charged to expense as they are incurred. Costs that are expensed in any given year may require disclosure separately in the company's income statement depending on the materiality of the amount. (EITF is a group established in 1984 to assist the FASB in the early identification of emerging issues affecting financial reporting and of problems in implementing authoritative pronouncements.

**5)** If a company determines that it should make Y2K disclosure, applicable rules or regulations should be followed. If a company has not made an assessment of its Y2K issues or has not determined whether it believes it has material issues, the staff believes that disclosure of this *known uncertainty* is required.

***Materiality the deciding factor.*** In addition, the staff believes that the determination as to whether a company's Y2K issues should be disclosed should be based on whether they are *material* to a company's business, operations, or financial condition, regardless of whether the enterprise is in the process of doing something to counteract the problem or has established contingency plans. The mere fact that they are aware of the problem and are trying to do something about it does not guarantee that disaster will not strike with the millennium.

If the Year 2000 issues are determined to be material, without regard to corrective measures, the nature and potential impact of the Year 2000 issues as well as these corrective measures should be disclosed. As part of this disclosure, the staff expects, at the least, the following topics will be addressed:

1) The company's general plans to address the Year 2000 issues relating to its business, its operations (including operating systems), and, if material, its relationships with customers, suppliers, and other constituents; and its timetable for carrying out those plans.

2) The total dollar amount that the company estimates will be spent to remediate its Year 2000 issues, if such amount is expected to be material to the company's business, operations, or financial condition. It must also reveal any material impact these expenditures are expected to have on the company's results of operations, liquidity, and capital resources.

In a fairly humorous, or possibly cautionary, mood, "the staff" suggests that these disclosures "must be reasonably specific and meaningful, rather than standard boilerplate."

***Foreign company disclosure requirements.***    The SEC requires that foreign private issuers also follow the guidance in this bulletin. In particular, these issuers should consider the disclosure requirements of Form 20-F, Item 1, "Description of Business," and Item 9, "Management's Discussion and Analysis of Financial Condition and Results of Operations," as mentioned above.

## Application of FASB 5, *Accounting for Contingencies*

In addition to any special rules, regulations, or guidance offered relating to Y2K problems, the SEC points out that FASB literature also includes FASB 5, *Accounting for Contingencies.* The standard defines a contingency as an existing condition, situation, or set of circumstances involving uncertainty as to possible gain or loss contingency. When a loss contingency exists, the loss may range from probable to reasonably possible to remote. (In other words, it's anybody's guess just how bad this millennium problem may or may not be.) In the meantime:

1) An accrual is required if the loss is probable and can be reasonably estimated.

2)  If the contingency is not probable, or cannot be estimated, disclosure should be made when there is at least a reasonable possibility that a loss or additional loss may have been incurred. The disclosure should indicate the nature of the contingency and should give an estimate of the possible loss or range of loss or the disclosure should state that such an estimate cannot be made.

It would appear that a pending failure of an entity's computer system in the year 2000 would constitute a contingency that would require consideration by entities and their auditors that would fall under the accounting and disclosure requirements of FASB 5.

## Disclosure by Investment Companies and Investment Advisers

Under the Investment Advisers Act of 1940 and the Investment Company Act of 1940, investment advisers and investment companies may be required to make appropriate disclosure to clients and shareholders if operational or financial obstacles are presented by Y2K. Disclosure is necessary if it is materially misleading to shareholders to omit the information.

The Investment Company Act provides that it is unlawful for investment companies to omit from registration statements and other public filings "any fact necessary in order to prevent the statements made therein, in light of the circumstances under which they were made, from being materially misleading."

Open-end investment companies (mutual funds) are required by this Act to describe in their registration statements the experience of their investment advisers and the services that the advisers provide. Therefore, these investment companies may need to disclose the effect that the Year 2000 issue would have on their advisers' ability to provide the services described in their registration statements.

The anti-fraud provisions of the Investment Advisers Act generally impose on investment advisers an affirmative duty, consistent with their fiduciary obligations, to disclose to clients or prospective clients, material facts concerning their advisory or proposed advisory relationships.

If the failure to address the Year 2000 issue could materially affect the advisory services provided to clients, an adviser who will not be able to or is uncertain about his or her ability to address Y2K issues has an obligation to disclose such information to clients and prospective clients. This disclosure must be made in a timely manner so that the clients and prospective clients may take steps to protect their interests.

Investment companies and investment advisers who determine that Year 2000 disclosure is required should also follow the guidelines on disclosure discussed earlier.

## Temporary Legislation on Y2K

The Securities and Exchange Commission is soliciting comment on a proposed temporary rule under the Securities Exchange Act of 1934 that would require all registered transfer agents that are not banks to file with the Commission at least one report regarding its Year 2000 readiness. The initial report would be due no later than 45 days after the Commission adopts this rule with follow-up reports due on August 31, 1998, and on August 31, 1999. The follow-up reports would include an attestation by an independent public accountant that would give the accountant's opinion whether there is a reasonable basis for the transfer agent's assertions in the reports. Additionally, the Commission is issuing an advisory notice on its transfer agent record retention and record keeping requirements relating to the Year 2000.

***Securities industry readiness.***   The SEC is evaluating the ability of participants in the U.S. securities industry to manage and prevent Y2K problems. The Commission has identified six stages involved in the preparation for Y2K:

1) Awareness of potential problems.
2) Assessment of what steps the transfer agent must take to avoid possible problems.
3) Implementation of any steps needed to avoid them.
4) Internal testing of software designed to avoid perceived problems.
5) Integrated or industry-wide testing of software designed to avoid problems (including testing with other financial institutions and customers).
6) Implementation of *tested* software that will avoid Y2K hang-ups.

The internal and integrated testing stages are the most difficult, and likely will require the most resources. At the time of the Commission staff's June 1997 "Year 2000 Report" to Congress, most members of the securities industry were engaged in the assessment and remediation phases of the Year 2000 effort. At the request of Congress in June 1997, the Commission staff prepared a comprehensive report to Congress describing, in part, the extent to which the securities industry is preparing to avoid Year 2000 Problems. The result is titled, "Report to the Congress on the Readiness of the United States Securities Industry and Public Companies to Meet the Information Processing Challenges of the Year 2000." Similar reports are required for 1998 and 1999.

Additionally, beginning in the third quarter of 1996, the Commission's Office of Compliance Inspections and Examinations included a Year 2000 examination module in its examinations of broker-dealers and transfer agents.

***The transfer agent's role.***   The release focuses on the readiness of registered transfer agents to address the Year 2000 date change. Because accurate output from computer programs is vital to a transfer agent's operations, every transfer agent currently should be taking steps to avoid Year 2000 problems. For example, a transfer agent with Y2K concerns could experience, among other things, problems with computer programs:

1) Not accepting securities transfers.
2) Having difficulty calculating dividend payment dates for equity securities.
3) Having difficulty computing interest payment and maturity dates for debt securities.

Transfer agents present special considerations for the Commission because, unlike other entities regulated under the Exchange Act, transfer agents have no self-regulatory organization (SRO) to assist them and the Commission in achieving Year 2000 objectives.

(SROs are the organizations responsible for "industry rules," as distinguished from the regulatory agencies like the SEC and the Federal Reserve Board. SROs include all of the national securities and commodities exchanges, and the National Association of Securities Dealers (NASD), which represents the firms operating the over-the-counter market.)

Therefore, information about progress in dealing with Year 2000 problems must be obtained directly from the transfer agents by the SEC. All transfer agents for securities registered pursuant to Section 12 of the Exchange Act must register with the Commission. However, the federal banking agencies (like the Federal Reserve Board) provide the "appropriate regulatory agency" (ARA) for registered bank transfer agents. The Commission is coordinating its Year 2000 activities with the banking regulators to achieve complete coverage of transfer agents, and still avoid duplication of efforts.

## INTERNATIONAL ORGANIZATION OF SECURITIES COMMISSIONS

Isolation from the outside business and financial world is no more possible than it is from the political world; therefore, there are international business and financial bodies as well as political ones. The international body whose aim is to maintain and develop just, efficient, and sound markets is the International Organization of Securities Commissions (IOSCO), of which the U.S. Securities and Exchange Commission is a member.

## Two Problems: Millennium and Leap Year

Their Technical Committee on Year 2000 may have issued the most quotable statement on the problem, "At midnight on December 31, 1999, unless the proper modifications have been made, the program logic in the vast majority of the world's computer systems will start to produce erroneous results because, among other things, the systems will incorrectly read the date 01/01/00 as being January 1 of the year 1900 or another incorrect date. In addition, systems may fail to detect that the Year 2000 is a *leap year*.

"Problems also can arise earlier than January 1, 2000, as dates in the next millennium are entered into Year 2000 noncompliant programs. Year 2000 problems could have negative repercussions throughout the world's financial systems because of the extensive interrelationship and information sharing between U.S. and foreign financial firms and markets."

This may appear to be a strange time to worry about leap year, but some have considered it the "other" Year 2000 problem. To even things out between the solar year and the calendar year, the Gregorian calendar provides that century years are *not* leap years unless they are evenly divisible by 400; therefore, 1700, 1800 and 1900 were *not* leap years, but 2000 *is!* But would a computer know—or care?

The Technical Committee of the IOSCO is concerned that securities market participants and related parties should be adequately addressing the risks associated with Year 2000 in sufficient time. They realize that there are competing resource demands on firms and regulators alike, but they emphasize that failure to confront this problem may have very serious, even catastrophic, consequences for firms and markets worldwide. The Technical Committee therefore exhorts (they cannot mandate) all IOSCO members and market participants in their jurisdictions to take all appropriate and necessary action to address this critical matter.

## It's a Risky Business

It has been estimated that without corrective measures (which have, admittedly, begun apace) 90% of all computer applications worldwide would malfunction. But IOSCO underscores the fact that the Year 2000 problem is not simply a technology issue, but a core business and regulatory concern. As such, it requires the attention and support at the highest levels within all affected organizations. If one entity has problems, many will be affected. The risks that the Year 2000 poses must be carefully identified and addressed. The following risks should be considered, at a minimum:

1) *Completion risk:* Priorities must be established and a business plan developed in the event that all computer processes cannot be converted in time.

2) *Implementation risk:* Adequate planning must consider that projects may be delayed or encounter unforeseen problems.

3) *Relationship risk:* All external system relationships (e.g., vendors, counterparties, agents, clients, regulators) must be evaluated for their potential effect on the organization if these external systems are not ready in time.

4) *Contingency risk:* The organization must identify reasonably foreseeable operational disruptions that could occur even if it believes that all of its internal and external systems are Year 2000 compliant.

5) *Legal risk:* The organization must evaluate what liabilities it will incur if its systems are not ready in time, including the likelihood that market authorities will not accept a failure to prepare for Year 2000 as an excuse for noncompliance with regulatory requirements.

# Chapter 19
## Independent Contractor or Employee?

Whether a person is an employee or independent contractor has been an area of uncertainty for many years. In August 1996, during the 104th Congress, changing and strengthening the "safe harbor" provisions were enacted as part of the *Small Business Jobs Protection Act*. The changes allow small businesses to rely on previous IRS actions and determinations to avoid reclassification of independent contractors as employees. The legislation does, however, still leave open the key question of what exactly is an independent contractor.

To make the definition of an independent contractor as clear as possible under current law, the IRS issued a training manual for IRS personnel on the independent contractor issue; introduced procedures for facilitating rapid determinations and appeals; and reduced penalties where a business acts in good faith to classify its independent contractors.

## WORKER CLASSIFICATION

With the exception of statutory employees, work classification is based upon a common law standard for determining whether the worker is an independent contractor or employee. That standard essentially asks whether the business has the right to *direct and control the worker*. The courts have traditionally looked to a variety of evidentiary facts in applying this standard, and the IRS has adopted those facts to assist in classifying workers.

## Accountant's Concern?

When conducting an audit, the auditor needs to assist taxpayers in identifying all of the evidence relative to their business relationships with workers. Many taxpayers may not be aware of what information is needed to make a correct determination of worker classification. This is especially true of small business owners who may not be aware of the relief available under Section 530 of the Revenue Act of 1978, resulting from worker reclassification. An auditor's examination should actively consider Section 530 during an examination, including furnishing taxpayers with a summary of Section 530 at the beginning of an examination.

Essentially, an accountant's responsibility is similar to an IRS tax examiner's responsibility as set forth by the Treasury Department which states:

"The examiner has a responsibility to the taxpayer and to the government to determine the correct tax liability and to maintain a fair and impartial attitude in all matters relating to the examination. The fair and impartial attitude of an examiner aids in increasing voluntary compliance. An examiner must approach each examination with an objective point of view."

## Determining Factors

Officially termed the *worker classification issue,* the focus is centered on three main areas that the IRS has concluded are primary categories of evidence to draw a distinction between an employee and an independent contractor. The essence of the distinction is whether or not the employer has the right to direct and control the worker. The three areas are:

1)  Behavioral control.
2)  Financial control.
3)  Relationship of the parties.

Those three areas provide evidence that substantiates the right to direct or control the details and means by which the worker performs the required services. Training is important in this context. Significant are such workplace developments as evaluation systems and concern for customer security in conjunction with business identification. All relevant information must be considered and weighed to determine whether a worker is an independent contractor or an employee.

Virtually every business will impose on workers, whether contractors or employees, some form of instruction. How else would a worker know what he or she is supposed to do, what duties to perform? This fact alone, however, is not sufficient evidence to determine a worker's status. As with every relevant fact, the problem is to determine whether the employer has retained the right to control the *details* of a worker's performance, or instead has given up the business's right to control those details. Accordingly, the weight of evidence in any case depends on the *degree* to which instructions apply with respect to *how the job gets done rather than to the end result.*

## Behavioral Control

Behavioral control concerns whether there is a right to direct or control how the worker performs the specific task for which he or she is engaged. Instructions and training are the main factors in considering the degree of behavioral control.

The degree of instruction depends on the scope of instructions, the extent to which the business retains the right to control the worker's compliance with the instructions, and the effect on the worker in the event of noncompliance. All these provide useful clues for identifying whether the business keeps control over the manner and means of work performance, or only over a particular product or service. The more detailed the instructions are that the worker is required to follow, the more control the business exerts over the worker, and the more likely the business retains the right to control the methods by which the worker performs the work. Absence of detail in instructions reflects less control.

Although the presence and extent of instructions is important in reaching a conclusion as to whether a business retains the right to direct and control the methods by which a worker performs a job, it is also important to consider the weight to be given those instructions if they are imposed by the business only in compliance with governmental or governing body regulations. If a business requires its workers to comply with established, municipal building codes related to construction, for example, the fact that such rules are imposed by the business should be given little weight in determining the worker's status. However, if the business develops more stringent guidelines for a worker in addition to those imposed by a third party, more weight should be given to these instructions in determining whether the business has retained the right to control the worker.

The nature of a worker's occupation also affects the degree of direction and control necessary to determine worker status. Highly trained professionals such as doctors, accountants, lawyers, engineers, or computer specialists may require very little, if any, training and instruction on how to perform their services for a particular business. In fact, it may be impossible for the business to instruct the worker on how to perform the services because it may lack the essential knowledge and skills to do so. Generally, professional workers who are engaged in the pursuit of an independent trade, business, or profession in which they offer their services to the public are independent contractors, not employees. In analyzing the status of professional workers, evidence of control or autonomy with respect to the financial details of how the task is performed tends to be especially important, as does evidence concerning the relationship of the parties.

An employment relationship can also exist when the work can be done with a minimal amount of direction and control, such as work done by a store clerk, or gas station attendant. The absence of a *need* to control should not be confused with the absence of the *right* to control. The right to control as an incident of employment requires only such supervision as the nature of the work requires. The key fact to consider is whether the business retains the *right* to direct and control the worker, regardless of whether the business actually exercises that right.

Evaluation systems are used by virtually all businesses to monitor the quality of work performed by workers, whether independent contractors or employees. In analyzing whether a business's evaluation system provides evidence of the right to control work performance, or the absence of such a right, an auditor should look for evidence of how the evaluation system may influence the worker's behavior in performing the details of the job.

If an evaluation system measures compliance with performance standards concerning the details of how the work is to be performed, the system and its enforcement are evidence of control over the worker's behavior. However, not all businesses have developed formal performance standards or evaluation systems. This is especially true of smaller businesses.

Training is the established means of explaining detailed methods and procedures to be used in performing a task. Periodic or ongoing training provided by a business about procedures to be followed and methods to be used indicates that the business wants the services performed in a particular manner. This type of training is strong evidence of an employer-employee relationship.

## Financial Control

Financial control concerns the facts which illustrate whether there is a *right* to direct or control how the worker's activities are conducted.

Factors to be considered are the business aspects of the worker's activities; significant investment, if any; unreimbursed expenses; services available to the relevant market; method of payment; and opportunity for profit or loss. These factors can be thought of as bearing on the issue of whether the recipient has the right to direct and control the means and details of the business aspects of how the worker performs services.

A significant investment is evidence that an independent contractor relationship may exist. It should be stressed that a significant investment is not necessary for an independent contractor. Some types of work simply do not require large expenditures. Even if large expenditures, such as costly equipment, are required, an independent contractor may rent the equipment needed at fair rental value. There are no precise dollar limits that must be met in order to have a significant investment. The size of the worker's investment and the risk borne by the worker are not diminished merely because the seller or lessor receives the benefit of the worker's services.

The extent to which a worker chooses to incur expenses and costs impacts his or her opportunity for profit or loss. This constitutes evidence that the worker has the right to direct and control the financial aspects of the business operations. Although not every independent contractor needs to make a significant investment, almost every independent contractor will incur an array of business expenses either in the form of direct expenditures or in the form of fees for pro rata portions of one or several expenses. Businesses often pay business or travel expenses for their employees. Independent contractors' expenses may also be reimbursed. An independent contractor can contract for direct reimbursement of certain expenses, or can seek to establish contract prices that will reimburse the contractor for these expenses. Attention should center on *unreimbursed* expenses, which better distinguish independent contractors and employees, inasmuch as independent contractors are more likely to have unreimbursed expenses. If expenses are unreimbursed, then the opportunity for profit or loss exists. Fixed ongoing costs that are incurred regardless of whether work is currently being performed are especially important. However, employees may also incur unreimbursed expenses in connection with the services they perform for their businesses. Relatively minor expenses incurred by a worker, or more significant expenses that are customarily borne by an employee in a particular line of business, would generally not indicate an independent contractor relationship.

An independent contractor is generally free to seek out business opportunities, as independent contractors' income depends on doing so successfully. As a result, independent contractors often advertise, maintain a visible business location, and are available to work for the relevant market. An independent contractor with special skills may be contacted by word of mouth and referrals without the need for advertising. An independent contractor who has negotiated a long-term contract may find advertising equally unnecessary, and may be unavailable to work for others for the duration of a contract. Other independent contractors may find that a visible business location does not generate sufficient business to justify the expense. Therefore, the absence of these activities is a neutral fact.

The method of payment can be helpful in determining whether the worker has the opportunity for profit or loss. A worker who is compensated on an hourly, daily, weekly, or similar basis is guaranteed a return for labor.

This is generally evidence of an employer-employee relationship, even when the wage or salary is accompanied by a commission. In some lines of business, such as law, it is typical to pay independent contractors on an hourly basis. Performance of a task for a flat fee is generally evidence of an independent contractor relationship, especially if the worker incurs the expenses of performing the services. A commission-based worker can be either an independent contractor or employee. The worker's status will depend on the worker's ability to realize a profit or incur a loss as a result of services rendered.

The ability to realize a profit or incur a loss is probably the strongest evidence that a worker controls the business aspects of services rendered.

Also to be considered is whether the worker is free to make business decisions that affect his profit or loss. If the worker is making decisions that affect the bottom line, the worker likely has the ability to realize profit or loss. It is sometimes thought that because a worker can receive more money working longer hours or receive less money by working less, he has the ability to incur a profit or loss. This type of income variation, however, is also consistent with employer status and does not distinguish employees from independent contractors.

Not all financial control facts need be present for the worker to have the ability to realize profit or loss. For example, a worker who is paid on a straight commission basis, makes business decisions, and has unreimbursed business expenses, likely would have the ability to realize a profit or loss, even if the worker does not have a significant investment and does not market her services.

## Relationship of the Parties

There are other facts that recent court decisions consider relevant in determining worker status. Most of these facts reflect how the worker and the business perceive the relationship to each other. It is much more difficult to link the facts in this category directly to the right to direct and control *how* work is to be performed than the categories discussed above. The relationship of the parties is important because it reflects the parties' *intent* concerning control. Courts often look at the intent of the parties because the intent is most often stated in their contractual relationship. A written agreement describing the worker as an independent contractor is viewed as evidence of the parties' intent that a worker is an independent contractor. However, a contractual designation, in and of itself, is not sufficient evidence for determining worker status. The facts and circumstances under which a worker performs services determine a worker's status. The *substance* of a relationship, not a label, governs the worker's status. The contract may be relevant in ascertaining methods of compensation, expenses that will be incurred, and rights and obligations of each party with respect to *how* work is to be performed. In addition, if it is difficult, if not impossible, to decide whether a worker is an independent contractor, the intent of the parties, as reflected in the contractual designation, is an effective way to resolve the issue.

Questions sometimes arise concerning whether a worker who creates a corporation through which to perform services can be an employee of a business that engages the corporation. If the corporate formalities are properly followed, and at least one nontax business purpose exists, the corporate form is generally recognized for both state law and federal law, including federal tax purposes. Disregarding the corporate entity is generally an extraordinary remedy, applied by most courts only in cases of clear abuse, so the worker will usually not be treated as an employee of the business, but as an employee of the corporation. (It should be noted that the fact that a worker receives payment for services from a business through the worker's corporation does not automatically require a finding of independent contractor status with respect to those services.)

*Employee benefits.*   Providing a worker with employee benefits has traditionally been linked with employee status and, therefore, can be an important factor in deciding an independent contractor-employee relationship. If a worker receives employee benefits, such as paid vacation days, paid sick days, health insurance, life or disability insurance, or a pension, this constitutes some evidence of employee status. The evidence is strongest if the worker is provided with employee benefits under a tax-qualified retirement plan, 403(b) annuity, or cafeteria plan, because by statute, these benefits can be provided to employees only. If an individual is excluded from a benefit plan because the worker is not considered an employee by the business, this is relevant though not conclusive in determining the worker's status as an independent contractor. If the worker is excluded on some other grounds, the exclusion is irrelevant in determining whether the worker is an independent contractor or an employee. This is because none of these employee benefits is required to be provided to employees. Many workers whose status as bona fide employees is unquestioned receive no employee benefits, as there is no requirement that all workers be covered.

*Termination rights.*   The circumstances under which a business or a worker can terminate their relationship have traditionally been considered useful evidence bearing on the status the parties intended the worker to have. However, in order to determine whether the facts are relevant to the worker's status, the impact of modern business practices and legal standards governing worker termination must be considered. A business's ability to terminate the work relationship at will, without penalty, provides a highly effective method to control the details of how work is performed, and indicates employee status. On the other hand, in the traditional independent contractor relationship, the business could terminate the relationship only if the worker failed to provide the intended service, which indicates the parties' intent that the business does not have the right to control how the work was performed. In practice, businesses rarely have complete flexibility in discharging an employee. The business may be liable for pay in lieu of notice, severance pay, "golden parachutes," or other forms of compensation when it discharges an employee. In addition, the reasons for which a business can terminate an employee may be limited, whether by law, by contract, or by its own practices.

A worker's ability to terminate work at will was traditionally considered to illustrate that the worker merely provided labor and tended to indicate an employer-employee relationship. In contrast, if the worker terminated work, and the business could refuse payment or sue for nonperformance, this indicated the business's interest in receiving the contracted product or service, which tended to indicate an independent contractor relationship. In practice, however, independent contractors can enter into short-term contracts for which nonperformance remedies are inappropriate; or they may negotiate limits on their liability for nonperformance. Typical examples are professionals, such as doctors and attorneys, who can terminate their contractual relationship without penalty.

Businesses can successfully sue employees for substantial damages resulting from their failure to perform the services for which they were engaged. As a result, the presence or absence of limits on workers' ability to terminate the relationship, by themselves, no longer constitutes useful evidence in determining worker status. A business's ability to refuse payment for unsatisfactory work continues to be characteristic of an independent contractor relationship.

***Permanent/indefinite relationship.*** The existence of a permanent relationship between the worker and the business is relevant evidence in determining whether there is an employer-employee relationship. If a business engages a worker with the expectation that the relationship will continue indefinitely, rather than for a specific project or period, it is a factor that is generally considered evidence of an intent to create an employment relationship.

A relationship that is created with the expectation that it will be indefinite should not be confused with a long-term relationship. A long-term relationship may exist between a business and either an independent contractor or an employee. The relationship between the business and an independent contractor can be long-term for several reasons:

1) The contract may be a long-term contract.

**2)** Contracts can be renewed regularly due to superior service, competitive costs, or lack of alternative service providers.

A business can also have a relationship with an employee that is long-term, but not indefinite. This could occur if temporary employment contracts are renewed, or if a long-term, but not indefinite, employment contract is entered into. As a result, a relationship that is long-term, but not indefinite, is a neutral fact that should be disregarded.

A temporary relationship is a neutral fact that should be disregarded. An independent contractor will typically have a temporary relationship with a business, but so too will employees engaged on a seasonal project, or on an "as needed" basis. The services performed by the worker, and the extent to which those services are a key aspect of the regular business of the company, are germane. In considering this, it should be remembered that the fact that a service is desirable, necessary, or even essential to a business does not mean that the service provider is an employee. The work of an attorney or paralegal is part of the regular business of a law firm. If a law firm hires an attorney or paralegal, it is likely that the law firm will present the work as its own. As a result, there is an increased probability that the law firm will direct or control the activities. However, further facts should be examined to see whether there is evidence of the *right* to direct or control before a conclusion is reached that these workers are employees. It is possible that the work performed is part of the principal business of the law firm, yet it has hired workers who are outside specialists and may be independent contractors.

## CHECKLIST

The 20 factors indicating whether an individual is an employee or an independent contractor follow:

**1)** *Instructions.* An employee must comply with instructions about when, where, and how to work. Even if no instructions are given, the control factor is present if the employer has the right to control how the work results are achieved.

**2)** *Training.* An employee may be trained to perform services in a particular manner. Independent contractors ordinarily use their own methods and receive no training from the purchasers of their services.

**3)** *Integration.* An employee's services are usually integrated into the business operations because the services are important to the success or continuation of the business. This shows that the employee is subject to direction and control.

4)  *Services Are Rendered Personally.* An employee renders services personally. This shows that the employer is interested in the methods as well as the results.

5)  *Hiring Assistants.* An employee works for an employer who hires, supervises, and pays workers. An independent contractor can hire, supervise, and pay assistants under a contract that requires their contractor to provide materials and labor and to be responsible only for the result.

6)  *Continuing Relationship.* An employee generally has a continuing relationship that may exist even if work is performed at recurring although irregular intervals.

7)  *Set Hours of Work.* An employee usually has set hours of work established by an employer. Independent contractors generally can set their own work hours.

8)  *Full-Time Required.* An employee may be required to work or be available full-time. This indicates control by the employer. An independent contractor can work when and for whom he or she chooses.

9)  *Work Done on Premises.* An employee usually works on the premises of an employer, or works on a route or at a location designated by an employer.

10)  *Order or Sequence Set.* An employee may be required to perform services in the order or sequence set by an employer. This shows that the employee is subject to direction and control.

11)  *Reports.* An employee may be required to submit reports to an employer, which shows that the employer maintains a degree of control.

12)  *Payments.* An employee generally is paid by the hour, week, or month. An independent contractor is usually paid by the job or on a straight commission.

13)  *Expenses.* An employee's business and travel expenses are generally paid by an employer. This shows that the employee is subject to regulation and control.

14)  *Tools and Materials.* An employee is normally furnished significant tools, materials, and other equipment by an employer.

15)  *Investment.* An independent contractor has a significant investment in the facilities used in performing services for someone else.

16)  *Profit or Loss.* An independent contractor can make a profit or suffer a loss.

17)  *Works for More than One Person or Firm.* An independent contractor is generally free to provide services to two or more unrelated persons or firms at the same time.

18)  *Offers Services to General Public.* An independent contractor makes services available to the general public.

**19)** *Right to Fire.* An employee can be fired by an employer. An independent contractor cannot be fired as long as results are produced that meet the specifications of the contract.

**20)** *Right to Quit.* An employee can quit a job at any time without incurring liability. An independent contractor usually agrees to complete a specific job and is responsible for its satisfactory completion, or legally is obligated to make good for failure to complete it.

# Chapter 20

## International Federation of Accountants

Founded in 1977, the International Federation of Accountants (IFAC), with headquarters in New York, consists of 142 national accountancy bodies from 103 countries with over two million members.

### IFAC and IASC Relationship

By 1982, it became obvious to the leadership of IFAC and the International Accounting Standards Committee (IASC), located on Fleet Street in London, that their particular bailiwicks needed to be clearly established in order to avoid confusion concerning their respective roles. It was agreed that the IASC should be the sole international body to set *financial accounting and reporting standards*. IFAC, on behalf of the accountancy profession, also agreed to contribute a certain portion of the IASC budget. Thus, the IASC, primarily through the IASC Board, develops, issues and promotes worldwide acceptance of international standards on financial accounting and reporting.

At the same time, IASC agreed to IFAC's role as the worldwide organization for the accountancy profession and accepted IFAC member bodies into the IASC. It was further established that IFAC would nominate 13 countries to sit on the IASC Board, with 4 other seats to be selected at IASC's discretion. Since 1995, IFAC has also funded the cost of one Board seat so that certain emerging market nations, otherwise unable to afford the cost, could participate in the IASC Board.

The Board of IFAC considers the following to be among their most important tasks:

**1)** Develop auditing initiatives.

**2)** Develop guidance and standards relating to education, ethics, management accounting, information technology and the public sector.

**3)** Give consideration to professional issues such as accountant's liability and the liberalization of professional services.

**4)** Act as primary spokesman on professional accountancy issues.

## Two Separate International Organizations

IFAC emphasizes that the international accountancy profession could be considered to have two primary standard-setting bodies: IFAC and the IASC. The organizations have common memberships in that the 142 national accountancy bodies from 103 countries that are full members of IFAC are *ipso facto* members of IASC (the associate and affiliate IFAC members are not officially IASC members). However, as pointed out above, they are two separate and distinct organizations with two agendas.

*Associate* members are national organizations whose members work in a support role to the accountancy professions, and newly formed accountancy bodies that have not yet met the full membership criteria.

*Affiliate* members are international organizations that represent a particular area of interest or a group of professionals who frequently interact with accountants.

There is considerable mutual support for one another's objectives. IFAC member bodies, in addition to their responsibility to promote and use IFAC guidance, are committed to promote and implement IASC pronouncements. There is also regular contact and coordination between the two organizations at the leadership level.

This arrangement has worked for the last 15 years or so. In addition, each organization appears to believe that it provides the necessary degree of independence for the IASC Board to set accounting standards, but also ensures the commitment of the accountancy profession in helping to see that these standards are actually implemented in international practice.

## Comparison to U.S. Organizations

The IFAC likens their and the IASC's role on the international scene to those of the AICPA (with a nod to the Institute of Management Accountants [IMA] and the Institute of Internal Auditors [IIA]) and the FASB, respectively. The FASB is completely independent of the profession and sets accounting standards. AICPA, etc., are the professional accountancy bodies and set standards and guidelines for accountants. They also comment on FASB pronouncements and support the FASB by providing representation to the Financial Accounting Foundation (FAF) Board of Trustees, but there is no control by the profession over the FASB.

## ORGANIZATIONAL STRUCTURE

The organization of IFAC is based on the Assembly, which is made up of one representative from each membership accounting body. The Assembly elects the Council which, in turn, selects an Executive Committee to advance the organization's policies and to appoint and oversee special task forces and seven standing committees.

The IFAC Council recently expanded its agenda by appointing task forces to work in the following areas:

1) **Anti-Corruption.** This task force will deal with anti-corruption and the accountant's role in both the public and private sectors. With the widespread awareness of the impact of corruption upon the social and economic life of both developed and, particularly, developing nations, comes the awareness that the accountancy profession must face up to its responsibility to aid in eradicating corruption.

   The task force is charged with preparing a guidance paper for the member bodies detailing how accountants should handle instances of corruption of which they become aware. It has also been suggested that encouraging increased disclosure and transparency in the public and private sectors, as well as promoting the development of common global accounting and auditing standards, could aid in combating fraud.

2) **Small- and Medium-Sized Enterprises (SME).** Recognizing that the growth of small businesses contributes to the economic well-being of many countries, IFAC is focusing greater attention on this constituency. A task force will recommend the development of guidance for both practitioners and SME advisors and owners.

3) **Quality Assurance.** Maintaining highly effective quality control systems enhances the profession's ability to serve the public interest. To further its mission of serving the public interest, a new IFAC task force will expand the existing statement on quality control systems for all aspects of the profession.

4) **Structure and Organization.** The environment in which IFAC operates today is significantly different from that in which it has operated over the past ten years. A task force will consider the changing environment and take a fresh look at IFAC's system of guidance, structure, and resources to determine if it is properly positioned for the twenty-first century.

## TECHNICAL ACTIVITIES

Technical activities of the IFAC are carried on by several committees in addition to the special task forces.

1) ***Ethics Advisory Group.*** As a result of the work of this committee, a revision of the *Code of Ethics for Professional Accountants* was recently issued. However, because of the growing acceptance of the code as fundamental guidance for accountants practicing worldwide, and as a model for a national accounting and auditing framework, IFAC considers revision and further guidance to be an ongoing process. Among the measures in the revision and exposure drafts are:

   a) Clarification of rules affecting confidentiality. Emphasis is placed on the belief that the rules of confidentiality must be balanced by the public's need to know certain information. It is agreed that professional accountants must respect the confidentiality of a client's or employer's affairs. However, instances may arise in which professional, legal, or ethical considerations overrule the need for confidentiality. An effort is being made to clarify when public interest may take precedence over the confidentiality of specific information.

   b) Guidance for accountants who employ nonaccountants. Taking the stand that accountants are ultimately responsible for any service performed for their client, whether by a lawyer, actuary, or appraiser, IFAC is suggesting guidance on the applicability of the code to nonaccountants.

   c) Separation of ethical issues into sections relating to:
   • All accountants.
   • Those in public practice.
   • Those employed in commerce, industry, the public sector, and education.

   d) Guidance when accountants are asked to give a second opinion. The code requires that they contact the original or existing accountant to obtain all relevant facts and information about the client. The assumption is that the objectivity of the second opinion could be open to question if it were not based on thorough research and investigation.

   e) Guidance relating to auditor independence and rotation concerns. The code cautions that accountants in public practice should rotate senior personnel when retained on long-term engagements. Otherwise, the use of the same auditor over an extended period could lead to the appearance of a lack of independence.

**f)** Stipulation that the *quality* of an audit must not suffer because an accountant has drastically underbid a competitor in order to gain a client.

**g)** Recommendation that IFAC member bodies and professional accounting institutes provide support, and hotlines to answer queries relating to ethical dilemmas.

**2)** ***Public Sector Committee (PSC).*** Work of this committee resulted in a published report on accrual accounting for governmental bodies. The Occasional Paper No. 3, entitled *Perspectives on Accrual Accounting,* consists of articles by accountants, economists, academics, administrators, and politicians relating to the question of reforming accounting methods for public sector entities.

As a result of governments throughout the world contracting out many of their normal services, the traditional use of cash basis accounting for financial reporting may now not be the best method to show the entity's true financial condition. Articles in this paper give a wide range of opinions on and experience in the use of accrual-based reporting to measure the assets and liabilities of governments.

The United Nations International Monetary Fund (IMF), the World Bank, and several regional development banks have pledged $1 million to support the PSC's Standards Project to produce a basic set of authoritative statements on financial reporting by governments. The multi-year project is divided into two phases:

**a)** Establishment of a core of accounting standards applicable under each of the accounting bases which governments typically use—cash, modified cash, modified accrual, and accrual.

**b)** Examination of the application of international accounting standards to the public sector.

In line with this latter phase, the committee will work closely with the International Accounting Standards Committee in the belief that the more consideration given to public sector issues in formulating International Accounting Standards (IASs) for the private sector, the easier it will be to harmonize the two sets of standards in the long run.

The first phase of IFAC's multi-year project to develop these governmental accounting standards and guidelines worldwide is progressing with the committee's exposing for comment a *Guideline for Governmental Financial Reporting.* Copies of the paper have been widely distributed. This is a big step in the group's aim to contribute to better decision making, financial management, and accountability by all governmental bodies.

The second phase of the project will consist of the development of a core set of recommended accounting standards for governments, also focusing on the four bases of accounting. They will be based on existing International Accounting Standards.

3) **Financial and Management Accounting Committee (FMAC).** Annually, this committee publishes *Articles of Merit,* award-winning articles selected from IFAC member body journals. Articles are chosen by a panel of three judges, members of FMAC, in a "blind" selection process. Articles submitted are judged on the basis of having made, or having the potential to make, "a distinct and valuable contribution to the advancement of management accounting."

In addition, the committee publishes special studies, guidelines, and the results of research in the area of management accounting. It also disseminates information through international forums and seminars on these issues.

4) **International Auditing Practices Committee (IAPC).** This committee's task is to upgrade auditing and related services standards globally by developing benchmark statements on varied auditing and attest functions to increase the credibility of financial statements. This endeavor is centered around IFAC's codification of International Standards on Auditing (ISAs) and Related Practices.

One of the committee's most important tasks involves working with *The Reporting on the Credibility of Information.* As trade in goods and services spreads over the globe, the demand for reliable information spreads even faster. Thus, IFAC, through this committee, is attempting to provide guidance on assuring the credibility of financial information with accountants assuming the role as the "primary care" providers. Building on the framework of existing auditing procedures and practices, the aim is to examine how and when these practices are effective in reporting on the reliability of information and how they can be improved and expanded. Another of their major areas of interest at present is the development of a statement, *Going Concern.* IFAC believes that additional standards and guidance are needed to pinpoint management's and the auditor's responsibilities in relation to the going concern assumption in preparing and auditing financial statements.

5) **Information Technology Committee (ITC).** As its title indicates, this group is charged with keeping the worldwide accounting community abreast of the latest developments and applications relating to information technology (IT). It encourages member bodies to keep up to date on available hardware and software and the relationship between IT and the accounting profession.

At a recent international meeting, the committee focused on the use of IT in developing countries, and approved a research program and budget. The initial research will involve determination of the current usage of IT in these countries and identification of the type and level of assistance that would be appropriate in developing economies.

Since being formed in 1995, the committee has begun formulating a series of guidelines to help management cope with rapidly expanding technological developments. The first guideline to be approved is *Managing Security in Information and Communications.* It emphasizes the growing importance of closely managing the risks related to information technology.

6) *Education Committee.* In the effort to bring about global accounting standards and mutual recognition agreements related to professional accounting services, this committee recommends the necessary elements for the education and training of all accounting professionals. Further, emphasis is placed on the importance and quality of continuing professional education (CPE) programs.

7) *Membership Committee.* IFAC increases its membership through this committee by checking on the accountancy profession in various countries, particularly those with developing economies. It provides guidance and assistance to groups attempting to increase the professional level of their members in order to attain the level of competency to meet IFAC membership requirements.

## IFAC HOLDS DEVELOPMENT SUMMIT

A forum on the development of the accountancy profession was organized by IFAC in conjunction with the World Bank and regional development agencies in 1998. Its purpose was to discuss how they could most effectively combine resources, expertise, and experience to enhance the quality of the accounting profession in countries where there is no organized profession as such.

As a result of this forum, a working group has been set up to develop a basis for a more permanent Coordination Committee to include members from all interested groups.

The aims of the forum and the follow-up committees include:

1) Identifying the common basic needs of accountancy framework and capability that would meet the needs of *donor agencies,* as well as both *foreign* and *domestic* investors.

2) Identifying where these needs are greatest.

3) Organizing the combined resources of the profession, local and national governments, and development agencies to meet these needs.

4) Avoiding duplication of effort in the various forms of and sources of assistance.

IFAC points out that although the specific needs of individual countries may differ, generic approaches that can be used and then adapted to particular needs may be the best method of "attack." Coordinated efforts could result in more efficient and cost-effective solutions

## IFAC AND THE YEAR 2000 (Y2K) ISSUE

The organization as a whole, and specifically the Information Technology Committee and the International Auditing Practices Committee, are intent on avoiding a worldwide dislocation of business with the arrival of the Year 2000. Becoming Y2K compliant in their computer systems is presenting significant problems and great costs to businesses and governments. As has become increasingly apparent, many computer systems cannot recognize the Year 2000 because the year has been programmed with two digits and not four—and therein lies the problem.

IFAC and the Committees have published articles, issued press releases, and prepared an International Auditing Practices Statement (IAPS) to increase international awareness of the problems. In addition, they have published an *International Audit Risk Alert on the Year 2000 Issue* to pinpoint some of the problems.

### Significant Risks to the Entity

They point out that organizations face a number of risks that need to be considered by management, the accountants, and auditors in connection with current audits. Some of the risks to be considered by management include:

1) Costs of systems' modifications to make them Year 2000 compliant.
2) Impact, if any, on financial statements, particularly with respect to forward-looking financial information used as a basis for financial reporting, such as warranty and slow-moving inventory calculations.
3) Loss of insurance, particularly where the insurer drops or indicates that business interruption insurance does not cover the Year 2000 problem.
4) Customer and supplier impacts of the Year 2000 on the entity.
5) Impact, if any, on management's going concern assessments, particularly where the cost of modifying the systems is high and the entity does not appear to have the resources to do so.
6) Disclosures of Year 2000 issues, particularly those required by regulatory bodies, the IASC, or national accounting disclosures.

## Role of Auditors in Y2K

The International Federation of Accountants points out that of particular concern for auditors is the impact that Y2K may have on the *going concern* assessment on business entities. For individual organizations, these are the tasks associated with identifying any problems and then putting appropriate steps in place to address them. In addition, the exclusion of the Year 2000 from many insurance policies in some countries also adds considerable risk to the personal liability of company directors.

Auditors will need to consider documenting the extent of their responsibilities with regard to the Y2K issue in an engagement letter or other form of communication to their clients.

*Auditors* may need, among other things, to:

1) Determine whether the Y2K issue has any effect on accounting estimates or classifications using future dating of the Year 2000 or beyond, and whether the financial statements need to be adjusted.

2) Determine whether there are any financial statement accounting disclosures required by national regulators, the IASC, or national accounting disclosure requirements, and whether these disclosures have been made in the financial statements. An example might be the disclosure of the amount spent in the current year on Y2K costs where these are material to the financial statements.

3) Review disclosures made by the entity outside the financial statements for Y2K information indicating possible material inconsistencies or material misstatements of facts in accordance with international rulings.

4) Determine if there is any need to modify the auditor's report with respect to lack of information, or with respect to the going concern assumption.

# Index